SPURGEON
A Life

SPURGEON
A Life

Alex DiPrima

Reformation Heritage Books
Grand Rapids, Michigan

Spurgeon: A Life
© 2024 by Alex DiPrima

All rights reserved. No part of this book may be used or reproduced in any manner whatsoever without written permission except in the case of brief quotations embodied in critical articles and reviews. Direct your requests to the publisher at the following addresses:

Reformation Heritage Books
3070 29th St. SE
Grand Rapids, MI 49512
616-977-0889
orders@heritagebooks.org
www.heritagebooks.org

Unless otherwise indicated, Scripture quotations from the King James Version. In the public domain.

Printed in the United States of America
24 25 26 27 28 29/10 9 8 7 6 5 4 3 2 1

Library of Congress Cataloging-in-Publication Data

Names: DiPrima, Alex, author.
Title: Spurgeon : a life / Alex DiPrima.
Description: Grand Rapids, Michigan : Reformation Heritage Books, [2024] | Includes bibliographical references.
Identifiers: LCCN 2024009816 (print) | LCCN 2024009817 (ebook) | ISBN 9798886861150 (hardcover) | ISBN 9798886861167 (epub)
Subjects: LCSH: Spurgeon, C. H. (Charles Haddon), 1834-1892. | Baptists—Great Britain—Clergy—Biography
Classification: LCC BX6495.S7 D274 2024 (print) | LCC BX6495.S7 (ebook) | DDC 286/.1092 [B]—dc23/eng/20240430
LC record available at https://lccn.loc.gov/2024009816
LC ebook record available at https://lccn.loc.gov/2024009817

To Robert Fisher,

pastor, mentor, and friend

Remember them…who have spoken
unto you the word of God.

—Hebrews 13:7

Contents

Foreword

Why is Charles Spurgeon so endlessly fascinating? His enduring popularity proves that he is. Most come to him because they hear of his reputation as a preacher, and then they find something above and beyond. For Spurgeon was not simply a large presence in the pulpit. He was, quite simply, an extraordinary man.

Indeed, there was something supernatural in the combination of his qualities. On the one hand, he was nothing like the stereotypical Victorian; he was lively and cheerful. His writings ripple with mirth. On the other hand, he was not frivolous but joyfully earnest. He was also a bighearted man of deep affections. Still today, his printed sermons and lectures throb with passion. He was a deeply kind and tender man. He was no pushover but a lion of conviction and courage. While joyful and resolute, he was not a triumphalist. Indeed, he struggled acutely with much pain and depression. And yet he never comes across as gloomy. And perhaps this is what draws people: they see in Spurgeon a man who was so gloriously and unusually *alive*.

He expressed his vivid humanness through his unique character. He had his own personality. But the more you look, the more it is obvious: his vitality and greatness of soul were the fruit of a deep knowledge of a fascinating Savior. That is why he is so captivating; he lucidly commends and reflects Jesus Christ. We are so drawn to him because he was so drawn to Christ. His great view of Christ humbled him, and yet it made him great in his Christlikeness. And isn't that what we want and need today? We need preachers who will lift Christ high, and we need Christians who are more like Christ.

That is why this crisp and up-to-date portrait of the man by Alex DiPrima is so welcome. It is clear, it is compelling, it is uplifting, and it is edifying. In other words, it embodies Spurgeon. More than that: just as Spurgeon did in his life and ministry, it placards Jesus Christ as a truly glorious Savior in whose light we are humbled, delighted, and made whole. So take and read, for through Spurgeon you will see much of Christ, and in beholding Him, you will be transformed into His most wonderful likeness.

Michael Reeves
President and Professor of Theology
Union School of Theology

Acknowledgments

As I publish this biography, I am aware of the great debt of gratitude I owe to many friends and helpers who have assisted me in bringing it to life. Fellow Spurgeon scholars Geoff Chang and Ray Rhodes were regular conversation partners throughout the writing of this book. I am grateful to Geoff Chang in particular for reviewing the manuscript and providing important feedback that helped me to tell Spurgeon's story more accurately. I am thankful to Nathan Finn, who was an early encourager of the project and also kindly reviewed the finished manuscript. I would like to thank Michael Reeves for contributing a lovely foreword and an endorsement of my work.

Robert Fisher provided the most substantive and useful feedback on the early drafts of the biography. His love, friendship, counsel, encouragement, and support stand behind every good thing I have ever done. It is my joy to dedicate this book to him.

Lydia Schaible has again proven herself an adroit and skillful editor as well as a kind and gracious friend. She helped to improve my writing significantly and provided me with timely encouragement along the way. I am grateful also to my friend Hunter Hobart, who humbly served as my "ideal reader," gave me valuable feedback, and helped me to clarify the aims of the book.

I am again indebted to my publishers at Reformation Heritage Books. It has been a delight to work with them. To Joel Beeke, David Woollin, Jay Collier, and Annette Gysen—thank you for supporting this project and helping me bring it to completion. Thanks belongs to Branden Preedy for furnishing me with many of the images found in this book.

Finally, I want to express my deepest gratitude to my wife, Jenna, for the unending support, inspiration, and love she freely gives me. I wrote the second half of this book during her long fight with breast cancer. Chapter 11 on Spurgeon's suffering took on special significance for me as I watched her suffer faithfully through the arduous rounds of treatment. Our hope in the world to come was never brighter than during those difficult months, and we both found immense help in Spurgeon. We feel we can truly say with him "that the worst days I have ever had have turned out to be my best days and when God has seemed most cruel to me he has then been most kind."

Introduction

On April 19, 1854, Charles Haddon Spurgeon formally accepted a call to pastor one of the most historic churches in the middle of the largest city in the world. He was only nineteen years old, had never gone to college, and had received no formal ministerial training. He had lived his entire life in the secluded and bucolic environs of the English countryside. Nothing about his family lineage presaged an especially bright future. His education was unspectacular, and he had never found himself in close proximity to great men or important events. He had begun preaching, almost by accident, at the age of sixteen through a local lay preachers' association in Cambridgeshire. Before accepting the call to London, Spurgeon had preached most of his sermons under the thatched roofs of country cottages, the old wooden ceilings of barns, and the open sky of the fields of East Anglia. And yet within just a few months of his arrival in the metropolis, newspapers across the city, and indeed the entire country, were printing reports such as this:

> An extraordinary sensation has recently been produced in London by the preaching of a young Baptist minister named C. H. Spurgeon. The crowds which have been drawn to hear him, the interest excited by his ministry, and the conflicting opinions expressed in reference to his qualifications and usefulness, have been altogether without parallel in modern times. What renders the present case remarkable is, the juvenility of the preacher,—his hold on the public being established before he had attained his twentieth year; and his first appearance

in London being that of a country youth, without any of the supposed advantages of a College education or ordinary ministerial training.[1]

A year later, the excitement had not abated:

> Never, since the days of George Whitefield, has any minister of religion acquired so great a reputation as this Baptist preacher, in so short a time. Here is a mere youth,—a perfect stripling, only twenty-one years of age,—incomparably the most popular preacher of the day. There is no man within her Majesty's dominions who could draw such immense audiences; and none who, in his happier efforts, can so completely enthrall the attention, and delight the minds of his hearers.[2]

It was clear a new force had entered the religious world of the nation. The curtain had opened on one of the most brilliant preaching careers in church history. London would witness a ministry whose storied success would defy belief if it was not so meticulously well-documented.

In defiance of the many prophecies and prognostications of his critics, Spurgeon would demonstrate exceptional staying power. The rustic and rough-hewn youth who first arrived in London in 1854 would minister there for thirty-eight years as the pastor of the largest Protestant church in Christendom until his death in 1892. In those years, he would execute a ministry of unparalleled success—one that seemed to elude rational explanation. Even by the end of his life, onlookers were still trying to grapple with what they had witnessed. In the week following his death, a Church of England journal recorded,

> Every now and then some one takes the world by storm. Without succeeding to anybody else's post, the newcomer makes for himself a definite place in the world's consciousness, and

---

1. *The Friend*, n.d., quoted in *C. H. Spurgeon's Autobiography, Compiled from His Diary, Letters, and Records by His Wife and His Private Secretary* (London: Passmore and Alabaster, 1898), 2:63.

2. *The Morning Advertiser*, February 18, 1856, quoted in *C. H. Spurgeon's Autobiography*, 2:72.

a recognised influence, for good or for ill, in some department of the world's work. He may be a statesman, soldier, poet, artist or preacher, but he is unique. That is the type of man whose influence lives on, and whose figure becomes historical. If we mistake not, Mr. Spurgeon belongs to this small class of persons whose career seems independent of circumstances just as their genius is independent of training.[3]

Sometimes in the history of the church, God simply raises up a man—a standard-bearer, a pathfinder, a trailblazer, a tribune, a bright and shining light—and places him in the middle of events. No material or logical account of the events can erase the certain awareness that one has observed a kind of supernatural intervention in the affairs of men. No study of origins, heredity, intellectual influences, natural events, or social and cultural circumstances can provide an entirely satisfying rationale for the thing. After such fruitless attempts are made, one must simply step back and say, "The hand of the Lord hath done this."

Spurgeon by the Numbers
Charles Spurgeon is a figure who towers over many others in the long line of godly men throughout Christian history. His storied preaching, copious writings, and millions of devoted followers are a testament to his extraordinary legacy. The sheer scope of his expansive ministry is enough to exhaust even the most hardworking, energetic, and high-capacity ministers today. One need only consider some of the astounding statistics related to his life and ministry to appreciate the singular place Spurgeon holds among church history's greatest preachers.

One might begin by considering Spurgeon from the standpoint of age. The record of personal achievements and spiritual milestones he attained while still in his childhood, adolescence, and early

---

3. *Record*, February 5, 1892, quoted in W. Y. Fullerton, *C. H. Spurgeon: A Biography* (London: William and Norgate, 1920), 73.

adulthood is in itself remarkable. He began devouring Puritan classics at the age of five or six years old. He was strikingly converted when he was only fifteen, began to preach regularly when he was sixteen, and took his first pastorate in a country village at just seventeen. He received a call to pastor perhaps the most prominent Baptist church in London when only nineteen years old, and by the time he reached the age of twenty, he had already preached over six hundred sermons. The first biography of Spurgeon, written by an American, appeared when he was only twenty-one years old.[4] By his midtwenties, he was pastoring the largest church in the entire Protestant world.

The numbers continue to impress as one considers the enormous size of his congregations. From the ages of seventeen to nineteen, Spurgeon grew a rural church in a small village from a few dozen members to over four hundred. When he arrived in London, the membership of the then New Park Street Chapel (later to change its name to the Metropolitan Tabernacle) numbered 232. By the end of his ministry in 1892, the membership of the church was 5,311 members.[5] The church added a total of 14,461 members over the course of his ministry, which amounts to an average of over one person per day. Nearly three-quarters of those new members were added through baptism.[6] Before he even reached his thirties, Spurgeon was regularly preaching morning and evening on Sundays to six thousand people gathered at both services. On many occasions he spoke to crowds of over ten thousand, and on one occasion he addressed an assembly of nearly twenty-five thousand people at the Crystal Palace. He regularly preached six to eight times per week and

---

4. E. L. Magoon, *"The Modern Whitfield": Sermons of the Rev. C. H. Spurgeon, of London; With an Introduction and Sketch of His Life* (New York: Sheldon, Blakeman, 1856).

5. These figures are recorded in the annual membership roles in the archives of the Metropolitan Tabernacle in London.

6. Geoffrey Chang, *Spurgeon the Pastor: Recovering a Biblical and Theological Vision for Ministry* (Nashville: B&H Academic, 2022), 110.

sometimes as much as ten to twelve times in a week. During his lifetime Spurgeon was estimated to have preached to over ten million people. He once said that never a week went by and seldom a day without letters coming in from individuals attributing their conversion to one of his sermons.[7]

Spurgeon also left behind a gigantic footprint in the arena of church planting. He helped to start nearly two hundred new churches in Britain alone.[8] It has been estimated that between 1865 and 1887, Spurgeon and his students founded over half of the new Baptist churches in England.[9] Spurgeon's influence in London, in particular, was extraordinary. Between 1865 and 1876, he helped to plant fifty-three of the sixty-two new Baptist churches in London.[10] Through the work of his famous Pastors' College, he trained nearly nine hundred men for pastoral ministry over the course of his life.[11] By his death in 1892, over 20 percent of all Baptist ministers serving in England and Wales had been trained by Spurgeon.[12]

The scope of Spurgeon's social ministries was equally extraordinary. By 1884 there were sixty-six benevolent ministries operating out of the Metropolitan Tabernacle, many of which Spurgeon personally founded, funded, or chaired.[13] These ministries included

7. C. H. Spurgeon, "Twenty Years," *Sword and the Trowel* (January 1875): 6.

8. Mike Nicholls, *C. H. Spurgeon: The Pastor Evangelist* (Didcot, UK: Baptist Historical Society, 1992), 175–77.

9. Peter J. Morden, *C. H. Spurgeon: The People's Preacher* (Farnham, UK: CWR, 2009), 151.

10. Nicholls, *C. H. Spurgeon: The Pastor Evangelist*, 98.

11. David W. Bebbington, "Spurgeon and British Evangelical Theological Education," in *Theological Education in the Evangelical Tradition*, ed. D. G. Hart and R. A. Mohler Jr. (Grand Rapids: Baker, 1996), 221.

12. Kenneth D. Brown, *A Social History of the Nonconformist Ministry in England and Wales 1800–1930* (Oxford: Clarendon, 1988), 33, 98; and J. H. Y. Briggs, *The English Baptists of the Nineteenth Century* (Didcot, UK: Baptist Historical Society, 1994), 3:88–90.

13. *Memorial Volume, Mr. Spurgeon's Jubilee: Report of the Proceedings at the Metropolitan Tabernacle on Wednesday and Thursday Evenings, June 18th and 19th, 1884* (London: Passmore and Alabaster, 1884), 7–8; and C. H. Spurgeon, "Mr. Spurgeon's Jubilee Meetings," *Sword and the Trowel* (July 1884): 373.

an orphanage, evening classes for working-class people, subsidized housing for poor widows, a clothing bank, several street missions, and ministries to children, prostitutes, police officers, and the blind. In addition to being considered the greatest preacher of the age, he was also known as one of London's leading philanthropists.

What of his literary endeavors? Spurgeon published more words in English than any other Christian ever. His published sermons now span seventy volumes, and their reach is virtually impossible to estimate. Some have suggested that by the beginning of the twentieth century, they had sold over one hundred million copies, though the total number was surely far higher due to the numerous copies that had been reproduced and distributed all over the world.[14] Spurgeon published roughly 150 books in less than forty years, including his devotional classics *Morning by Morning*[15] and *Evening by Evening*,[16] a collection of his addresses on pastoral ministry called *Lectures to My Students*,[17] and his massive commentary on the Psalms titled *The Treasury of David*.[18] Beginning in 1865, he also published a monthly magazine called *The Sword and the Trowel* that was in continual circulation throughout the rest of his life and enjoyed a regular readership of fifteen thousand. Alongside these massive publishing endeavors, Spurgeon found time to pen approximately five hundred letters per week.

Few ministers in church history have embraced as broad a scope of evangelical work as Charles Spurgeon. Generations since have

---

14. Chang, *Spurgeon the Pastor*, 12; and J. C. Carlile, *C. H. Spurgeon: An Interpretive Biography* (London: Kingsgate, 1933), 233.

15. C. H. Spurgeon, *Morning by Morning: or, Daily Readings for the Family or the Closet* (London: Passmore and Alabaster, 1866).

16. C. H. Spurgeon, *Evening by Evening: or, Readings at Eventide for the Family or the Closet* (London: Passmore and Alabaster, 1868).

17. C. H. Spurgeon, *Lectures to My Students*, 3 vols. (London: Passmore and Alabaster, 1881–1894).

18. C. H. Spurgeon, *The Treasury of David: Containing an Original Exposition of the Book of Psalms; A Collection of Illustrative Extracts from the Whole Range of Literature; A Series of Homiletical Hints upon Almost Every Verse; And List of Writers upon Each Psalm*, 7 vols. (London: Passmore and Alabaster, 1869–1885).

looked at his life and ministry with a combination of awe and disbelief. His career would defy credibility if it were not so carefully chronicled by hundreds of eyewitnesses, journalists, and biographers. Indeed, various legends and fables have grown up around Spurgeon (perhaps no preacher has ever had more quotes falsely attributed to him), but in his case the truth was often even more impressive than the rumor.

Spurgeon the Preacher
Without question, the primary reason underlying Spurgeon's massive popularity was his extraordinary preaching. Other great men throughout church history have attained their influence by their scholarship, their writing, their theological contributions, their social activism, their exceptional leadership, their ability to organize and administrate, or their prominence in controversy. Spurgeon achieved his eminence principally as a preacher of the gospel. Preaching was the prevailing and defining activity of his life and contributed more than anything else to his monumental legacy.

The leading qualities of Spurgeon's preaching were his Christ-centeredness, his spiritual earnestness, and his popular style. In the first place, his sermons enjoyed such massive appeal because of their constant preoccupation with the person and work of Jesus Christ. The gospel of salvation for sinners through the incarnation, death, and resurrection of Jesus was always the keynote in his preaching. Spurgeon believed that if preaching was to be faithful to God's new covenant revelation of Himself in His Son the Lord Jesus, the redemptive events at the heart of the gospel must predominate over all else. Moreover, the preacher had a certain responsibility not only to proclaim Christ's person and work but to embody the heart and disposition of the Savior toward sinners in the preacher's own character and bearing. Thus, he believed, Christ and His gospel were to condition both the *matter* and the *manner* of preaching.

Second, Spurgeon's preaching was distinguished by its superlative quality of spiritual earnestness. Few preachers have labored more consistently and manifestly under the influence of the Holy Spirit's power than Charles Spurgeon. The evident anointing of God's Spirit on his preaching infused his sermons with a remarkable spiritual intensity and an arresting sense of the presence of God among the people. His preaching seemed to bring heaven to earth and God to man in ways that were almost tangible. Thousands would remark on the profound sense of conviction that animated Spurgeon and drove his message home to the heart. The sheer drama of his preaching could be so imposing as to affect within his hearers the most ardent feelings of awe, worship, reverence, fear, longing, conviction, hope, and joy.

Finally, his sermons were rendered so effective to so many thousands of people because of their popular style. Spurgeon did not speak in the stuffy and stultified prose of professors in the lecture hall, but in the frank and direct language of the common man on the street. He was eminently a preacher of the people. His sermons were marked by a kind of simplicity, clarity, and candor that were wonderfully refreshing to the masses of ordinary men and women who felt they had been discounted and forgotten by the religious establishment of the day. His sermons spoke directly to the heart of the people and engaged the concerns of their souls with familiar warmth and pastoral tenderness. He was a preacher *for them*. He took to himself the spiritual and emotional burdens of his hearers and made them his own. He endeavored to preach sermons that took into view the people's deepest needs and anxieties and sought to bring to them the hope of the gospel in ways that were genuinely and experientially useful to them. He spoke to his congregations with the kind of openness, sincerity, and forthrightness one would expect when being addressed by an old and dear friend. Such preaching was, in the best sense, relevant. It could also be positively exhilarating. The mid-Victorian context was oversaturated with cerebral sermons and sterile discourses that seemed far removed from the lives of everyday people. Within this context, Spurgeon's preaching came to the people of London with peculiar force and power and seemed to rouse them from their long spiritual slumber.

These qualities, along with others that will be identified in this biography, coalesced to make Spurgeon's preaching exceptionally compelling. He was unequaled among his contemporaries during his lifetime and has been without a match since. He stands altogether in a class of his own as a preacher of exceptional brilliance.

Spurgeon the Pastor-Theologian

Spurgeon was not a theologian in the classical sense. That is to say, he was not a credentialed professor of theology who taught divinity and penned extensive works on Christian doctrine. Nonetheless, he ought to be regarded as a theologian in a more general sense as a minister who studied theology carefully, contributed to theological discussions and debates, and articulated a theological vision for himself and his church that was historical, confessional, and pastoral. Spurgeon was well read in the early church fathers, the Reformers, the Puritans, and leading evangelical divines. He also read extensively in contemporary theological and exegetical literature and provided numerous reviews of much of what he read in the *Sword and the Trowel*. What's more, he established his own ministerial training college known as the Pastors' College, which educated students in systematic theology, church history, biblical languages, metaphysics, and classics, among other subjects. Spurgeon himself taught pastoral theology at the school and helped to oversee the college's curriculum.

Spurgeon's theology may be described as historic orthodox, Protestant, Calvinistic, Baptist, and evangelical. In the late 1880s, he mounted his most famous defense of evangelical orthodoxy in the Downgrade Controversy (considered in chapter 13). But as early as the 1860s, many were already looking to him as a leading spokesman for evangelical belief. He championed matters of central importance to evangelicals such as preaching the biblical gospel, the centrality of the cross, the necessity of new birth, and the inspiration and authority of the Bible. Beyond these more foundational doctrinal issues, Spurgeon was also willing to be quite vocal and outspoken about some of his personal theological distinctives. He happily identified with the Particular Baptist tradition and led his church to affirm the Second London Baptist Confession of 1689, which had been largely forgotten among Baptists of the day. He gloried in the Reformation, treasured his Puritan heritage, and celebrated Calvinistic doctrine in full public view.

Spurgeon's theology permeated his preaching. He believed fervently that faithful preaching should be rigorously doctrinal and that the preacher should make it his aim to steadily acquaint his people with the major doctrines of the Bible over time. He modeled this in his own preaching as he regularly unfolded important doctrines such as God's holiness, human depravity, the covenant of grace, the exclusivity of Christ, penal substitutionary atonement, divine sovereignty, effectual call, and the doctrine of the Holy Spirit. His preaching was rich in theological content and regularly brought before his hearers the most important and essential doctrines of the Christian faith.

Spurgeon might best be regarded as a pastor-theologian—one who sought to organize, integrate, and articulate his theology within the framework of a vibrant and multidimensional pastoral ministry. He developed his theology principally in his preaching, but it was also worked out in other arenas of his ministry. He deployed his theology chiefly to edify the people of God and to fortify the church's evangelistic witness. He believed theology ought to serve the spiritual formation of believers. Therefore, he equipped the members of his flock with a robust doctrinal vision that shaped their piety, enlarged their view of God and His grace, and helped them to live faithfully in the world as followers of Jesus.

Spurgeon the Man
What is perhaps still more striking about Spurgeon is that behind all his extraordinary fruitfulness as a preacher and a pastor, he was a deeply pious man. He studied experimental godliness, dedicated himself to prayer, and cultivated rich personal fellowship with God. Unassailable in integrity, zealous for good works, and unfailing in

public and private devotion, Spurgeon provided a compelling model to the many hundreds of ministers who admired his example and sought to follow in his trail. Spurgeon knew the test of a minister ultimately lay not in what he was before the gazing eye of the public but in who he was in private, hidden from the crowds, before the audience of One.

By all accounts, even those of his opponents, Spurgeon possessed unimpeachable character. In over forty years of public ministry, he lived entirely free from any form of moral scandal, and in 130 years since his death, his faithful testimony has never been stained or brought into disrepute. Spurgeon was known to be a man of unswerving virtue and piety. He was entrusted with staggering authority, leadership, and oversight by tens of thousands of people from the beginning of his adult life, and that trust went unbroken until his death nearly forty years later.

Spurgeon possessed many qualities approximating genius, and they were evident in him from an early age. His prodigious powers of attention, memory, and recall uniquely suited him for his calling and enabled him to attain heights of oratorical and literary ability beyond the reach of ordinary people. He was born with exceptional intellectual endowments and rhetorical gifts that, when accompanied by his tremendous insight into human nature, practically destined him for eminence among the preachers of his day. When it came to administrative brilliance, he was without peer. In natural leadership ability, he excelled. In every room, his was the dominant presence.

In his personality, Spurgeon was an intensely complex man who seemed to embody a striking mix of emotional and psychological contradictions. Though an extreme extrovert and a highly public figure, he could also be retiring, bookish, and inward by disposition. Though a man of abundant confidence, ebullience, and good humor, he struggled with depression all his life and could descend to points of despondency so low that it seemed at times he was sure of nothing at all. He possessed an unusually vast emotional capacity and could move from one pole of the emotional spectrum to the other with tremendous velocity. Spurgeon's astounding transparency about his emotional and spiritual vicissitudes is one of the reasons many today find him to be so relevant. He was truly authentic.

There is no denying Spurgeon was what we today might call a workaholic. He often worked sixteen-hour days and embraced a grueling routine of almost ceaseless activity. This habit was born in part from his temperament and in part from his view of the Christian life. Spurgeon held that a Christian is a worker, a servant, and a soldier and that Christ is his master. All of one's energy should be marshaled and directed toward serving the Lord to the utmost. This perspective played itself out in Spurgeon's life in his often working himself to the point of exhaustion and even severe sickness. From the late 1860s on, Spurgeon required extended annual retreats to the South of France for recovery and recuperation. His attitude toward his work surely contributed to his extraordinary ministerial output over the course of his life, but it also almost certainly played a part in his premature death at the age of fifty-seven.

Why Another Biography?

Spurgeon has been the subject of numerous biographies, but surprisingly few of significant quality. After his death in 1892, at least one new biography of him appeared in print every month for the next two years. Most of these accounts, written as they were by friends and acquaintances, are heavy on warm reminiscences but light on thoughtful analysis and interpretation. As is often the case with biographies that lack sufficient distance from the death of their subject, these accounts fail to assess Spurgeon's life and overall influence with adequate depth and historical insight. Of these early biographies, the best contribution is G. Holden Pike's (originally) six-volume work, *The Life and Works of Charles Haddon Spurgeon*.[19] It is far too long and cumbersome for a popular readership, however.

---

19. G. Holden Pike, *The Life and Works of Charles Haddon Spurgeon*, 6 vols. (London: Cassell, 1894).

A seminal work that appeared a few years later is what is usually referred to as Spurgeon's autobiography, compiled and edited by his wife, Susannah, and personal secretary, Joseph Harrald. Originally published in four volumes, the autobiography is the ultimate textbook for students of Spurgeon. It provides tremendous insight into his personal perspectives on his life, his ministry, his trials, his successes, his experiences of grace, and his walk with God. Again, at well over one thousand pages, it is not an especially accessible resource to most Christians today.

In the early twentieth century, two biographies stand out for their quality: W. Y. Fullerton's *C. H. Spurgeon: A Biography* (1920) and J. C. Carlile's *C. H. Spurgeon: An Interpretive Biography* (1933). Both authors knew Spurgeon personally and provided sympathetic and admiring portraits of the man that include several interesting anecdotes. Sadly, both are out of print today.

The first scholarly biography of Spurgeon appeared in 1982 with Patricia Kruppa's *Charles Haddon Spurgeon: A Preacher's Progress*,[20] which broke significant new ground in Spurgeon studies. But the biography is problematic in numerous ways and ultimately offers a distorted view of Spurgeon that cannot be commended as a fair or accurate portrait of the man. A decade later, Lewis Drummond put forth a massive biography titled *Spurgeon: The Prince of Preachers*.[21] Beyond its excessive length (nearly nine hundred pages), Drummond's work is seriously flawed, replicating numerous errors from previous accounts and introducing new ones of his own. Though in some way helpful, his biography cannot be safely endorsed as a reliable guide to Spurgeon's life.

---

20. Patricia Stallings Kruppa, *Charles Haddon Spurgeon: A Preacher's Progress* (New York: Garland, 1982).

21. Lewis A. Drummond, *Spurgeon: Prince of Preachers*, 3rd ed. (Grand Rapids: Kregel, 1992).

The best short biography of Spurgeon is Arnold Dallimore's fine treatment, simply titled *Spurgeon: A New Biography*.[22] Dallimore's work should be commended for providing a useful and edifying introduction to Spurgeon's life that is broadly accessible to a wider readership. Often when asked to recommend a single biography of Spurgeon, Dallimore's is the first I mention. Yet his account is also limited in certain respects.

First, Dallimore's biography unfortunately contains some errors and inaccuracies that, though few, impair our understanding of Spurgeon at crucial points. The clearest example of this is his account of the Downgrade Controversy, which contains some factual mistakes and confuses the order of events, leading to a somewhat flawed picture of this pivotally important episode in Spurgeon's life. Furthermore, his biography is now nearly forty years old. Thus, it does not take into view the explosion of interest in Spurgeon both at the popular and scholarly level since the 1980s.[23] There have been more doctoral dissertations written on Spurgeon in the last twenty-five years than there were in the previous century. Moreover, the contemporary resurgence of interest in Calvinism and Reformed theology, which became most visible in the early 2000s in the "young, restless, and reformed" movement, seems to have had a particular fascination with Spurgeon's ministry and theology. Conferences like Together for the Gospel, online platforms like the Gospel Coalition, and seminaries like the Southern Baptist Theological Seminary in Louisville, Kentucky, have lauded Spurgeon as a theological hero of sorts and have drawn considerable attention to his life and legacy.

---

22. Arnold Dallimore, *Spurgeon: A New Biography* (Edinburgh: Banner of Truth, 1985).

23. Some of the best published scholarly works on Spurgeon have appeared in the last twenty years and include Mark Hopkins, *Nonconformity's Romantic Generation: Evangelical and Liberal Theologies in Victorian England* (Eugene, Ore.: Wipf and Stock, 2006); Peter J. Morden, *Communion with Christ and His People: The Spirituality of C. H. Spurgeon* (Eugene, Ore.: Pickwick, 2013); and Thomas Breimaier, *Tethered to the Cross: The Life and Preaching of C. H. Spurgeon* (Downers Grove, Ill.: IVP Academic, 2020).

Furthermore, the launching of the Spurgeon Center at Midwestern Baptist Theological Seminary in Kansas City, Missouri, just in the last decade, has provoked new interest in Spurgeon as well. With its vast archival collections, hundreds of digital resources, and numerous conferences and events, the Spurgeon Center has become the global hub for Spurgeon studies. As a result of all of these developments, new books about previously underresearched aspects of Spurgeon's life and ministry are flying off the press.

Among newer books on Spurgeon, some stand out for special commendation. Peter Morden has provided a superb examination of Spurgeon's spirituality in his book *Communion with Christ and His People*.[24] Michael Reeves's *Spurgeon on the Christian Life* offers an illuminating examination of the core tenets of Spurgeon's thought.[25] Ray Rhodes has written a fine treatment of the Spurgeon marriage in *Yours, till Heaven*.[26] Geoff Chang's *Spurgeon the Pastor* is a superlative study of Spurgeon's vision for pastoral ministry and church life.[27] I myself have made an effort at contributing to this growing body of literature in my book *Spurgeon and the Poor*, which explores Spurgeon's understanding of the relationship between the gospel and social ministry.[28] Each of these books has charted new ground in the arena of Spurgeon studies. Needless to say, in the 130 years since Spurgeon's death, we are still learning new things about him!

The biography in your hands is my attempt to provide a new portrait of Spurgeon that makes some improvements over previous accounts of his life and also takes into view many of the new

---

24. Peter J. Morden, *Communion with Christ and His People: The Spirituality of C. H. Spurgeon* (Eugene, Ore.: Pickwick Publications, 2013).

25. Michael Reeves, *Spurgeon on the Christian Life: Alive in Christ* (Wheaton, Ill.: Crossway, 2018).

26. Ray Rhodes Jr., *Yours, till Heaven: The Untold Love Story of Charles and Susie Spurgeon* (Chicago: Moody, 2021).

27. Geoffrey Chang, *Spurgeon the Pastor: Recovering a Biblical and Theological Vision for Ministry* (Nashville: B&H Academic, 2022).

28. Alex DiPrima, *Spurgeon and the Poor: How the Gospel Compels Christian Social Concern* (Grand Rapids: Reformation Heritage Books, 2023).

studies and new data now available to historians and researchers. I have also endeavored to write within the context of the resurgent popular interest in Spurgeon, which grew rapidly beginning in the 1990s and continues apace at the time of this volume's publication. I have aimed at a warm, accessible, and edifying introduction to Spurgeon's life. I intend it not primarily for the academy but for the church. My aim is not merely to inform but to edify and encourage. I wrote this biography for my friends, my family, my church, my community, and the wider Christian world. I wrote it for a new generation of Christians who may not yet be well acquainted with the life of Charles Haddon Spurgeon. I hope it will make its way into the hands of pastors and laypeople alike, of those who typically enjoy history and those who don't, and of people familiar with Spurgeon and especially those who aren't.

There are a few features of this biography that I hope will immediately stand out to the reader. The first is that I attempt a chronological narrative that is meant not only to be practically useful for organizing the major events and episodes of Spurgeon's life but also to serve as an interpretive account that helps readers gain insight into Spurgeon's thought, character, and personality. Second, I aim to spotlight Spurgeon the man, with the hope that he emerges from this narrative as a living and breathing person—one whom readers can know, access, and touch and with whom they can empathize. Finally, as will become clear, I have not hesitated to draw what I regard to be important lessons from Spurgeon's life for Christians today. At times I am content to allow these lessons to be implicit, and at other points I do not resist the urge to make them explicit.

I ask my readers to remember that this volume is meant to be an introduction to Spurgeon's life. As such, I have aimed to keep it to a manageable size conducive to my ends. Thus, I have had to leave a great deal of material behind so that the book would not become too overgrown and unwieldy. The process of determining what material to exclude has been exceedingly painful. I can only console myself with the hope that readers will eventually go beyond this volume to other books that will open up dimensions of Spurgeon's life and work in greater depth.

My desire and prayer are that this consideration of Spurgeon's life will excite greater appreciation for this extraordinary man of God, as well as a deeper love for the glorious Savior who captivated Spurgeon's heart and life. Spurgeon was altogether absorbed in the person and work of Jesus Christ. His entire life and ministry were devoted to the singular object of preaching the gospel of the cross and calling sinners everywhere to place their hope and trust in the blood of Christ. This biography, then, aims to help readers look through Spurgeon to behold the Lord Jesus in His matchless perfection, His all-sufficiency, and His tender love toward needy sinners.

1

Essex Lad

Who we are and who we were will always be, in some way, indissolubly linked. Our past is a key to our present and a kind of prophecy about our future. That is why the further we go into the future, the more we desire a greater acquaintance with our past and the more insight we gain into our present.

In May 1891 Charles Spurgeon traveled by carriage over fifty miles from his home in south London to rural Essex to visit the village where he was raised. Though he was in poor health, he insisted on making the journey to the home of his ancestors. He would die less than a year later on January 31, 1892. Inspired by this visit, Spurgeon penned a personal memoir of his early childhood days called *Memories of Stambourne*.[1] This short book, later adapted to become part of Spurgeon's autobiography compiled by his wife, Susannah, and his personal secretary, Joseph Harrald, provides tremendous insight into Spurgeon's childhood. He felt he had to make this journey and write this book because he realized what many often come to understand only in their older age—insight into one's childhood can unlock all kinds of secrets and, in a sense, introduce us to ourselves. As one of Spurgeon's favorite poets, William Wordsworth, put it, "The child is father of the man."

---

1. C. H. Spurgeon, *Memories of Stambourne* (New York: American Tract Society, 1891).

Spurgeon Country

Stambourne, where Spurgeon spent his earliest boyhood days, was a humble hamlet nestled in the fields and meadows of the county of Essex in the heart of East Anglia. The English novelist H. G. Wells provided this charming description of Essex:

> There is a gap in the suburbs of London. The suburbs of London stretch west and south, and even west by north, but to the north-eastward there are no suburbs; instead there is Essex. Essex is not a suburban county; it is a characteristic and individualised country which wins the heart.... Once you are away from the main Great Eastern lines, Essex still lives in the peace of the eighteenth century, and London, the modern Babylon, is, like the stars, just a light in the nocturnal sky.... This country is a part of the real England—England outside London and outside manufacture. And it's the essential England still.[2]

Essex constituted a low-lying rural region far away from the hustle and bustle of the main metropolitan centers of England. As a boy, Spurgeon would have felt himself far removed from city life and the major affairs of men. He grew up around the humble and honest people of the country, whose daily anxieties seldom rose above concern for their chickens' egg production. His pleasant upbringing in these environs would always prejudice him against the city and leave him regularly pining after the green pastures and quiet woods of his boyhood days. The evangelical poet and hymn writer William Cowper famously declared, "God made the country and man made the town." As one who reveled in God's absolute sovereignty and providence over all things, Spurgeon might have critiqued this line on theological grounds. Nonetheless, the poetic sentiment of Cowper's statement would have resonated with Spurgeon. For Spurgeon, the country of East Anglia would always be home in a way the city never could be.

---

2. H. G. Wells, *Mr. Britling Sees It Through* (New York: Macmillan, 1916), 6, 30.

The Spurgeon family had been associated with that region of the country for centuries. As best we can tell, there were Spurgeons in Essex going back to the days of the boy king Edward VI, who came to the throne in 1547 at the age of nine. Under his rule, Archbishop Thomas Cranmer reshaped English religious life, bequeathing to the newly established Church of England its seminal texts, the Thirty-Nine Articles and the Book of Common Prayer.[3] Until that time, England had been a Roman Catholic country, but through the help of Cranmer and others, the nation embraced reformation. Though England briefly reverted to Catholic rule under Mary I (known to history as Bloody Mary), and though Cranmer would die a martyr's death in Oxford under Mary's reign, the Anglican Church would eventually be reestablished under Elizabeth I and would endure thereafter. The state church in England would be a truly Protestant church at last, and Cranmer's doctrinal and liturgical standards would continue to shape the national church's life and worship for centuries to come.

A Puritan Heritage

Spurgeon's family would never identify with the Church of England. The Spurgeons were Nonconformists through and through. The Nonconformists (sometimes referred to as Dissenters) were those Protestants in England who refused to give their allegiance to the

---

3. The terms *Church of England*, *Anglican Church*, and *established church* are essentially synonymous and refer to the state church in England. The Church of England officially broke off from the Roman Catholic Church in 1534 after Parliament passed the Act of Supremacy, which made King Henry VIII the "Supreme Head of the Church in England." But the Church of England remained basically Roman Catholic in character until Henry's death in 1547. From 1547 to 1553, under the reign of Edward VI, the Church of England began to look more properly Protestant in character. Mary I's reign from 1553 to 1558, however, violently wrenched the church back to its earlier Catholicism. After Mary's death, her half sister, Elizabeth I, took the throne in 1558, and the Church of England became thoroughly and abidingly Protestant through the second Act of Supremacy and what came to be known as the Elizabethan Religious Settlement. Elizabeth's long and prosperous reign of over four decades solidified England's Protestant commitment.

Anglican Church. They were the Presbyterians, the Congregationalists, the Baptists, and other denominational bodies who could
not in good conscience affirm all the articles of the state church
or simply objected to the idea of a state church in the first place.
This divide between official Anglicanism and the other Protestant
denominations in England would become the most significant
divide in English religious life from the early seventeenth century
to the present day. Generally speaking, the Church of England
looked down on Nonconformity. Nonconformists, for their part,
resented Anglicanism.

For centuries Nonconformists were, as they saw it, second-class
citizens in England, denied certain rights enjoyed by their Anglican counterparts, such as the opportunity to serve in Parliament or
the freedom to pursue an education at England's elite universities.
This is to say nothing of the compulsory tax they were required to
pay to support the erection and maintenance of the Anglican par-
ish churches. In the seventeenth century, the man Spurgeon believed
to be his great-grandfather's great-grandfather, Job Spurgeon, even
spent a few months in prison simply for attending a Nonconformist
meeting.[4] "The record of his family," writes Patricia Kruppa, "was for
Spurgeon a source of personal inspiration and a constant reminder of
the tyranny of religious establishments."[5] When Spurgeon was born
in 1834, Nonconformists had just been granted the right to serve
in political office a few years earlier. It would not be until 1871 that
the final restrictions were lifted for Nonconformists seeking degrees
from Oxford and Cambridge, those oldest and most prestigious of
England's universities. Spurgeon would have to wait until 1880 to be
granted the right to bury his church members in public graveyards
without being required to use the Anglican burial rites.[6] Though
Spurgeon would acknowledge that he had many Christian brothers

---

4. Fullerton, *C. H. Spurgeon: A Biography*, 2.
5. Kruppa, *Charles Haddon Spurgeon: A Preacher's Progress*, 11.
6. C. H. Spurgeon, "The Burials' Bill," *Sword and the Trowel* (October 1880): 506.

and sisters among the established church, he would nonetheless wrestle with that body and advocate for its official disestablishment throughout his entire life.

Nonconformity was in Spurgeon's background and in his blood. He gloried in his Nonconformist heritage and felt keenly the disadvantages he labored under as a Dissenter. He would always maintain the kind of pride that is the unique possession of those who feel they have been persecuted simply for being in the right. He felt as though he inherited an ancient nobility sired by conviction without any shred of compromise. He once remarked, "I had far rather be descended from one who suffered for the faith, than bear the blood of all the emperors in my veins."[7] Spurgeon felt his Nonconformity deeply, and he bristled as he endured regular reminders of the distinction between him and those who called the Church of England their mother. He would never relent from the certainty that he was right, and they were wrong.

In the centuries before Spurgeon's birth, East Anglia had become a Puritan stronghold in England.[8] The Puritans, most of whom eventually became Nonconformists, sought to purify the Church of England by laboring for the further reform of the church's life, worship, and doctrine.[9] Puritanism's birth can be dated roughly to the beginning of Elizabeth I's reign in 1558. Disappointed with the Elizabethan Religious Settlement, the Puritans advocated for a fuller reformation of the Anglican Church. Their concern was that though England had become a Protestant country, reform had not yet had its full effect on the nation. They looked longingly at the progress of reformation on the Continent in places like John Calvin's Geneva and Martin Bucer's Strasbourg. After a tumultuous century that saw

---

7. Fullerton, *C. H. Spurgeon: A Biography*, 2.

8. Morden, *Communion with Christ and His People*, 20–21.

9. For an introduction to the Puritan movement, see Joel Beeke and Michael Reeves, *Following God Fully: An Introduction to the Puritans* (Grand Rapids: Reformation Heritage Books, 2022); and J. I. Packer, *A Quest for Godliness: The Puritan Vision of the Christian Life* (Wheaton, Ill.: Crossway, 1990).

widespread persecution of the Puritans, a civil war that engulfed the entire nation, and a brief Puritan reign under the Lord Protector, Oliver Cromwell, the Puritans were finally outed as religious ren-egades in 1662 after the passing of the Act of Uniformity.[10] Puritan ministers were ejected from their churches, and from then on, their influence in England radically diminished. But their ideals were still in the air in the Essex countryside at the time of Spurgeon's birth. East Anglia had at one time been the home of Puritan greats such as John Owen, Thomas Goodwin, and "Roaring" John Rogers. Just as Puritanism had descended on London from the east country in the seventeenth century, so in the nineteenth century the cause would be renewed, this time by a single preacher whose advent was entirely unhailed and unforeseen.

Birth and Move to Stambourne

Charles Haddon Spurgeon was born on June 19, 1834, in Kelvedon, Essex, to John and Eliza Spurgeon. He was the first of seventeen chil-dren, only eight of whom survived infancy.[11] Though Spurgeon rarely commented on the premature death of his siblings, it nonetheless must have shaped his sense of the brevity of life, the reality of death, and the urgency of eternity. Spurgeon's father, John, earned a living as a clerk in a coal merchant's office. He also served churches as a Con-gregationalist lay preacher, which often involved itinerating around the countryside, sometimes for many miles, to fulfill a distant preach-ing engagement. Eliza devoted herself to the care and nurture of her

---

10. The Act of Uniformity required all England's ministers to subscribe to the primary confessional documents of the Church of England, particularly the Book of Common Prayer. The Puritans could not do this in good conscience and were thus legally barred from serving in their churches until the Act of Toleration in 1688.

11. Morden, *C. H. Spurgeon: The People's Preacher*, 15. It was not uncommon for children to die in infancy in the Victorian era; the infant mortality rate was right around 30 percent the year Spurgeon was born. To lose nine children out of seven-teen, however, would have been quite unusual and far beyond the normal experience of most families.

children. Her extraordinary influence on Charles was a major force in his spiritual formation, but this is to get ahead of the story.

The home in Kelvedon, Essex, where Spurgeon was born on June 19, 1834

When Spurgeon was about fourteen months old, in 1835, his parents sent him to live with his grandparents in the village of Stambourne.[12] He would live there until age six. Spurgeon's long removal to Stambourne seems to be the result of a severe financial crisis facing his parents. Before becoming a clerk, John Spurgeon was a grocer. In 1835 he embarked on a new business venture, opening a grocery store in Raleigh, Essex. He encountered tremendous challenges, however, in his efforts to get the business up and running. By January 1837, John was in dire financial straits. His business had utterly failed, and he was unable to pay his creditors, leading him to forfeit his house and all his earthly possessions in an effort to pay off his loans. In the end, he was forced to spend six weeks in jail in Chelmsford from January 30 to March 14, 1837, while he continued to settle his debts. When he was released, he and his family were

---

12. Morden, *C. H. Spurgeon: The People's Preacher*, 15.

utterly destitute. The Spurgeons would slowly rebuild their lives in Colchester, however, where John was given honest work as a clerk, and over time the family was able to recover some level of basic financial stability.[13]

Spurgeon's mother,
Eliza Spurgeon

Spurgeon's father,
John Spurgeon

Charles never mentioned the difficulties his family faced during these years, likely because he wished to hide his father's shame and protect the family's reputation. Moreover, he simply was not present in the home during this time of great difficulty since he was living with his grandparents in Stambourne. Though the crisis of these early years represented a painful trial for the Spurgeon family, Charles would always trace the sovereign purposes of God in his removal to his grandparents' home and would view this chapter of his upbringing as pivotal in setting the course for the rest of his life.

Spurgeon described Stambourne as giving him "a sense of being out of the world, and having nothing particular to do,"[14] which offered

---

13. Geoffrey Chang, "New Insights into the Formative Influence of Spurgeon's Early Years," *Themelios* 47, no. 3 (December 2022): 500–512.

14. Spurgeon, *Memories of Stambourne*, 16.

the perfect setting for the boy to create some of his most cherished childhood memories. Recollecting these early days, he reminisced,

> Oh, the old house at home! Who does not love it, the place of our childhood, the old roof-tree, the old cottage? There is no other village in all the world half so good as that particular village!… We like to see the haunts of our boyhood. There is something pleasant in those old stairs where the clock used to stand; and in the room where grandmother was wont to bend her knee, and where we had family prayer. There is no place like that house after all.[15]

Even at the end of his life, Spurgeon was able to recount the precise positioning of the furniture and the details of the pictures that hung on the wall of the little manse at Stambourne over fifty years earlier. Throughout his life, Spurgeon would live in large houses, preach in massive auditoriums, and visit the stately homes of some of the great men of the day. Yet the cramped rooms and narrow halls of the humble manse would always remain the most hallowed ground to him.

Charles's grandfather, James Spurgeon, was a Congregationalist preacher who pastored a small congregation that met in the village meetinghouse next door to the manse. James was born the year America declared its independence, and he moved to Stambourne in 1810 to pastor the church, which he faithfully shepherded for over a half century

Spurgeon's grandfather, James Spurgeon

until his death in 1864.[16] Spurgeon's grandmother, Sarah, along with his Aunt Ann, shared the role of mother to Spurgeon while he stayed in his grandparents' home.

---

15. *C. H. Spurgeon's Autobiography*, 1:13.
16. Spurgeon, *Memories of Stambourne*, 54–55.

The enormity of James's influence on Charles cannot be over-stated. During Spurgeon's boyhood, no one loomed larger in his world than his grandfather. In the section of his autobiography that treats these years, Spurgeon recounts with warmth and affection many happy memories. He tells of pleasant evenings at the dinner table when James would lead the household in family devotions. These occasions often included a healthy dose of inquisitive questions from Charles over whatever biblical text was considered that evening. Spurgeon loved opportunities to accompany his grandfather in his pastoral work, and it is easy to imagine young Charles eagerly taking up the role of the old man's little assistant.

From a spiritual standpoint, it was James's preaching that most affected Spurgeon. Evidently James was an able preacher who delivered his sermons with a sense of both pastoral tenderness and evangelical fervor. Spurgeon wrote, "Buildings may perish, and new shrines may succeed them; but no earthly house will accommodate a sounder or more useful ministry than that of my grandfather."[17] Spurgeon's accounts of his grandfather's sermons, which he would have heard as a small child, remind us of an important lesson Christians today can perhaps forget: children develop their earliest notions of subjects such as God, sin, eternity, judgment, Christ, grace, and salvation at early ages. Once formed, these associations are hard to alter. Spurgeon's own impressions of these grand issues took their form chiefly through his grandfather's preaching, and they shaped his inner world. Reverence for the holiness of God, conviction of sin, and a hunger for salvation in Christ came early for him precisely because he was introduced to serious Bible preaching at a young age. His grandfather's sermons awakened within Spurgeon an appetite for spiritual things and proved foundational to all that Spurgeon would ever be and do in service to Christ's kingdom. One wonders how many more children would develop such spiritual longings for

---

17. *C. H. Spurgeon's Autobiography*, 1:31.

the things of God if they were exposed to similar preaching at an early age.

Yet there was at least one more gift of special magnificence that James Spurgeon bequeathed to his grandson while he lived under his grandparents' roof. James was a lover of books and owned a respectable library that contained many volumes by the Puritans. Some of these volumes he kept in a dark little den in the manse. It was in this small den that Spurgeon was introduced to men who, through their writings, would become some of his most treasured companions throughout the rest of his life. He wrote, "Here I first struck up acquaintance with the martyrs…next with Bunyan and his 'Pilgrim'; and further on, with the great masters of Scriptural theology, with whom no moderns are worthy to be named in the same day…. Out of that darkened room I fetched those old authors when I was yet a youth, and never was I happier than when in their company."[18]

So it was, as only a young boy, that Spurgeon began to develop an admiration for Puritan authors. This appreciation for the Puritans would eventually become one of the hallmarks of his entire life and ministry and would one day lead the British prime minister William Gladstone to pronounce Spurgeon the "Last of the Puritans."[19] Spurgeon would eventually have one of the largest Puritan libraries in the world and would become one of the main standard-bearers for Puritan theology in the nineteenth century.[20] But at this early stage, it was simply a boy's delight at the discovery of hidden treasures in a dark, forgotten den in a remote corner of the world.

---

18. *C. H. Spurgeon's Autobiography*, 1:23.

19. Christian T. George, "A Man Behind His Time," in *The Lost Sermons of C. H. Spurgeon: His Earliest Outlines and Sermons Between 1851 and 1854*, ed. Christian T. George (Nashville: B&H Academic, 2016), 1:18. For a consideration of Spurgeon's Puritanism, see Morden, *Communion with Christ and His People*, 16–46.

20. Spurgeon had roughly twelve thousand volumes in his personal library, which featured hundreds of books by Puritan authors. Today, about half of Spurgeon's library (all that has survived), including many of his most treasured Puritan books, is housed at the Spurgeon Library on the campus of Midwestern Baptist Theological Seminary in Kansas City, Missouri.

A Portrait of a Boy

Though it could certainly be said that Spurgeon was somewhat bookish as a child, he was by no means dull. As a boy Spurgeon was precocious, confident, and spirited. He was unusually zealous in the pursuit of a cause that gripped his small heart, and he could be quite bold, even before adults and authority figures. These traits were all manifestly displayed in an episode that might have portended something of his future in ministry. A member of James Spurgeon's congregation named Thomas Roads liked to frequent the local pub, much to the grief of his pastor. Observing his grandfather's distress over the straying member of his flock, Charles announced, "I'll kill old Roads, that I will!" Though James rebuked his grandson for such a heinous declaration, Spurgeon nonetheless protested, "I shall do nothing bad; but I'll kill him though, that I will." All James could do was chide his grandson for speaking so, but he nonetheless remained puzzled as to the boy's intentions. Then one day Spurgeon walked into the house and declared, "I've killed old Roads; he'll never grieve my dear grandpa anymore." James was naturally shocked and alarmed and insisted that Spurgeon tell him what he had done. All Spurgeon could say was, "I've been about the Lord's work, that's all."

Soon after, "old Roads" showed up at his pastor's home, and all became clear. Roads recounted,

> I was a-sitting in the public just having my pipe and mug of beer, when that child comes in — to think an old man like me should be took to task, and reproved by a bit of a child like that! Well, he points at me with his finger, just so, and says, "What doest thou here, Elijah? Sitting with the ungodly, and you a member of a church, and breaking your pastor's heart. I'm ashamed of you! I wouldn't break my pastor's heart, I'm sure." And then he walks away. Well, I did feel angry, but I knew it was all true, and I was guilty, so I put down my pipe, and did not touch my beer, but hurried away to a lonely spot, and cast myself down before the Lord, confessing my sin and begging for forgiveness. And I do know and believe the Lord in mercy

pardoned me; and now I've come to ask you to forgive me; and I'll never grieve you any more, my dear pastor.[21]

Youthful courage and pluck were characteristic of Spurgeon throughout his teenage years and into his twenties. When affected with a sense of righteousness, Spurgeon could be extraordinarily determined in the pursuit of his cause. If he felt he was on the side of truth, he believed he had every right to proceed undaunted and resolute. This childhood trait would display itself at a number of crucial points in Spurgeon's ministry.

Alongside his boyish confidence, Spurgeon possessed a playful curiosity and adventurous nature. He loved to go exploring in the woods behind the Stambourne meetinghouse and delighted in the occasional village fox hunt. When the manse was overcome by an infestation of rats, Spurgeon proudly hunted them for his grandfather for a shilling a dozen. When he later returned home to his parents' house in Colchester, he loved to be the ringleader in his siblings' games.

Though Spurgeon was confident, adventurous, and playful, he also possessed a more quiet and sensitive side and could be unusually cautious for a young boy growing up in the country. He was often anxious in the presence of large animals and did not feel comfortable riding horses. He did not enjoy playing sports with other boys and preferred to read or go off exploring on his own. He took pleasure in solitude and said, "To be quite alone was my boyish heaven."[22] His father remembered, "He was always reading books—never digging in the garden or keeping pigeons, like other boys. It was always books and books. If his mother wanted to take him for a ride, she would be sure to find him in my study poring over a book."[23] He felt intimidated by large assemblies and would often become overwhelmed by too much company. For most of his life, he would get nervous

---

21. *C. H. Spurgeon's Autobiography*, 1:24.
22. *C. H. Spurgeon's Autobiography*, 1:30.
23. Pike, *Life and Works of Charles Haddon Spurgeon*, 1:17.

crossing busy streets and was often anxious in large crowds (something the Prince of Preachers never had a chance of avoiding).[24]

Moreover, as a child, Spurgeon possessed a vivid imagination and could sometimes torture himself with highly realistic visions of hell and eternal torment. These ideations would often produce the most intense inner anxieties of the soul. In the grace and providence of God, it was precisely these inward reflections that eventually led him to cry out to God for mercy and salvation. This quality could sometimes hurt as well as help him, however. When put to its best use, Spurgeon's keen interiority could nurture the most intimate communion with God and profound insights into the spiritual realm. At its worst, it could become a kind of morbid introspection that could at times sap Spurgeon of his sense of the love of God and his assurance of salvation. Positively, this trait contributed greatly to his effectiveness as a preacher, as he was able to draw on deep spiritual intuitions and insights to help his hearers go deeper with God. Negatively, it could abet his severe struggles with melancholy and depression. It is precisely this aspect of Spurgeon's personality that makes him relatable to so many today. His inward disposition, psychological vulnerability, and familiarity with the range of emotional vacillations that are so much a part of human experience have the effect of making him accessible even to people today who are more than a century removed from him.

The storied Victorian novelist Charles Dickens was a contemporary of Spurgeon. His books were wildly popular even in his own day, and Spurgeon owned a complete set of his works. If there is anything to be gleaned from Dickens's novels, it is that children are capable of deep feeling, and their earliest experiences often shape them in profound ways. Whether it was in *Great Expectations*, *David Copperfield*, or *Oliver Twist*, Dickens, in a manner ahead of his time, dignified childhood and emphasized the personhood of children, who were too often seen as incidental members of society in

---

24. Kruppa, *Charles Haddon Spurgeon: A Preacher's Progress*, 34.

Victorian England. Like the children in Dickens's novels, Spurgeon had a complex and rich inner life as a boy and was capable of powerful feelings and profound emotions, even as a small child.

The overall portrait we get of Spurgeon in these early years is of a boy who was spiritually serious, sincere, and earnest. He was adventurous and confident and yet was in some ways cautious and insecure. He loved to read, delighted in nature, and could be profoundly affectionate and loyal toward those he loved. He had an immense capacity to feel and nursed exceptionally deep thoughts of the world and the God who made it. Though the adult Spurgeon would likely be classified as an extrovert (one who draws energy and stimulation from being in the company of others), the boy had the tendency at times to retreat within himself and could be extraordinarily introverted when it suited him.[25]

Eliza Spurgeon

At the age of six, Spurgeon returned to his parents' home, then in Colchester. The Spurgeon family, which had grown by three more children by this time, was now on more solid financial footing. Spurgeon's father was extraordinarily busy in his efforts to provide for the family, and it was left to his mother to care for the children's daily needs.

It's here that we should take stock of the tremendous impact of Eliza Spurgeon on her children, and Charles in particular. In later days, Spurgeon would often highlight the extraordinary influence of his mother on his life. She played a pivotal part in shaping his earliest impressions of the grace of God. Over the years Spurgeon would offer a number of touching tributes to her. In a typical strain, he once wrote,

> I cannot tell you how much I owe to the solemn words of my good mother.... It was the custom on Sunday evenings, while we were yet little children, for her to stay at home with us, and

---

25. Morden, *Communion with Christ and His People*, 20–21.

then we sat round the table and read verse by verse, and she explained the Scripture to us.... Certainly I have not powers of speech with which to set forth my valuation of the choice blessing which the Lord bestowed on me in making me the son of one who prayed *for* me, and prayed *with* me. How can I ever forget her tearful eye when she warned me to escape from the wrath to come?... How can I forget when she bowed her knee, and with her arms about my neck, prayed, "Oh that my son might live before Thee!"[26]

On another occasion when Spurgeon was asked the secret to his success he said, "I can tell you two reasons why I am what I am: my mother and the truth of my message."[27] Eliza's second son, John Archer Spurgeon, who would one day serve as Charles's co-pastor at the Metropolitan Tabernacle in London, said of his mother, "She was the starting point of all the greatness any of us, by the grace of God, have ever enjoyed."[28]

Perhaps one of the greatest tokens of Eliza's faithfulness as a Christian mother was that all eight of her surviving children professed faith in Christ and commended the faithful example of their mother in leading them to Jesus. Spurgeon's father, John, also testified to Eliza's faithful witness before her children, recalling how impressed he was as he "heard her pray for them one by one by name."[29]

Eliza Spurgeon's legacy to her son Charles was to give to him the most dignified and noble view of Christian mothering and female piety. Many of Spurgeon's spiritual heroes were women, and this began with his own mother, whom he esteemed as highly as any

---

26. *C. H. Spurgeon's Autobiography*, 1:68–69.

27. Carlile, *C. H. Spurgeon: An Interpretive Biography*, 24.

28. G. Holden Pike, *James Archer Spurgeon, D.D., L.L.D.: Preacher, Philanthropist, and Co-Pastor with C. H. Spurgeon at the Metropolitan Tabernacle* (London: Alexander and Shepheard, 1894), 20.

29. George Carter Needham, *The Life and Labors of Charles H. Spurgeon: The Faithful Preacher, the Devoted Pastor, the Noble Philanthropist, the Beloved College President, and the Voluminous Writer, Author, Etc., Etc.* (Boston: D. L Guernsey, 1887), 28.

other Christian he ever met. She was heavenly-minded, sensitive to the things of God and the concerns of eternity, and spiritually earnest in her pursuit of holiness. God used these very qualities to excite Spurgeon's growing interest in spiritual things, and they cultivated within him both a seriousness with regard to the state of his soul and an eagerness to have the hope that his mother possessed. Eliza gave to her son the greatest possible gift a mother could give: she made Christ and His gospel appear lovely to him.

Spurgeon's father also had a positive influence on the young boy, but our pictures of him are fewer and dimmer. John Spurgeon was often away working and preaching. He relied on his wife to provide most of the spiritual nurture in the home while he struggled to provide materially for the family. Spurgeon nonetheless maintained a close bond with his father throughout his life and looked to him for spiritual guidance, particularly during his teenage years.

The Move to Cambridge

Though his family faced financial challenges, Spurgeon received as fine an education as a boy of his social standing could hope to receive. In 1849, after attending various schools in Colchester and Maidstone, Spurgeon was sent to board at Newmarket Academy just outside of Cambridge. When Spurgeon arrived, he had just turned fifteen years old. Cambridge and its surrounding environs would provide the scenes for some of the most critical events of his young life.

Spurgeon was a superb student at Newmarket and was especially gifted in science and mathematics. He also achieved a basic proficiency in Latin and Greek. He stood out among his peers and received the enthusiastic commendation of his schoolmasters and teachers. He would eventually become a tutor to younger students, which was an opportunity he relished. Academics came naturally to Spurgeon, and he possessed many qualities that seemed to destine him for eminence and fame. His winsome personality, exceptional mental acuity, and extraordinary rhetorical gifts (which were soon to manifest) were all harbingers of approaching greatness. It is likely that Spurgeon would have succeeded at almost anything he set his mind to in the world of scholarship or industry. What R. T. Kendall said of Martyn Lloyd-Jones in the twentieth century might easily have been said of Spurgeon in the nineteenth century: "We are talking about a genius—a man who might well have become Prime Minister had he gone into politics."[30] But Spurgeon's greatness ultimately did not lie in the political world. That arena would never have any appeal for him.

Later in his life, Spurgeon would associate his time at Newmarket primarily with progress in the things of God rather than in academics. His days in Cambridgeshire were not ultimately preparatory for a career as either a brilliant scholar or politician, but rather they readied him for a lifetime of following Christ and serving Him as a minister of the gospel. The next four years in Cambridge were in many ways the beginning of the rest of his life. He arrived there a boy, spiritually lost and unsure what his future would hold. He would depart a man, transformed by the grace of God and well on his way to becoming the greatest preacher of the age.

---

30. R. T. Kendall, foreword to *Preaching and Preachers*, by Martyn Lloyd-Jones, 40th anniversary ed. (Grand Rapids: Zondervan, 2012), 11–12.

2

"Look and Live"

Spurgeon's childhood was deeply shaped by the gospel. The good news—the message about what God has done in Christ to make a way of salvation for sinners through His incarnation, death, and resurrection—permeated the world in which Spurgeon was reared. It seemed as though he took in gospel preaching with his mother's milk. His grandfather's sermons were rich with evangelical truth and often included fervent gospel appeals. Spurgeon's parents, especially his mother, explained the gospel to him on many occasions and pleaded with their son to close with Christ and embrace the Savior as God's provision for his sins. Spurgeon himself said, "I confess to have been tutored in piety, put into my cradle by prayerful hands, and lulled to sleep by songs concerning Jesus."[1] Yet it wasn't until Spurgeon was fifteen years old that he finally turned from his sin and believed the gospel. One might wonder why, with such an upbringing, it took so long for Spurgeon to embrace the good news.

From one angle, the answer is straightforward. The apostle Paul says in 1 Corinthians 2:14, "But the natural man receiveth not the things of the Spirit of God: for they are foolishness unto him: neither can he know them, because they are spiritually discerned." According to this text, we could simply say Spurgeon was, for years, naturally blind to the truth. He had not yet been born again and given the gifts of repentance and faith and therefore was still in bondage to sin.

1. *C. H. Spurgeon's Autobiography*, 1:102.

Yet from another angle, humanly speaking, one can trace an inward struggle within Spurgeon that delayed his response to the gospel and precipitated a spiritual crisis within him. What was going through his mind and heart in the years leading up to his conversion? What hindered him for years from believing the gospel for himself, and what were the factors that finally led to his conversion?

Doubt and Despair

Spurgeon left behind a substantial memoir of these years in his auto-biography, which documents a protracted spiritual struggle that preceded his conversion in 1850.[2] Particularly from the ages of ten through fifteen, Spurgeon wrestled with intense doubt and despair over the state of his soul. He wrote,

> For five years, as a child, there was nothing before my eyes but my guilt; and though I do not hesitate to say that those who observed my life would not have seen any extraordinary sin, yet as I looked upon myself, there was not a day in which I did not commit such gross, such outrageous sins against God, that often and often have I wished I had never been born.... I reckoned that the most defiled creature, the most loathsome and contemptible, was a better thing than myself, for I had grossly and grievously sinned against Almighty God.[3]

Spurgeon's comments should not be taken as an indication that he committed especially heinous sins as a boy, but rather that he felt the ordinary sins of his life to be exceedingly wicked and enough to separate him from God forever. Even though he struggled so profoundly with a sense of sin and fear of eternal punishment, it does not appear he confided in anyone, not even his parents. He said,

> Children are often very reticent to their parents. Often and often have I spoken with young lads about their souls, and they have told me they could not talk to their fathers upon such

2. *C. H. Spurgeon's Autobiography*, 1:75–96.
3. *C. H. Spurgeon's Autobiography*, 1:80–81.

matters. I know it was so with me. When I was under concern of soul, the last persons I should have elected to speak to upon religion would have been my parents,—not through want of love to them, nor absence of love on their part; but so it was. A strange feeling of diffidence pervades a seeking soul, and drives it from its friends.[4]

Spurgeon grew up with a sensitive conscience. He felt his sin keenly and would regularly confess it freely without any prompting from others. So strong was his sense of sin that he would often cry himself to sleep over thoughts of his native sinfulness and the impending judgment of God against his sin. After such restless nights, he would awake in the morning and immediately reach for solid evangelical books to provide him with hope for his poor soul. He often turned for solace to Puritan classics, such as Joseph Alleine's *Alarm to the Unconverted* or Richard Baxter's *Call to the Unconverted*, and said of these books, "I read and devoured them when under a sense of guilt."[5]

But even though Spurgeon read many good, gospel-centered books and heard many sermons full of gospel truth, he still felt himself enslaved to sin and trapped underneath the judgment of God. His descriptions of this period of torturous introspection mirror those of Christian from Bunyan's *Pilgrim's Progress*, who struggled underneath the massive burden of sin that was on his back. The quotes below capture something of Spurgeon's despair:

When but young in years, I felt with much sorrow the evil of sin. My bones waxed old with my roaring all the day long. Day and night God's hand was heavy upon me. I hungered for deliverance, for my soul fainted within me. I feared lest the very skies should fall upon me, and crush my guilty soul. God's law had laid hold upon me, and was showing me my sins. If I slept

4. *C. H. Spurgeon's Autobiography*, 1:68.
5. *C. H. Spurgeon's Autobiography*, 1:80.

at night, I dreamed of the bottomless pit, and when I awoke, I seemed to feel the misery I had dreamed.[6]

Was there ever a bond-slave who had more bitterness of soul than I, five years a captive in the dungeons of the law, till my youth seemed as if it would turn into premature old age, and all the buoyancy of my spirit had vanished?[7]

Often, during the day, when I had a little time for quiet medita-tion, a great depression of spirit would come upon me because I felt that sin,—*sin*,—sin had outlawed me from my God.... I went to the house of God, and heard what I supposed was the gospel, but it was no gospel to me. My soul abhorred all man-ner of meat; I could not lay hold upon a promise, or indulge a well-grounded hope of salvation. If anyone asked me what would become of me, I must have answered, "I am going down to the pit." If anyone had entreated me to hope that mercy might come to me, I should have refused to entertain such a hope. I used to feel that I was in the condemned cell.[8]

A Theology of Sin

Some readers may pass off these sentiments as the melodramatic exaggerations of youth. Before accepting this portrayal, however, two things must be understood. First, we must remember that Spur-geon wrote these descriptions much later in life. He put them down after many years of reflection on these adolescent experiences and only after he had time to work out a mature understanding of what was going on internally during this time before his conversion. Thus, the quotations above represent his seasoned thoughts on what this period of his life was like.

Second, these quotes, dark as they are, highlight some important aspects of Spurgeon's mature theology of sin, wrath, and judgment.

---

6. *C. H. Spurgeon's Autobiography*, 1:79–80.
7. *C. H. Spurgeon's Autobiography*, 1:82.
8. *C. H. Spurgeon's Autobiography*, 1:85.

Spurgeon believed in the native depravity of the human heart, and thus he saw himself as a wretched sinner in need of the grace of God. He wrote these statements in recognition of the Bible's plain teaching regarding the human condition outside of Christ. Spurgeon embraced what the apostle Paul wrote in Ephesians 2:1–3: "And you hath he quickened, who were dead in trespasses and sins; wherein in time past ye walked according to the course of this world, according to the prince of the power of the air, the spirit that now worketh in the children of disobedience: among whom also we all had our conversation in times past in the lusts of our flesh, fulfilling the desires of the flesh and of the mind; and were by nature the children of wrath, even as others." Spurgeon saw himself in these words. He believed them both theologically and experientially. He never found evidence lacking in the Bible for the doctrine of total depravity, nor did he want for evidence in his own life.

Spurgeon believed not only in human depravity and sin but also in the doctrine of divine wrath and eternal punishment for the wicked outside of Christ. He believed the orthodox doctrine of hell, which he understood to be the just penalty reserved for those who die in their sins. As one who knew himself to be a lost sinner, Spurgeon saw himself as being under God's just condemnation and believed he would inherit the righteous punishment for his sins—namely, eternal hell. Thus, for Spurgeon, sin was the source of all his misery and made him accountable before a holy God whom he was not prepared to meet. He therefore saw his situation as grave and desperate.

To a generation that has long forgotten how to talk about the doctrines of human depravity, divine wrath, and everlasting punishment, this kind of seriousness regarding sin will seem foreign. Moreover, to many today who seem allergic to any kind of sober introspection, Spurgeon's descriptions of his inner life will seem morbid and depressing. But to those who read the Bible honestly and search their hearts sincerely, Spurgeon's attitude toward his sin is the proper response to the scriptural realities of human wickedness and divine judgment. Spurgeon saw himself through the lens of the Bible, and what he saw was a desperate sinner in need of salvation.

How did Spurgeon come to have this view of himself and his spiritual state outside of Christ? Some may assume this was simply a matter of course for children growing up in England in the 1800s and that all children in those days were natively serious and intro-spective. But this would be fiction. The fundamental influences that enabled Spurgeon, even as a child, to see his spiritual condition for what it was were not characteristic of his era nor were they the expe-rience of every boy growing up in England in the mid-nineteenth century. The reason Spurgeon was so profoundly sobered over the state of his soul was because he was taught from an early age the pure and unvarnished truth about his spiritual condition outside of Christ. His parents and grandparents did not shield him from the realities of sin and everlasting punishment but rather taught him these truths from an early age. They did not expose him to these doctrines because they wished to give him a gloomy outlook on life. Rather, out of genuine love, they warned him of the realities of sin and of the wrath to come, and they pointed him to Christ as God's provision for salvation. They knew that apart from a genu-ine realization of his own sinfulness, he would never look to Christ for forgiveness and everlasting life. Thus, they instructed him in the truth even as a young boy, in order that he would believe on Christ and be saved.

Spurgeon's family genuinely believed in eternal realities and in life beyond the grave, and they acted like it. They were heavenly-minded and spoke often of the unseen realm. Growing up in this context, it was not long before Spurgeon was awakened to the truth concerning his spiritual state. One of his biographers, J. C. Carlile, notes, "He was brought up among those who talked about the deeper experiences of the soul as commonplace."[9] Being reared in this envi-ronment had the effect of alerting Spurgeon to realities beyond what

---

9. Carlile, *C. H. Spurgeon: An Interpretive Biography*, 34.

he could touch with his hands and see with his eyes. In a word, it alerted him to God and to eternity.

Struggling On

These inner strivings shaped Spurgeon's perspective on his spiritual state and contributed to the gloom he felt over his sin. Spurgeon struggled on in doubt and despair for five years, and though he continued to hear the message of salvation in Jesus Christ, he failed to lay hold of it. Something about the simplicity of trusting in Christ for the forgiveness of his sins made salvation seem strangely out of his reach:

> How often have I thought that, if he had said, "Bare your back to the scourge, and take fifty lashes"; I would have said, "Here I am! Come along with your whip, and beat as hard as you please, so long as I can obtain peace and rest, and get rid of my sin." Yet that simplest of all matters—believing in Christ crucified, accepting His finished salvation, being nothing, and letting Him be everything, doing nothing but trusting to what He has done,—I could not get a hold of it.[10]

Even on occasions when it occurred to Spurgeon to call out to God for mercy and forgiveness, something always seemed to hinder him from doing so freely. He thought himself unworthy to hope in God's grace and seemed to view it as a kind of sinful presumption to pray to God for deliverance. He thought to himself, "What, *I* approach the throne? Such a wretch as *I* lay hold on the promise? *I* venture to hope that God could look on me? It seemed impossible."[11] And even if he did pray, he felt he had no right to believe God would be willing to hear him. "I thought that the heavens were brass above me, and that if I cried never so earnestly, the Lord would shut out my prayer. I durst not pray, I was too guilty; and when I did dare to pray, 'twas hardly prayer, for I had no hope of being heard."[12]

---

10. *C. H. Spurgeon's Autobiography*, 1:90.
11. *C. H. Spurgeon's Autobiography*, 1:73.
12. *C. H. Spurgeon's Autobiography*, 1:78.

This same feeling of hopelessness cast a pall over Spurgeon's Bible reading. He had the experience, familiar to many before they come to faith, of reading the Bible and finding in it only evidence of his condemnation. "I used to read the Bible through," he said, "and the threatenings were all printed in capitals, but the promises were in such small type I could not for a long time make them out; and when I did read them, I did not believe they were mine; but the threatenings were all my own."[13]

So onward Spurgeon went, feeling himself to be the most helpless and hopeless soul on earth. Though occasional distractions could briefly quiet his sorrows and silence his conscience, he would always eventually recede into the same turmoil of soul. But he knew he must find a way out of the cycle of sin and shame that dominated his life. His acute awareness of his sin had crowded out all his prospects for joy and any hope he had of a fulfilled and satisfied life apart from Jesus. There was no comfort for him in atheism (though he briefly contemplated it), no escape to be found in the fleeting pleasures of the world, and no solution in his own efforts at doing good. All was fruitless and empty. Every door seemed shut to him. "But I did know this," he said, "that I could not remain as I was; that I could not rest happy unless I became something better, something purer than I was."[14]

Conversion

Spurgeon's internal wrestling persisted until January 6, 1850, when Spurgeon experienced the new birth. He had recently returned to his parents' home in Colchester during the winter break at Newmarket Academy. We must imagine a fifteen-year-old Spurgeon, his mind free from the ordinary hustle and bustle of the school term. A new year was upon him, and his whole life lay ahead. Fifteen-year-old boys in England at this time were probably just beginning to think

---

13. *C. H. Spurgeon's Autobiography*, 1:85.
14. *C. H. Spurgeon's Autobiography*, 1:91.

about a vocation and the possibility of a college education. Spurgeon perhaps felt perplexed and overwhelmed as he wondered where his peculiar personality and gifts would find their place in the world. Whatever his thoughts about his future, we know his mind and heart were still trapped under the weight of his sin. The future was not a bright prospect to him, but a burden. A cloud of gloom and judgment hung over his head, thicker than the snow clouds in the Essex sky that morning.

Plagued with anxieties, spiritual and otherwise, Spurgeon set out that Sunday morning, likely to attend a church service in a neighboring town. But he left his home in the midst of a terrible blizzard. He began to hike up the long ascending street leading to the church where he intended to worship that day. But as he encountered the snow and ice, he realized it would be fruitless to attempt to reach his original destination. Even though it would be only a short walk back

to his home, he decided he would still try to attend a place of worship that morning, hoping to hear some word of comfort to soothe his sorrowful condition. He decided to turn into Artillery Street and entered the local Primitive Methodist Chapel, which was just a short walk from his house. The tiny gathering that greeted him did not make for an impressive congregation. Spurgeon was one of only a small band of people assembled for worship, no more than a dozen or so.

The interior and exterior of the Primitive Methodist Chapel, Artillery Street, Colchester, where Spurgeon was converted

As Spurgeon recounts, the minister who was scheduled to preach was nowhere to be found, presumably hindered by the storm from joining his congregation that morning. Before long, however, a poor and humble man from among the assembly stepped into the pulpit and began to preach. Though a few different men would later claim to have preached the sermon, Spurgeon could never identify with any certainty the man who preached that day. The preacher chose for his text Isaiah 45:22, "Look unto me, and be ye saved, all the ends of the earth: for I am God, and there is none else." Years later Spurgeon would comment that the sermon was poorly delivered and not the kind of message one would expect to be used of God to achieve any great good. The man, who possessed little evident gift or learning, preached with a deep Essex accent and stammered and stuttered the whole way through. Yet he was God's appointed instrument to bring the message of salvation to Spurgeon.

For a while it seemed all the preacher could do was repeat the words of the text over and over. But as his message picked up momentum, he looked at the young man in the back of the chapel and began speaking directly to him. Spurgeon recounted the moment:

> Just fixing his eyes on me, as if he knew all my heart, he said, "Young man, you look very miserable.... And you will always be miserable—miserable in life and miserable in death—if you don't obey my text; but if you obey now, this moment, you will be saved." Then lifting up his hands, he shouted, as only a Primitive Methodist could do, "Young man, look to Jesus Christ. Look! Look! Look! You have nothing to do but look and live."... I saw at once the way of salvation.... There and then the cloud was gone, the darkness had rolled away, and that moment I saw the sun; and I could have risen that instant, and sung with the most enthusiastic of them of the precious blood of Christ, and the simple faith which looks alone to Him.[15]

---

15. C. H. *Spurgeon's Autobiography*, 1:106.

And so it was, with a look to the Savior, that Spurgeon experienced salvation. His sins were forgiven as he placed his faith in Christ, receiving from Him justification and redemption through His blood. The overwhelming sense of guilt and despair that had dominated his mind and heart was gone in an instant. The terrors of hell could no longer reach him. He had found freedom from sin's penalty and power and knew the full pardon from sin that can come only through trust in the gospel. He had come to taste of everlasting life in Christ, which seemed to immediately drive away all the darkness and doubt of the preceding five years.

Spurgeon would never get over the wonder of that day when he first came to faith in Christ. He would recount the story hundreds of times over the course of his life, often using the account in his sermons and evangelistic appeals to the lost.[16] In his story Spurgeon saw something of a paradigm for evangelical conversion. He realized that he first had to feel the weight of God's law upon him and come to a place of conviction and sorrow over his sin. His sense of desperation over the state of his soul was necessary to bring him to the point of repentance and faith. Though he would later regret that he did not go to Christ immediately, he nonetheless recognized the hand of God in those five years in which the Lord was slowly leading him to seek the Savior.

One component to Spurgeon's conversion that would continue to have abiding significance to him was the role of preaching in bringing him to faith. He testified, "The revealed Word awakened me; but it was the preached Word that saved me; and I must ever attach peculiar value to the *hearing of the truth*, for by it I received

---

16. Eric Hayden has observed that Spurgeon gave an account of his conversion in every one of the fifty-six volumes of the *Metropolitan Tabernacle Pulpit* and did so an average of five times per volume, quoted in "The Conversion of Charles Haddon Spurgeon: January 6, 1850," by Geoff Thomas, Banner of Truth (January 1, 2000), accessed August 20, 2022, https://banneroftruth.org/us/resources/articles/2000/the-conversion-of-charles-haddon-spurgeon-january-6–1850/.

the joy and peace in which my soul delights."[17] The apostle Paul wrote that "faith cometh by hearing, and hearing by the word of God" (Rom. 10:17). And so it was with Spurgeon. He would always view preaching as God's appointed means of convicting sinners and pointing them to Christ for salvation. Conversion experiences like his would occur hundreds of times as Spurgeon preached the gospel and called sinners to look only to Christ for rescue. The power of preaching in his life, both as a small child coming under conviction and as a young man coming to faith, would fuel Spurgeon's efforts to preach the gospel to sinners for the rest of his life.

Early Discipleship and Baptism

That evening, Spurgeon joyfully reported his experience of conversion at the Primitive Methodist Chapel to his parents. Their gladness over their son's salvation was immense and exuberant. "Oh! There was joy in the household that day," Spurgeon wrote, "when all heard that the eldest son had found the Saviour, and knew himself to be forgiven."[18] After Spurgeon returned to Newmarket Academy in Cambridge, he carried on a regular correspondence with his parents that documented his early spiritual experiences. He depended on John and Eliza for prayer and encouragement and often solicited their advice with respect to challenges and opportunities that he faced as a young Christian.

Spurgeon's early spiritual zeal could hardly be contained. He immediately threw himself into a host of Christian activities. He said, "I could scarcely content myself even for five minutes without trying to do something for Christ."[19] Just a month after his conversion, in February 1850, he eagerly began distributing tracts to homes all over Newmarket. He called this his "little effort."[20] He took over a district that contained thirty-three homes from two women who had

---

17. *C. H. Spurgeon's Autobiography*, 1:104.
18. *C. H. Spurgeon's Autobiography*, 1:109.
19. *C. H. Spurgeon's Autobiography*, 1:181.
20. Needham, *Life and Labors of Charles H. Spurgeon*, 41.

previously carried on the work. His visits to these homes involved more than simply dropping off a tract in the mailbox. Spurgeon would often meet with people to provoke spiritual conversation for the good of those he visited. He assumed a pastoral bearing toward these people, praying regularly for them, taking an interest in their spiritual welfare, and seeking to meet their practical needs as he had opportunity. He longed to see the fruit of conversion through his labors, saying, "Oh, that I could see but one sinner constrained to come to Jesus!"[21] This compassion for sinners would soon funnel into a desire to preach the gospel. Spurgeon's eagerness to preach to people and to pastor them came almost immediately upon his conversion. Carlile states, "That early experience in the little chapel at Colchester decided almost everything for Spurgeon."[22] It was almost as though his calling to faith in Christ and his calling to preach the gospel were one and the same to him.

By April he joined the membership of the local Congregationalist church in Newmarket (there was no Baptist church in the town). Though Spurgeon grew up in a Congregationalist family and had been baptized as an infant, he had come to Baptist convictions while still a boy through his reading of the New Testament.[23] He thus believed his infant baptism to be invalid and that the Bible required him to be baptized as a believer. But Spurgeon wanted to secure his parents' blessing before being baptized. For several weeks he wrote back and forth with his parents, soliciting their approval of his baptism. He felt as though he was withholding obedience from Jesus and that he could not serve Him with a clear conscience unless he received baptism as a believer. Eventually his parents consented, and Spurgeon excitedly made plans to be baptized. His mother said, "Ah, Charles! I often prayed the Lord to make you a Christian, but I never asked that you might become a Baptist." Spurgeon playfully

---

21. *C. H. Spurgeon's Autobiography*, 1:121.

22. Carlile, *C. H. Spurgeon: An Interpretive Biography*, 51.

23. *C. H. Spurgeon's Autobiography*, 1:48–50; and Morden, *Communion with Christ and His People*, 79–84.

replied, "Ah, mother! The Lord has answered your prayer with his usual bounty, and given you exceeding abundantly above what you asked or thought."[24]

Spurgeon was baptized on May 3, 1850. The baptism was organized by a local Baptist minister named W. W. Cantlow and took place eight miles outside of Cambridge in the River Lark before a host of witnesses. Spurgeon's baptism was a triumphant moment for him as a young Christian. It seemed to seal his commitment to Christ and his identification with His church and motivated him to give himself to Christ with even greater ardor and zeal. He confessed to struggling with feelings of fear and timidity in his Christian life before his baptism, even in the moments just before being baptized. But all that seemed to change as he entered the river. Writing of his baptism, he said,

> The wind blew down the river with a cutting blast, as my turn came to wade into the flood; but after I had walked a few steps, and noted the people on the ferry-boat, and in boats, and on either shore, I felt as if Heaven, and earth, and hell, might all gaze upon me; for I was not ashamed, there and then, to own myself a follower of the Lamb. My timidity was washed away; it floated down the river into the sea, and must have been devoured by the fishes, for I have never felt anything of the kind since. Baptism also loosed my tongue, and from that day it has never been quiet. I lost a thousand fears in that River Lark, and found that "in keeping His commandments there is great reward."[25]

Temperatures were probably in the low fifties that morning, and Spurgeon, soaking wet, had to walk eight miles back to Newmarket. Yet such an inconvenience was unlikely to diminish his sense of privilege and wonder at being a child of God and a baptized member of the church. His commitment to Christ was now complete; hereafter, he would withhold nothing from Him.

---

24. *C. H. Spurgeon's Autobiography*, 1:69.
25. *C. H. Spurgeon's Autobiography*, 1:152.

In the days following his baptism, Spurgeon began to give himself to two ministries that would thereafter remain close to his heart. First, Spurgeon started to teach Sunday school regularly at his local church. He counted the opportunity to commend Christ to children week by week an extraordinary privilege, and he engaged in it with singular devotion. For the rest of his life, he would champion Sunday school ministry as being one of the most noble and profitable ways of serving Christ.[26]

The second ministry that began to occupy a special place in Spurgeon's life at this time was prayer. His early letters and diary entries are filled with references to his attendance at the regular prayer meetings of the church. He loved to gather for prayer with other believers, even if such gatherings sometimes numbered no more than a half dozen older saints. He considered an hour or two in such company for this purpose to be a heavenly engagement.[27]

A Surprising Friend and Mentor
While at Newmarket Academy, Spurgeon developed a friendship that he would forever treasure. Spurgeon's extraordinary spiritual earnestness as a new convert attracted the notice of a humble and godly woman named Mary King. Mary served as the cook at Newmarket, and over the next two years she would play a pivotal role in Spurgeon's early spiritual development. In truth, she functioned as a kind of mother in the faith to him. Spurgeon was drawn to Mary because of her evident piety and her enthusiasm for the doctrines of grace, which by this time he had come to love. They would often talk

---

26. Spurgeon published his thoughts on the importance of Sunday school ministry and other ministries to children in a collection of addresses; see C. H. Spurgeon, *"Come, Ye Children": A Book for Parents and Teachers on the Christian Training of Children* (London: Passmore and Alabaster, 1897).

27. Spurgeon often spoke and wrote on the priority of prayer. His most significant treatment of the subject is found in a collection of addresses he gave on the occasion of the regular prayer meetings at the Metropolitan Tabernacle. See C. H. Spurgeon, *Only a Prayer Meeting: Forty Addresses at the Metropolitan Tabernacle and Other Prayer Meetings* (London: Passmore and Alabaster, 1901).

together about the things of God, and both were refreshed by one
another's friendship. Mary found Spurgeon's youthful Christian zeal
a breath of fresh air. Spurgeon found in Mary a seasoned faith worthy
of imitation. Later in life, Spurgeon wrote of her, "She was a good old
soul [and] liked something very sweet indeed, good strong Calvinistic doctrine.... Many a time we have gone over the covenant of grace
together, and talked of the personal election of the saints, their union
to Christ, their final perseverance, and what vital godliness meant;
and I do believe I learnt more from her than I should have learned
from any six doctors of divinity of the sort we have nowadays."[28]

Mary saw potential in young Charles and was surely cognizant
of his unusual gifts that were beginning to manifest as he neared
adulthood. Spurgeon was a new Christian with few close friends and
spiritual influences, and he needed someone who could disciple him
in his young faith. Though an unlikely spiritual guide and mentor,
Mary filled a significant void in Spurgeon's life, and she, more than
any other person, influenced his spiritual formation at this crucial
stage. Many years later, while Spurgeon was pastoring in London,
he received word that Mary had declined in health and needed aid.
On hearing this, he eagerly arranged to assist her and ended up
supporting her financially for the rest of her life, all to honor her
extraordinary investment in his early days as a new Christian.[29]

A New Work Begins

By the time Spurgeon reached his sixteenth birthday on June 19,
1850, he had been a Christian for six months and a baptized member of his local church for about six weeks. He had just moved from
Newmarket to Cambridge to come under the tutelage of Mr. Leeding,
who was a former teacher of Spurgeon when he was in Colchester.[30]
Though still a student, Spurgeon was nonetheless busily employed

---

28. *C. H. Spurgeon's Autobiography*, 1:53.
29. *C. H. Spurgeon's Autobiography*, 1:54–55.
30. Fullerton, *C. H. Spurgeon: A Biography*, 43.

in Christian work of all sorts. He regularly engaged in evangelism and tract distribution all over Cambridgeshire; taught Sunday school at his new church, St. Andrew's Street Baptist Church; and was a committed attender of worship gatherings and prayer meetings. His young piety grew with each passing day, and he eagerly stepped into every opportunity for Christian service that presented itself to him. God was preparing a new work for Spurgeon, however—one he neither anticipated nor sought. It was a work that would engage him for the rest of his life. In Cambridge, in the winter of 1850–51, England's greatest preacher would make his start.

3

A Preacher Is Born

Throughout the centuries, church history's greatest preachers have come to prominence in a host of different ways. Some had their beginnings in leading universities and seminaries. Others were connected with great men or historic churches. Some had their start through dramatic events or climactic episodes that thrust them into the spotlight. None of these factors were at play in Spurgeon's case. His was a most inauspicious start. His background, rearing, and education in no way signaled the glory that was to come. Everything about Spurgeon's life up until the winter of 1850–51 was relatively quiet, uneventful, and foreseeable. Though he certainly possessed extraordinary gifts and singular zeal for the things of God, especially for someone so young, few recognized in him the marks of a preaching prodigy. But within a few years, in 1856, the first biography of Spurgeon would appear, written by an American who celebrated him as the "Modern Whitfield."[1] But in late 1850, nothing in Spurgeon's life warranted such fanfare. His star had not yet risen, and his destiny was still unknown. But all that was about to change.

The story of Spurgeon's emergence as one of the greatest preachers of the age is unlike those of some of Britain's pulpit geniuses of previous centuries. Hugh Latimer and Nicolas Ridley found their voices through the tumultuous events of the English Reformation,

---

1. Magoon, *"The Modern Whitfield."* Only a year later, another biography would appear; see G. J. Stevenson, *A Sketch of the Life and Ministry of the Reverend C. H. Spurgeon* (New York: Sheldon, Blakeman, 1857).

which for many years favored preachers of a more evangelical persuasion. Most of the leading Puritans came up through England's elite institutions in Oxford and Cambridge. Scotland's great preachers, such as Knox and Rutherford, were bred in the universities of St. Andrews and Edinburgh and were also aided in their course by dramatic national events. Whitefield and Wesley were itinerant ministers who built a following through preaching in Britain's great cities and cultural centers in the days of the Great Awakening. Spurgeon's beginnings did not take place in elite universities or great metropolitan centers, nor was he aided by events of profound national significance. Rather, Spurgeon made his start in country cottages, fields, and barns in the forgotten little villages of England's east country.

Spurgeon's First Sermon

Upon relocating to Cambridge in June of 1850, Spurgeon joined the membership of the historic St. Andrew's Street Baptist Church in the heart of the university town. The church was situated a stone's throw from Emmanuel College, Cambridge, which was often described in the early seventeenth century as the great "nursery of the Puritans." Spurgeon's earliest days as a preacher took place under Emmanuel's yawning shadow, which surely would have delighted the Puritans who had once crowded its sacred halls. Just down the street from Emmanuel, St. Andrew's Street Baptist Church had been founded in 1721 and boasted among its ministers Robert Robinson, the composer of the hymn "Come Thou Fount of Every Blessing," and Robert Hall Jr., a great preacher in his own right.

When Spurgeon first arrived in Cambridge, the church was still known for its vibrant evangelical ministry. This included the church's lay preachers' association, which was a society of men who agreed to preach as needed in homes, chapels, and fields in the villages surrounding Cambridge. Participation in the association did not require ordination, a college degree, or any kind of licensure to preach. All that was required was a willingness to preach to small congregations in various settings and a basic ability to preach the gospel with faithfulness and clarity. Lay preachers' associations like the one at St. Andrew's were common in Spurgeon's day, especially in the country, where access to sound preaching was harder to come by. This was the optimal environment for sixteen-year-old Spurgeon to have his first experiences with preaching.

Spurgeon's first sermon occurred in this context almost by accident.[2] As the story goes, the lay preachers' association was managed by James Vinter. One Saturday afternoon, Vinter asked Spurgeon to go the next evening to a nearby village called Teversham, just a couple miles east of town. Vinter told Spurgeon a young man who was not experienced in preaching was to minister there, and he would appreciate company on the journey. In hindsight, Spurgeon discerned the clever phrasing of Vinter's request, which was carefully worded both to mislead and to technically be true. The next evening Spurgeon accompanied a young man slightly older than he to a cottage in Teversham where a small band of Christians was gathered to hear the word preached. As the pair traveled the country lanes on the way to the cottage, Spurgeon eventually expressed his hope and expectation that God would help his companion in the preaching that evening. Immediately, his friend made clear that he had never preached in his life and had no intention of doing so and that he had

---

2. The precise date of Spurgeon's first sermon is a matter of debate. Christian George has a date of August 1850 in the timeline section that opens the first volume of the *Lost Sermons of C. H. Spurgeon*, 1:xxxvi. Mark Hopkins dates the first sermon in the following month, September 1850; see *Nonconformity's Romantic Generation*, 127. But there may be reason to suspect a date as late as January 1851. Two pieces of evidence support this theory. First, Spurgeon did not even join the membership of St. Andrew's Street Baptist Church until October 3, 1850. Is it likely James Vinter would have asked a nonmember to preach in the church's lay preachers' association, especially one so young and unproven? A second piece of evidence lies in the clear dating of the fourth sermon Spurgeon ever preached as February 9, 1851, the sermon being included and so dated in the first set of Spurgeon's personal sermon notebooks; see *C. H. Spurgeon's Autobiography*, 1:213. One gets the impression Spurgeon began preaching regularly immediately after he preached his first sermon, though this is not conclusive. Thus, a gap of several months between his first sermon and his fourth sermon seems unlikely.

agreed only to accompany Spurgeon, who was the one expected to preach that evening. "This was a new view of the situation," Spurgeon thought, "and I could only reply that I was no minister; and that even if I had been, I was quite unprepared."[3] His companion assured him, however, that there would not be a sermon that evening unless Spurgeon was the one to preach it.

Teversham Cottage,
where Spurgeon preached his first sermon

Spurgeon finally resigned himself that this would be the occasion of his first sermon, even if all he had was a few frantic minutes to prepare. Reflecting on the event years later, he said,

> I felt that I was fairly committed to do my best. I walked along quietly, lifting up my soul to God, and it seemed to me that I could surely tell a few poor cottagers of the sweetness and love of Jesus, for I felt them in my own soul. Praying for Divine help, I resolved to make the attempt…. I would trust the Lord to open my mouth in honor of His dear Son. It seemed a great risk and a serious trial; but depending on the power of the Holy

3. *C. H. Spurgeon's Autobiography*, 1:200.

Ghost, I would at least tell out the story of the cross and not allow the people to go home without a word.[4]

Spurgeon preached from 1 Peter 2:7, "Unto you therefore which believe he is precious," and made it through the sermon without incident. The sermon did not spark revival, nor did it immediately thrust Spurgeon onto the public scene as an up-and-coming preacher, but it was nonetheless evident to those who were present that there was something more to this young man. After the message, an old lady asked Spurgeon, "How old are you?" to which he replied, "I am under sixty." "Yes, and under sixteen!" was the woman's response.[5]

Thus began a preaching career unparalleled in England's history. The preaching first heard that evening in a small country cottage would soon fill the largest halls in London. Though Spurgeon would learn to preach with greater depth and skill as time went on, the fundamental message would remain the same; whenever he preached, he would seek to "tell out the story of the cross." This would be the theme of his message for the next four decades.

"The Boy Preacher of the Fens"

Spurgeon's first preaching experience was perhaps something like Bach's first encounter with the organ or Michelangelo's first efforts with a mallet and chisel, in the sense not only that in preaching Spurgeon discovered the work of his life but also that this was manifestly a matter of personal destiny. As cliché as it may sound, Spurgeon was simply born to preach. This was unmistakable among the small hamlets and villages of Cambridgeshire, and in a short time it would become evident to the entire world.

At this stage, Spurgeon began to preach as much as he could, itinerating all over the East Anglian countryside. Over the next three and half years, before his arrival in London, he would preach over

---

4. *C. H. Spurgeon's Autobiography*, 1:200–201.
5. *C. H. Spurgeon's Autobiography*, 1:202.

six hundred sermons.[6] He often filled pulpits in various country chapels on Sundays and also preached midweek in a variety of settings, including in the open air, to as many as would listen to him. As the months rolled on, he developed a reputation as the famed "boy preacher of the Fens." The Fens refers to a marshy, rural region known as the Fenlands, associated chiefly with the rustic environs around Cambridgeshire and Lincolnshire. Spurgeon's notoriety in these counties was based not only on his youth but on the extraordinary quality of his preaching, marked as it was by a potent combination of evangelical earnestness and sublime theology.

These two facts—Spurgeon's extreme youth and the high caliber of his preaching—present the student of history with something of a quandary. Simply put, how could someone so young and inexperienced preach with such evident gift and theological depth? One need only survey the collections of outlines and manuscripts in any volume of *The Lost Sermons of C. H. Spurgeon* to get a sense of the extraordinary quality of his earliest sermons, all of them preached when he was still a teenager.

There are a few factors related to Spurgeon's background that can help us make at least some sense of the preaching phenomenon he was even as a youth. First, it must be remembered that Spurgeon was spiritually intense even from his earliest days, and he was what some have described as an "old soul" in the things of God. Eternal realities dawned on him at a young age while he lived in his grandparents' home in Stambourne. He grew up experiencing serious preaching from both his grandfather and his father. He read books filled with rich doctrine by Puritan authors, and he gave himself eagerly to the study of divinity while still a child. His boyhood environment was filled with the ethos of devout evangelical piety and exalted Reformed theology, which conspired to make him a young man of considerable depth and spiritual substance.

---

6. Eric W. Hayden, "Did You Know?," *Christian History* 29, no. 1 (1991): 2.

Second, Spurgeon was extraordinarily bright. He benefited from a solid middle-class education, was tremendously well read, and seemed to possess innate mental and intellectual endowments that bordered on genius. He was an attentive student of the English language, of nature, and of experience, and he marshaled his knowledge of these fields with exceptional mastery. His mind was well stocked with all the requisite resources to make him a thoughtful and compelling communicator.

Third, Spurgeon benefited from great models in preaching. He made himself the apprentice of many eminent preachers who came before him. Spurgeon regarded George Whitefield as his primary model and said he endeavored to "follow his glorious track."[7] He had the highest esteem also for John Wesley, whom he estimated as second only to Whitefield.[8] Other influences at this early stage of Spurgeon's preaching career included Charles Simeon, the storied preacher of Cambridge; John Angell James of London; and William Jay of Bath. Spurgeon not only read the sermons of these men and others but, in some cases, would actually borrow from their outlines in the crafting of his own sermons.

Apart from these social and historical factors, the answer to Spurgeon's extraordinary success as a preacher, even as a teenager, must be found in the activity of the Spirit of God. Throughout his life Spurgeon believed that God alone makes preachers. Any preacher can grow and learn as he goes along, but there must be for every true preacher some measure of gift and ability that God alone supplies. Furthermore, Spurgeon believed there was an obvious difference between preaching that is done in human strength, and preaching that is done in the power of God. In true preaching God owns both the man and the message. There is a kind of divine anointing of the preacher by the Holy Spirit, and the ministry of the word is

---

7. *C. H. Spurgeon's Autobiography*, 2:66; see also William Williams, *Personal Reminiscences of Charles Haddon Spurgeon* (London: Religious Tract Society, 1895), 180.

8. *C. H. Spurgeon's Autobiography*, 1:176.

accompanied with unction and power that can be traced only to God. This is what Spurgeon experienced time and again, even in his early preaching. God had manifestly gifted Spurgeon for the work of preaching, and in His providence and grace, He used his preaching for the salvation and edification of thousands. Any explanation for the extraordinary success of Spurgeon's preaching that does not include this most crucial element will be wide of the mark. Spurgeon was mighty in preaching because God's hand was on him in an awesome and mysterious way.

The Call to Waterbeach

On October 3, 1851, Spurgeon filled the pulpit of Waterbeach Baptist Chapel, located just a few miles north of Cambridge. He was warmly received and immediately invited back to preach the following week. By the end of the second sermon, the congregation had heard all they needed to hear, and they extended a formal call to Spurgeon to become their pastor. Though he was only seventeen and still unsure about his future, he felt drawn to this needy church and was also moved with love and compassion for the unconverted people of the village. He agreed to accept the invitation, and thus Spurgeon began his first pastorate when he was only seventeen.

When Spurgeon arrived at Waterbeach, church services attracted only a few dozen people. By the end of his brief pastorate there, the church was filled to overflowing with over four hundred people in attendance.[9] Surely some people were drawn to the little chapel by the novelty of the boy preacher, but most came because of the remarkable depth and fervency of his preaching. One of the Waterbeach deacons said of Spurgeon, "He talked amazingly, like a man a hundred years old in Christian experience."[10] J. C. Carlile wrote, "In truth, it was amazing how deep and varied his spiritual experience appeared to all who knew him. It was not simply that he read experimental

9. Morden, *C. H. Spurgeon: The People's Preacher*, 44.
10. Carlile, *C. H. Spurgeon: An Interpretive Biography*, 78.

theology with unflagging interest and profit, but that he himself was so sensitised in spirit that he took on the experiences of others and lived them until they became his own."[11] Spurgeon indeed had the maturity of someone much older, and it came through in his preaching. The richness and depth of his sermons were the product of a near walk with God, a profound knowledge of the Scriptures, and an extraordinary insight into the human condition; all three were manifest to a degree that was rare in one so young. It did not take long for the people of the little chapel to realize that they had something spectacular in their midst.

Waterbeach Baptist Chapel,
where Spurgeon pastored from late 1851 to early 1854

As for the village of Waterbeach, Spurgeon viewed it as his mission field. He wanted to see the people of the village supernaturally changed at the heart level, leading to genuine life change. In a word, he wanted to see revival. And according to Spurgeon's accounts of his days in Waterbeach, this was indeed his experience. He wrote,

> In a short time, the little thatched chapel was crammed, the biggest vagabonds of the village were weeping floods of tears, and those who had been the curse of the parish became its blessing.

11. Carlile, *C. H. Spurgeon: An Interpretive Biography,* 85.

Where there had been robberies and villainies of every kind, all round the neighborhood, there were none, because the men who used to do the mischief were themselves in the house of God, rejoicing to hear of Jesus crucified. I am not telling an exaggerated story, nor a thing that I do not know, for it was my delight to labor for the Lord in that village. It was a pleasant thing to walk through that place, when drunkenness had almost ceased, when debauchery in the case of many was dead, when men and women went forth to labor with joyful hearts, singing the praises of the ever-living God; and when, at sunset, the humble cottager called his children together, read them some portion from the Book of Truth, and then together they bent their knees in prayer to God. I can say, with joy and happiness, that almost from one end of the village to the other, at the hour of eventide, one might have heard the voice of song coming from nearly every roof-tree, and echoing from almost every heart. I do testify, to the praise of God's grace, that it pleased the Lord to work wonders in our midst. He showed the power of Jesu's name, and made me a witness of that gospel which can win souls, draw reluctant hearts, and mould afresh the life and conduct of sinful men and women.[12]

From the beginning, Spurgeon witnessed remarkable fruitfulness in his ministry at Waterbeach. Through his preaching, men and women found Christ, and the village itself underwent a kind of transformation. The excitement over his preaching never abated but only intensified over the course of his two-year ministry there.

The Village Pastor

Though much about his ministry in Waterbeach was extraordinary, Spurgeon enjoyed many of the fairly conventional elements of a normal village pastorate. He kept a busy preaching schedule, ministering the word at least twice on the Lord's Day and sometimes midweek in Waterbeach and in neighboring villages as well. Throughout the week he regularly visited his church members for encouragement,

---

12. *C. H. Spurgeon's Autobiography,* 1:228.

exhortation, and prayer. Children, the elderly, the poor, and the sick were the special objects of his attention and care. As part of his basic oversight of the church, Spurgeon interacted regularly with the deacons and enjoyed a healthy collaboration with them in the church's ministry. He always held the highest view of the ministry of deacons, which he first developed while at Waterbeach and maintained throughout his years in London. Spurgeon said of the Waterbeach deacons, "[They] were in my esteem the excellent of the earth, in whom I took great delight. Hard-working men on the week-day, they spared no toil for their Lord on the Sabbath; I loved them sincerely, and do love them still. In my opinion, they were as nearly the perfection of deacons of a country church as the kingdom could afford."[13]

Among the more ordinary experiences Spurgeon had in his first pastorate were some of the typical challenges, trials, and discouragements that are familiar to many men in ministry. Spurgeon learned at a young age how to console a grieving family who had lost a child in infancy. He knew what it was like to pray with individual members suffering with chronic and terminal health issues. He had frequent meetings with backsliding Christians, members struggling with doubt and despair, and those enduring severe trials and hardships of various kinds. Like all true pastors, Spurgeon carried with him the griefs and sorrows that weighed on his church members. He genuinely cared for the flock at Waterbeach and endeavored to enter into their lives as a loving and sympathetic pastor.

Perhaps the greatest grief Spurgeon experienced while at Waterbeach, one that caused him "many bitter tears," was the apostasy of the man he thought to be his first genuine convert. Thomas Charles was an agricultural laborer, who, according to Spurgeon, had been "the ringleader in all that was bad" and the "terror of the neighborhood."[14] One day, feeling a sense of his sin and guilt, he came to hear Spurgeon preach, much to the surprise and alarm of the congregation.

---

13. *C. H. Spurgeon's Autobiography*, 1:255–56.
14. *C. H. Spurgeon's Autobiography*, 1:238.

On hearing the gospel, he professed to experience something of real repentance and faith and began to evidence a changed life. "He gave up his drinking and swearing," Spurgeon said, "and was in many respects an exemplary individual." The man eagerly started to serve the church and even engaged in Sunday school ministry in surrounding villages. Spurgeon recounted that after a few months, however, "he returned to his old habits, and any thoughts of God and godliness that he had ever known, seemed to die away."[15]

On the whole, though he experienced discouragement along the way, Spurgeon enjoyed these days as some of the happiest of his life. He loved his people, and they loved him. Though the congregation could afford to pay him only forty-five pounds a year (a paltry sum even in those days, and hardly enough for even a single man to live on), the church supported him in other ways, such as providing him with a regular supply of produce, bread, and other forms of hospitality.[16] Spurgeon said, "My congregation is as great and loving as ever. During all the time that I have been at Waterbeach, I have had a different house for my home every Sabbath day. Fifty-two families have thus taken me in; and I have still six other invitations not yet accepted. Talk about the people not caring for me, because they give me so little! I dare tell anybody under heaven 'tis false! They do all they can."[17]

Though many of the elements of Spurgeon's ministry were typical, there were other aspects that were unusual, if not wholly unique. At least two are worth noting. The first was Spurgeon's exceptional zeal in the work of pastoring. He never did anything by halves, especially when engaged in work for the Lord. He was serving his master and his master's people. This required his most earnest efforts. Thus, it was not unusual for Spurgeon to preach three times on the Lord's Day and to have weeks in which he was called on to preach every

---

15. C. H. *Spurgeon's Autobiography*, 1:238.
16. C. H. *Spurgeon's Autobiography*, 1:253.
17. C. H. *Spurgeon's Autobiography*, 1:248–49.

day. While the pastor of Waterbeach, he still itinerated with the lay preachers' association and often traveled several miles, sometimes in the pouring rain, to fulfill a preaching engagement.[18]

A second extraordinary aspect of Spurgeon's ministry was the singular response to his preaching, which attracted people from all over the region in unprecedented numbers. He celebrated numerous conversions and baptisms while at Waterbeach, and his fame spread throughout the surrounding villages and towns as a preacher of exceptional ability. Spurgeon's brother, James Archer Spurgeon, captured something of the enthusiasm over Spurgeon's preaching around this time:

> When I drove my brother about the country to preach, I used to think then, as I have thought ever since, what an extraordinary preacher he was. I began to admire him, and I went on doing it more and more the longer I knew him. Oh, what wonderful unction and power I remember in some of those early speeches of his!… He seems to have leaped full-grown into the pulpit. It was wonderful. I can still remember distinctly some of his early sermons. Their breadth and brilliance, and the power that God's Holy Spirit evidently gave to him, made them perfectly marvelous. I have since traced not more genius than impressed me then, but more breadth, more depth, more spirituality, more of God's own Word, as to the knowledge both of the letter of it and of its inner meaning; but I thank God that my first impressions of my brother are among the brightest and the best, and I have found no cause to change my opinion from that time to this, that he was a God-made man and a God-sent man to his age, and by the grace of God he was faithful to that mission all through life.[19]

God's Providence in the Maid's Mistake

While Spurgeon was ministering to his flock at Waterbeach and itinerating throughout the Cambridgeshire countryside, he continued

---

18. Morden, *C. H. Spurgeon: The People's Preacher*, 40–41.
19. Pike, *James Archer Spurgeon*, 25.

his education under Mr. Leeding and also assisted him as a tutor to younger boys in his academy in Cambridge. Though Spurgeon was delightfully ensconced in his private studies and in his rural pastorate, he remained unsure about what course his future should take. It was evident enough by this time that Spurgeon had been born for the ministry. But one question still loomed large over his life as he approached his eighteenth birthday, and it caused him no small amount of anxiety. The question was whether or not he should enroll in college to continue his education and preparation for whatever vocation God would have for him.

Cambridge University would not have been an option for Spurgeon in the early 1850s. At that time, Nonconformists still could not receive degrees from Oxford and Cambridge. Nonetheless, there were by this time a number of colleges throughout England that would have suited someone of Spurgeon's status quite well. One of the leading options among Nonconformists at that time was Stepney College, later to change its name to Regent's Park College. Though it might have been assumed that Spurgeon would one day go to college, he never appeared to be keen on taking this next step, especially if it required him to abandon his flock at Waterbeach. And while all Spurgeon's friends and family thought he should attend college, he said, "I have no great desire for it; in fact, none at all."[20] It appears he found the demands of ministry satisfying enough and believed all the benefits he would gain from college could be achieved through practical experience and a course of self-education. But at the insistence of others, he agreed to give college serious consideration, even to the point of sitting for an interview.

The key event occurred just four months into Spurgeon's young pastorate at Waterbeach. On February 1, 1852, Dr. Joseph Angus, who was the head of Stepney College at the time, visited Cambridge and preached at St. Andrew's Street Baptist Church. Angus had formerly been the pastor of New Park Street Chapel for two years, a

---

20. C. H. *Spurgeon's Autobiography,* 1:244.

serendipitous fact, the relevance of which could only be appreciated a few years later.[21] Angus had heard of the boy preacher and was encouraged to schedule an interview with Spurgeon to discuss his future prospects at Stepney. An appointment was made for the two to meet at the house of Mr. Macmillan, a local publisher. In the mysterious providence of God, however, one of church history's most fateful "accidents" then occurred. Ever punctual, Spurgeon arrived on time for the meeting. The maid of the house directed him to a room where he sat by himself for over two hours waiting for Angus. Finally, Spurgeon mustered up the courage to ring the bell for the maid to inquire about Angus's whereabouts. To his alarm, he discovered that Angus had arrived shortly after he did and had been waiting in another room for several minutes before eventually having to depart to catch his train to London. The maid had mistakenly directed them to separate rooms and never alerted either one that the other had arrived. The meeting between Angus and Spurgeon never took place!

At first Spurgeon was seemingly troubled and disoriented by the maid's blunder, and he lamented the missed opportunity. But as he walked across Midsummer Common in Cambridge on his way to his next appointment that day, it seemed to him that a message from God came to his mind, unannounced and unbeckoned. It said, in the words of Jeremiah 45:5, "Seekest thou great things for thyself? Seek them not." As Spurgeon turned these words over in his head, he developed a different perspective on the ordeal. He later wrote,

> This led me to look at my position from another point of view, and to challenge my motives and intentions. I remembered the poor but loving people to whom I ministered, and the souls which had been given me in my humble charge; and, although at that time I anticipated obscurity and poverty as the result of the resolve, yet I did there and then solemnly renounce the offer of Collegiate instruction, determining to abide for a

21. Fullerton, *C. H. Spurgeon: A Biography*, 54.

season at least with my people, and to remain preaching the Word so long as I had strength to do it.[22]

Though Spurgeon had adopted this new resolution, the matter was not immediately put to rest. Evidently, John Spurgeon expected his son to go to college and even put pressure on him to do so. Spurgeon's autobiography contains a number of letters from Charles to John respectfully pleading his case for not going to college. In the end, though John desired for his son to attend Stepney, he eventually left the matter up to Charles, who chose to remain the pastor at Waterbeach while continuing his private education with Leeding. It appears Spurgeon never had the slightest regret about the decision. By the autumn of 1852 he could write to his mother, "I am more and more glad that I never went to College. God sends such sunshine on my path, such smiles of grace, that I cannot regret if I have forfeited all my prospects for it."[23] In later life he reflected on the maid's mistake and said that he had "a thousand times since thanked the Lord very heartily for the strange Providence which forced my step into another path."[24] Eventually tens of thousands of people would also have reason to thank God for this strange providence. For had Spurgeon attended college, it is possible London would never have come calling.

---

22. *C. H. Spurgeon's Autobiography*, 1:243.
23. *C. H. Spurgeon's Autobiography*, 1:248.
24. *C. H. Spurgeon's Autobiography*, 1:241–42.

4

The Call to London

On Sunday morning, November 27, 1853, Spurgeon awoke early in Cambridge and set out on the familiar six-mile route to Waterbeach to lead his congregation in the morning worship service. As was his custom upon arriving, Spurgeon took out his copy of the Baptist hymnal to select the hymns for that morning's service. The hymnal the church used had been prepared by the famous preacher John Rippon. For sixty-three years Rippon had been the pastor of the Baptist church in Carter Lane, London. Toward the end of Rippon's ministry, the church moved and changed its name to New Park Street Chapel.

Just as Spurgeon was preparing to select the hymns from Rippon's hymnal for the service, one of the deacons, Robert Coe, arrived and handed him a letter sent from the church Rippon had pastored just two decades earlier. The letter contained an invitation for Spurgeon to preach at New Park Street Chapel. The church was well known to Spurgeon, as it had a distinguished legacy stretching all the way back to the period of the English Revolution in the mid-seventeenth century. In 1650 a Baptist congregation began to gather in London despite persecution. Not until 1688, after the Act of Toleration was passed, would the congregation enjoy full freedom to worship publicly and to practice their faith according to Baptist convictions.

In the two centuries before the arrival of this letter in Waterbeach, the church had enjoyed the long tenure of three eminent Baptist preachers. The first was Benjamin Keach, who pastored the church from 1668 to 1704. Keach was an immensely influential early Particular Baptist and an original signatory of the Second London Baptist Confession of 1689. The second distinguished ministry lasted over fifty years and belonged to John Gill, who today is still regarded as one of the most significant theologians in Baptist history.[1] Gill pastored the church from 1719 to 1771. The third ministry of note in the church's history was that of the aforementioned John Rippon, who pastored the church from 1773 to 1836. Though a fine preacher in his own right, Rippon made his most lasting contribution in the hymnal he published in 1787, which became something of an evangelical classic.[2]

This storied congregation, with its illustrious heritage of venerable former ministers, looked now to a teenager from a tiny hamlet in the Cambridgeshire countryside. The idea seemed so irregular and unorthodox to Spurgeon that he assumed a mistake had been made:

> I quietly passed the letter across the table to the deacon who gave out the hymns, observing that there was some mistake and that the letter must have been intended for a Mr. Spurgeon who preached somewhere down in Norfolk. He shook his head, and remarked that he was afraid there was no mistake, as he always knew that his minister would be run away by some large church or other, but that he was a little surprised that the

---

1. John Gill is known for his abundant exegetical and theological writings, especially his systematic theology, *A Body of Doctrinal and Practical Divinity; or, A System of Practical Truths. Deduced from the Sacred Scriptures* (London: Whittingham and Rowland, 1815). Spurgeon had the highest esteem for Gill and referred to him as "the greatest scholar the church had yet chosen"; see *C. H. Spurgeon's Autobiography*, 1:308. Christian George has traced the influence of John Gill on Spurgeon's early sermons; see his note in *Lost Sermons of C. H. Spurgeon*, 1:70–71n3. Though he often lauded Gill, Spurgeon also maintained some moderate criticisms of him. For an example of these criticisms, see C. H. Spurgeon, *Commenting and Commentaries: Two Lectures Addressed to the Students of the Pastors' College, Metropolitan Tabernacle, Together with a Catalogue of Biblical Commentaries and Expositions* (London: Passmore and Alabaster, 1893), 8–10.

2. John Rippon, *A Selection of Hymns, from the Best Authors, Intended to Be an Appendix to Dr. Watts's Psalms & Hymns* (London: Thomas Wilkins, 1787).

Londoners should have heard of me quite so soon…. He shook his head very gravely; but the time had come for me to look out the hymns, therefore the letter was put away, and, as far as I can remember, was for the day quite forgotten.[3]

But the matter could not be put off, and a reply was required. Spurgeon responded the next day, indicating that he would be willing to preach on a Sunday in December. He expressed in his letter his great surprise that they should write to him and took pains to ensure they understood that he was only a youth, lest they should come to regret their invitation when they laid eyes on him. He wrote, "My last birthday was only my nineteenth," and "if you think my years would unqualify me for your pulpit, then, by all means, I entreat you, do not let me come."[4] The reply from New Park Street indicated that they were fully aware of his age and situation and were eager for him to come and preach to them on December 18. The Boy Preacher of the Fens would indeed pay a visit to the Londoners.

Victorian London

An acclaimed nineteenth-century British writer who has famously immortalized the sights, scenes, and smells of Victorian London in the popular imagination is the eminent novelist Charles Dickens. Numerous literary experts have suggested that London is the most important character in all Dickens's novels. Many of his greatest works, such as *David Copperfield*, *Bleak House*, and *Little Dorrit*, abound with descriptions of the city's crowded lanes, polluted streets, and colorless tenements. A well-known passage in *Oliver Twist* includes the following cheerless description of the capital city:

> It was market-morning. The ground was covered, nearly ankle-deep, with filth and mire; a thick steam, perpetually rising from the reeking bodies of the cattle, and mingling with the fog, which seemed to rest upon the chimney-tops, hung

---

3. *C. H. Spurgeon's Autobiography*, 1:317.
4. *C. H. Spurgeon's Autobiography*, 1:317.

heavily above…. Countrymen, butchers, drovers, hawkers,
boys, thieves, idlers, and vagabonds of every low grade, were
mingled together in a mass; the whistling of drovers, the bark-
ing of dogs, the bellowing and plunging of oxen, the bleating of
sheep, the grunting and squeaking of pigs, the cries of hawkers,
the shouts, oaths, and quarrelling on all sides; the ringing of
bells and roar of voices, that issued from every public-house;
the crowding, pushing, driving, beating, whooping, and yell-
ing; the hideous and discordant din that resounded from every
corner of the market; and the unwashed, unshaven, squalid,
and dirty figures constantly running to and fro and bursting in
and out of the throng; rendered it a stunning and bewildering
scene, which quite confounded the senses.[5]

This dismal scene depicted London as Spurgeon probably found it in
late 1853. The city was overcrowded, underfunded, and severely polluted. Peter Morden writes, "Disease was endemic; crime was rife;
poverty was widespread."[6] Certainly London knew nothing of the
rural charm and quiet beauty that lay fifty miles to its east.

Yet there was more to the story than the London of Dickensian
narrative. London was the center of manufacturing and trade, the
industrial heartbeat of a thriving nation. It was also the economic,
cultural, and political hub of the British Empire. In 1851, just a few
years before Spurgeon's arrival, Prince Albert, husband to Queen
Victoria, organized the Great Exhibition, which displayed before
the world the most extraordinary leaps of innovation and improve-
ment in the arenas of science, technology, and industry. Many were
the achievements of the age, and London made a show of them all.
Advancement and *progress* were the watchwords of the nineteenth
century. During Victoria's reign, the animal gave way to the engine,
the gas lamp to the lightbulb, and the hand stitch to the sewing
machine. The railway system expanded to cover the entire country

5. Charles Dickens, *Oliver Twist*, 2nd ed. (London: Richard Bentley, 1839),
2:21–22.

6. Morden, *C. H. Spurgeon: The People's Preacher*, 51.

and revolutionized the industrial life of the nation. Steamships propelled trade and made international travel more accessible. New developments in photography allowed the Victorians to document this era of rapid expansion.

The advances of this period contributed to a sense of confidence and optimism concerning human progress. As technological and industrial gains produced substantial improvements in the quality of life of the average Victorian, the nation became more sensitive to social problems such as poor working conditions, dirty water, and crowded living quarters. Toward the end of his life, Spurgeon described London as "that place where my fellow creatures love to congregate, and create sewage and influenza, coal-smoke and yellow fogs."[7] Many of the proposed social reforms of the era centered on these sorts of issues. For example, in London, the lack of an adequate sewage system brought about various cholera epidemics and eventually an unbearable summer that came to be known as the Great Stink of 1858.[8] These kinds of social maladies would not be tolerated by a nation breathing in the new air of industrial progress. Parliament soon moved to decisively address the crisis and approved plans to install London's first comprehensive sewage system.

In Spurgeon's day, London was the largest city in the world, with roughly three million inhabitants when Spurgeon first arrived in 1853.[9] That figure would double to six million by the time of his death in 1892. The population was growing at a rapid rate and with it, new construction that spread out in every direction. New roads, railways, and street lighting crisscrossed the endless maze of old and new neighborhoods. Judith Flanders writes, "London was, for most

---

7. Spurgeon, *Memories of Stambourne*, 7–8.

8. Stephen Halliday, *The Great Stink of London: Sir Joseph Bazalgette and the Cleaning of the Victorian Metropolis* (Gloucestershire: History Press, 2001); and Judith Flanders, *The Victorian City: Everyday Life in Dickens' London* (New York: St. Martin's Griffin, 2015), 223–25.

9. London was the largest city in the world for a century, from roughly 1825 to 1925. See Tertius Chandler and Gerald Fox, *3000 Years of Urban Growth* (New York: Academic Press, 1974), 364.

of the century, one never-ending building site."[10] Throughout his life, Spurgeon felt overwhelmed by the metropolis that seemed to him like an endless sprawl of humanity. In an 1875 article titled "London: A Plea," he wrote, "Traversing all parts of London very frequently, we are nevertheless lost in it. Has any living man any idea of the vastness of our metropolitan world? It is not a city, but a province, nay, a nation. Every now and then we find ourselves quite at sea in a locality which we thought we knew as well as our own garden."[11]

But it wasn't only London's massive size and scale that disheartened Spurgeon; it was its sinfulness and vice. He referred to it as "this wicked, wretched City of London"[12] and compared it to Sodom and ancient Corinth.[13] He certainly would have agreed with Dickens's Mr. Micawber from *David Copperfield*, who famously labeled London the "Modern Babylon."[14] Even after thirty-five years in the city, he still viewed London as morally ruined, writing in 1889,

> I confess I can never go through this huge city without feeling unhappy. I never pass from end to end of London without feeling a black and dark cloud, hanging like a pall over my spirit. How my heart breaks for thee, O sinful city of London! Is it not so with you, my brethren? Think of its slums, its sins, its poverty, its ungodliness, its drunkenness, its vice! These may well go through a man's heart like sharp swords. How Jesus would have wept in London.[15]

---

10. Flanders, *Victorian City*, 10.

11. C. H. Spurgeon, "London: A Plea," *Sword and the Trowel* (April 1875): 145.

12. C. H. Spurgeon, "The Blind Man's Eyes Opened; or, Practical Christianity," in *The Metropolitan Tabernacle Pulpit: Sermons Preached and Revised by C. H. Spurgeon* (Pasadena, Tex.: Pilgrim Publications, 1973), 29:675.

13. C. H. Spurgeon, "Beginning at Jerusalem," in *Metropolitan Tabernacle Pulpit*, 29:381; and C. H. Spurgeon, "A Prophetic Warning," *Sword and the Trowel* (October 1883): 522.

14. Charles Dickens, *The Personal History of David Copperfield, in Two Volumes* (London: Chapman and Hall, 1874), 1:186.

15. C. H. Spurgeon, "Jesus Wept," in *Metropolitan Tabernacle Pulpit*, 35:342.

To Spurgeon, the city embodied a thousand sorrows and piled up humanity's collective miseries into one massive heap. The seemingly never-ending expansion of industrialization and urbanization represented for him the corruption of a purer kind of existence, which he identified with the country. Kruppa writes, "He never shed his countryman's instinctive fear of cities, and he regretted that he had lived to see much of the countryside 'sucked into the vortex of London.'... He viewed the inevitable march of industrialism as a threat to the countryside, and believed that with the passing of the countryside, the character of society itself changed radically, for the destruction of rural society meant the destruction of pastoral virtues as well."[16]

Though Spurgeon was by nature and nurture a lover of the country, he nonetheless found himself for most of his life in the heart of the largest and densest city in the world. Many of the Lord's servants find themselves serving in places they would never choose for themselves and in contexts they do not especially like. Spurgeon reminds us that we need not like the place where we are called to serve. We need only to love the Lord of the place and the souls of those who live there.

The Country Boy Visits the City

It might be imagined that a youthful Spurgeon would look at London with a sense of adventure, perhaps even of wonder. In fact, his reaction was the opposite. When Spurgeon visited London to deliver his trial sermon at New Park Street Chapel, he felt acute dread and loneliness. Just a few hours in the urban jungle were enough to make him wish to retreat as soon as possible to his rustic refuge in the East Anglian countryside. His portrayal of that December visit is of a shy country boy, intimidated and lost amid the crowded streets that seemed to form an endless maze. As he gazed all around at London's majestic architecture, he felt dwarfed by the imposing edifices—so much the product of the baroque imagination of Christopher Wren.

---

16. Kruppa, *Charles Haddon Spurgeon: A Preacher's Progress*, 16–17.

The city's building landscape also bore the influence of the Gothic Revival with its pointed spires, angular arches, and stained-glass windows, creating an aesthetic that would have offended Spurgeon's Protestant sensibilities. In the midst of the city, Spurgeon stood out as a country bumpkin. Fullerton wrote, "His very clothes proclaimed his country breeding. He had a great satin stock round his neck, and in special honour of the occasion he produced a blue handkerchief with white spots."[17] Of that first night in London Spurgeon wrote,

> That Saturday evening in a London boarding-house was about the most depressing agency which could have been brought to bear upon my spirit. On the narrow bed I tossed in solitary misery, and found no pity. Pitiless was the grind of the cabs in the street, pitiless the recollection of the young city clerks, whose grim propriety had gazed upon my rusticity with such amusement, pitiless the spare room which scarcely afforded me space to kneel, pitiless even the gas-lamps which seemed to wink at me as they flickered amid the December darkness. I had no friend in all that city full of human beings, but felt myself to be among strangers and foreigners, and hoped to be helped through the scrape into which I had been brought, and to escape safely to the serene abodes of Cambridge and Water-beach, which then seemed to be Eden itself.[18]

Spurgeon's feelings of loneliness and alienation amid the seemingly limitless sprawl of humanity that he encountered in the city was not unusual. London seemed to provoke this kind of feeling in many people. The great author and essayist Thomas de Quincey, in his *Autobiographic Sketches* published the same year in which Spurgeon made this visit to London, conveyed a similar sentiment:

> No man ever was left to himself for the first time in the streets, as yet unknown, of London, but he must have been saddened and mortified, perhaps terrified, by the sense of desertion and utter loneliness which belong to his situation. No loneliness can

---

17. Fullerton, *C. H. Spurgeon: A Biography*, 60.
18. *C. H. Spurgeon's Autobiography*, 1:318.

be like that which weighs upon the hearts in the centre of faces never ending, without voice or utterance for him; eyes innumerable…and hurrying figures of men weaving to and fro, with no apparent purposes intelligible to a stranger, seeming like a mask of maniacs, or, oftentimes, like a pageant of phantoms.[19]

The following morning, as Spurgeon set out for the chapel, he might have looked on London as T. S. Eliot would a century later: "Unreal City, under the brown fog of a winter dawn."[20] The immediate locale around New Park Street Chapel offered Spurgeon little cheer. He described it as "dim, dirty, and destitute."[21] The church was located in a depressed part of the city just south of the River Thames, surrounded by factories and warehouses. The neighborhood routinely flooded and was often blanketed under a cloud of black smoke that billowed forth from the industrial buildings in the vicinity. The location was not only dirty and unsightly but also inconvenient, as access from the north across Southwark Bridge required travelers to pay a toll, limiting access from the north half of London.

When Spurgeon arrived at the chapel, he found the exterior of the building intimidating, and he imagined a congregation within that was "wealthy and critical" and nothing like his flock in Waterbeach, "to whom my ministry had been sweetness and light."[22] The congregation that actually greeted him that morning, though small (estimates ranged from eighty to two hundred in a hall that could seat twelve hundred), was friendly, gracious, and warmhearted and did much to soften Spurgeon's first impressions of London and the church.[23] As he navigated the halls around the chapel and visited the church vestry, he found himself in a veritable museum of Baptist

---

19. Thomas de Quincey, *Autobiographic Sketches* (Boston: Ticknor, Reed, and Fields, 1853), 208–9.

20. T. S. Eliot, *The Waste Land* (New York: Penguin Random House, 2021), 59.

21. *C. H. Spurgeon's Autobiography*, 1:315.

22. *C. H. Spurgeon's Autobiography*, 1:319.

23. W. Y. Fullerton estimated eighty people were present for that first sermon on December 18; see *C. H. Spurgeon: A Biography*, 60. G. Holden Pike estimated that there were two hundred; see *Life and Works of Charles Haddon Spurgeon*, 1:98.

history. He stopped to gaze up at a peculiarly impressive and austere portrait of Benjamin Keach and indulged a youthful impulse to sit in the chair that had once been occupied by the famous Dr. Gill. The thought of preaching in John Rippon's pulpit thrilled him.

Spurgeon's sermon that December morning came from James 1:17, "Every good gift and every perfect gift is from above, and cometh down from the Father of lights, with whom is no variableness, neither shadow of turning." The sermon was received with glad and enthusiastic hearts. It was evident to the small congregation that they had encountered something exceptional in the young preacher. When Spurgeon returned to preach again that evening, he found a much larger audience to hear him. Apparently those who were present in the morning service had excitedly spread the word among their friends and family about their visiting preacher, and many of those they invited came out to hear him preach that night. The effect of Spurgeon's preaching was immense and immediate. After the evening service, there was a profound sense of wonder that hovered over the congregation. Most of the members uncharacteristically lingered throughout the sanctuary, not knowing exactly what to do with themselves, but all felt something must be done immediately to secure the young preacher for another visit.[24] They had been living on former glory, but Spurgeon represented to them the opportunity of a new future.

New Park Street Chapel had begun to decline since the close of the ministry of John Rippon in 1836, and perhaps even earlier than that. Ever since the move to New Park Street in 1830, the church had struggled to recover its former vibrancy and renown among London churches. The move was not by choice but rather was forced because of plans for new roads in the vicinity of the old Carter Lane building. Though the congregation was compensated for the forced relocation, the result of the move would prove injurious to the church. Access to the building was now limited, and attendance declined. After the

---

24. Pike, *Life and Works of Charles Haddon Spurgeon*, 1:99.

long and fruitful ministries of Keach, Gill, and Rippon, the church struggled regularly with pastoral turnover. With the arrival of the nineteen-year-old from Cambridgeshire, however, the members of the church now had an overwhelming sense that their brightest days were before them.

The Call

The deacons of New Park Street Chapel invited Spurgeon to fill the pulpit again for three Sundays in January 1854 (January 1, 15, and 29). But before the final Sunday in January when Spurgeon was to preach, the church called a special meeting on Thursday, January 26, and passed a resolution to extend a formal call to Spurgeon to come and fill the pulpit on a six-month trial basis. In conveying the news of the resolution to Spurgeon, John Olney wrote,

> I am sure you will find the church render to you all the esteem and affection you will desire, and be ready to sustain you by their prayers and co-operation, and I am equally certain that you will not be lacking in your efforts to supply them with the Bread of Life, and the Good Wine of the Kingdom. I hope and pray that you may be led—by what appears to my mind, and I trust will appear to yours also, to be the guiding of Providence,—to accept the invitation of the church.[25]

As might be imagined, Spurgeon felt both honored and over-whelmed by the invitation. There is no evidence that he had ever entertained thoughts of pastoring in London before the initial invitation to preach at New Park Street, and every indication was that he had been entirely content to pastor in the country. He had an inward sense of the Lord's sovereign hand in these events, however, and seemed altogether resolute that he should accept the call. He wrote to the deacons of New Park Street, "Now my Heavenly Father drives me forth from this little Garden of Eden; and whilst I see that

---

25. *C. H. Spurgeon's Autobiography*, 1:347.

I must go out, I leave it with reluctance, and tremble to tread the unknown land before me."[26]

Though Spurgeon accepted the invitation, he nonetheless requested one amendment to the proposed plan—namely, that the six-month trial be shortened to three months. He did not make this request to expedite the timetable for a decision concerning his future or to pressure the church to make a quick determination. Rather, he felt that because of his relative youth and inexperience, he was in no position to impose on a congregation for as long as six months if they quickly discerned that he was not a good fit as their long-term pastor. He preferred that if the church arrived at such a judgment, he could quickly be out of their pulpit and on his way back to Waterbeach. It appears Spurgeon still felt underqualified for their consideration and was fully prepared if the trial period ended in disappointment. He also was not sure he would be able to endure the pressures of living in London and fully recognized he may prefer to return to Cambridgeshire, even if the church extended to him a formal call. Every indication is that he genuinely and honorably wanted to preserve a way for either party to decline a long-term commitment without any hint of having led the other on or let the other down.[27] He concluded his letter with a final entreaty: "And now one thing is due to every minister, and I pray you to remind the church of it, namely, that in private, as well as in public, they must all earnestly wrestle in prayer to the God of our Lord Jesus Christ, that I may be sustained in the great work."[28]

A New Kind of Preaching

Whether six months or three, the trial was never completed, for just two months after he arrived, on April 19, 1854, the church unanimously voted at a specially called meeting to invite Spurgeon to

---

26. *C. H. Spurgeon's Autobiography*, 1:348.

27. Pike, *Life and Works of Charles Haddon Spurgeon*, 1:100–101.

28. *C. H. Spurgeon's Autobiography*, 1:349.

be their permanent pastor. By that time the building was already bursting at the seams, and Spurgeon had become something of a metropolitan sensation. His preaching attracted scores of people from all over London who were eager to hear the gospel preached as they had never heard it before. Christ was offered to the common people with such bold and free expressions of the love of God toward sinners that they could not help but be drawn to it. The old gospel

Spurgeon in 1855

of the blood of Jesus sounded forth from the pulpit of New Park Street with a force and power that made divine grace seem like an almost tangible reality. That this message was announced by a youth of nineteen with such vigor, earnestness, and sincerity only served to intensify public interest and excitement. Spurgeon's preaching brought to his audience a cogent sense of the holiness of God, the exceeding sinfulness of man, the imminence of eternity, and the readiness of Christ to save. As Spurgeon preached, grown men wept freely, young and old were caught up in wonder, and hardened sinners became penitent believers.

No one who came to hear Spurgeon preach had seen his like in their lifetime. Many of the typical London preachers were stuffy and dry; Spurgeon was warm and popular. They were calm, composed, even cold; Spurgeon was vibrant, hot-blooded, and dynamic. Many of them were known for erudite and pedantic orations that were more fit for university halls; Spurgeon gave his congregations forceful and compelling preaching that brought the hearer to a point of decision.

This was wholly surprising in someone so young, so uncultured, and so physically unimpressive. Spurgeon was short, stout, and often appeared disheveled. There was nothing in his appearance to inspire one's attention or interest. Many people were surprised, and even disappointed, when they first laid eyes on him. Yet as soon as he rose to preach, "a transfiguring process began."[29] One person who heard Spurgeon when he first came to London said, "When he mounted the pulpit you might have thought of him as a hairdresser's assistant; when he left it, he was an inspired apostle."[30]

"How Earnestly They Prayed"

Prayer meetings found a great advocate in Charles Haddon Spurgeon. As a new convert, he started attending prayer meetings zealously in Newmarket and Cambridge and was faithfully present even when there were only a few others on hand to join with him in prayer.[31] While pastoring in Waterbeach, he gave prayer meetings the highest priority in the life of the church. He maintained this attitude toward prayer when he arrived in London. Throughout his life, Spurgeon held that one of the clearest evidences of the Holy Spirit's work in a person's heart is an abiding love of prayer.

The extraordinary vibrancy that was restored to the prayer meetings of New Park Street Chapel shortly after Spurgeon's arrival was one of the clearest indications to the members of the church that God's Spirit was once again at work in their midst. Spurgeon described the exhilaration of those early prayer meetings:

> I can never forget how earnestly they prayed. Sometimes they seemed to plead as though they could really see the Angel of the covenant present with them, and as if they must have a blessing from Him. More than once we were all so awe-struck with the solemnity of the meeting, that we sat silent for some moments while the Lord's power appeared to overshadow us; and all I

---

29. Carlile, *C. H. Spurgeon: An Interpretive Biography*, 111.
30. Fullerton, *C. H. Spurgeon: A Biography*, 84.
31. *C. H. Spurgeon's Autobiography*, 1:135, 141.

could do on such occasions was to pronounce the Benediction, and say, "Dear friends, we have had the Spirit of God here very manifestly tonight; let us go home and take care not to lose His gracious influences." Then down came the blessing; the house was filled with hearers, and many souls were saved. I always give all the glory to God, but I do not forget that He gave me the privilege of ministering from the first to a praying people. We had prayer-meetings in New Park Street that moved our very souls. Every man seemed like a crusader besieging in the New Jerusalem, each one appeared determined to storm the Celestial City by the might of intercession; and soon the blessing came upon us in such abundance that we had not room to receive it.[32]

The congregation found themselves caught up in one of those unique and thrilling periods that churches sometimes enjoy when experiencing the special blessing of God: an altogether extraordinary season distinguished by Spirit-anointed preaching, explosive growth, and vigorous prayer meetings that often extend late into the night.

Throughout his ministry Spurgeon would give special prominence to prayer meetings.[33] He viewed the prayers of the members of his congregation like the engine room of a great ship; they propelled the entire ministry of the church and supplied it with all its power. When asked by one eager American for the secret to his enormous success, Spurgeon replied, "My people pray for me."[34] The most lasting testament to Spurgeon's commitment to prayer meetings is contained in his popular volume *Only a Prayer Meeting*, which includes forty short addresses on prayer that he gave in the context of his church's prayer meetings over the years. The church enjoyed fellowship and joy in prayer together from the beginning of Spurgeon's ministry in London as hundreds gathered to pray at the church's weekly prayer meetings. Spurgeon would later write, "The prayer meeting often seems to be held close to Jerusalem's city wall;

---

32. *C. H. Spurgeon's Autobiography*, 1:361.
33. Morden, *Communion with Christ and His People*, 140–42.
34. Carlile, *C. H. Spurgeon: An Interpretive Biography*, 25.

it stands in a sort of border land between the celestial and the ter-restrial; it is a house and yet a gate, fruition and expectation in one, the house of God and the very gate of heaven."[35]

Exeter Hall

By the middle of the year, the deacons of New Park Street faced a difficult challenge as they found themselves regularly turning away people each Sunday because of capacity issues. In September the congregation voted to enlarge their building to accommodate the multitudes who descended on Southwark each Lord's Day to hear Spurgeon preach. While this renovation took place, the church would rent Exeter Hall in the Strand just north of the River Thames in central London, practically equidistant between St. Paul's Cathe-dral and Westminster Abbey. Exeter Hall had seats for four thousand and standing room for one thousand more. Even with nearly four times the capacity of New Park Street Chapel, it would not be long before the church again had to turn away people. Exeter Hall appar-ently introduced Spurgeon to numerous crowds who otherwise would not hear him when tucked away in a dirty neighborhood south of the Thames.

The New Park Street Chapel opened again on May 31, 1855. The main hall could now seat fifteen hundred with room for another five hundred crammed into hallways and classrooms. After the extraor-dinary crowds that had come to hear Spurgeon at Exeter Hall, it appeared the money spent on the enlargement at New Park Street was wasted. To stem the tide, the church decided to hold the Sun-day morning service at New Park Street Chapel and then return to Exeter Hall for the evening service. But the church's deacons realized this was not an acceptable long-term arrangement. The coming years would see the church move between a handful of massive venues, ultimately culminating in the erection of a new building of unprec-edented proportions.

---

35. C. H. Spurgeon, "Between Two," *Sword and the Trowel* (August 1868): 340.

Spurgeon preaching at Exeter Hall in early 1855

Cholera Strikes London

As the extraordinary year of 1854 drew to a close, a devastating trial visited South London, threatening to plunge the church into a state of crisis. Not even a year after Spurgeon arrived in London, he found himself ministering amid an unusually severe cholera epidemic that would ultimately take the lives of over ten thousand people. Cholera was a deadly disease typically spread through contaminated water. Many among Spurgeon's congregation fell prey to the disease, and Spurgeon was called on almost daily to minister to those who were sick. In recounting this difficult season of ministry, Spurgeon said, "During that epidemic of cholera, though I had many engagements in the country, I gave them up that I might remain in London to visit the sick and the dying. I felt that it was my duty to be on the spot in such a time of disease and death and sorrow."[36] Spurgeon was weighed down by both the death of so many of his beloved members and the fear that he himself would contract the disease, as it was believed in those days that cholera was contagious. He said, "Family after family summoned me to the bedside of the smitten, and almost

---

36. *C. H. Spurgeon's Autobiography*, 1:372.

every day I was called to visit the grave.... My friends seemed to be falling one by one and I felt or fancied that I was sickening like those around me. A little more work and weeping would have laid me low among the rest; I felt that my burden was heavier than I could bear. I was ready to sink under it."[37] Nonetheless, he labored on among those who were perishing and seemed prepared to face death if he, too, fell prey to the disease.

But one afternoon as he was returning home from yet another funeral, he saw a sign in a shopkeeper's window displaying the words of Psalm 91:9–10: "Because thou hast made the LORD, which is my refuge, even the most High, thy habitation; there shall no evil befall thee, neither shall any plague come nigh thy dwelling." Spurgeon received this text as the Lord's word to him, and he immediately derived strength from it. He continued to minister amid the epidemic in the confidence that God was with him to protect him.[38] Spurgeon never contracted cholera, and before long the plague subsided, but only after inflicting a painful toll on the church and the surrounding neighborhood. Through it all, Spurgeon proved himself to be a true shepherd of the flock and one who was ready to literally lay down his life in service to his congregation.

Winter soon set in, and Spurgeon's first year in London came to a close. Yet the curtains of his ministry were just opening, and the great drama of his momentous career had only just begun. It would have been impossible for him to know at that time, but he had just commenced one of the most extraordinary ministries in the annals of church history. Those who were truly aware of what was going on at New Park Street knew they were witnessing a genuine outpouring of God's saving power. Not all maintained this perspective, however. Spurgeon would learn of others who entertained more cynical views of the young preacher and were not shy about publishing their criticisms.

---

37. *C. H. Spurgeon's Autobiography*, 1:371.
38. *C. H. Spurgeon's Autobiography*, 1:372.

5

Opposition and Criticism

Spurgeon's first impressions of London were dismal and disenchanting, and there were some critics in London who developed similar views of Spurgeon. Though he was immediately received by many among the masses as a favored preacher of exceptional ability, not all shared this opinion. In fact, in his early years in London, Spurgeon ministered amid what he described as "a constant din of abuse" heaped on him by various quarters of the religious press.[1] For no sooner had Spurgeon entered the public eye than many of London's leading papers began to excoriate him as an arrogant, irreverent, and sensational preacher.[2]

The criticisms of Spurgeon started to mount in early 1855 and continued unabated throughout that year and into 1856. The services at Exeter Hall, which began in fall 1854, had greatly increased Spurgeon's visibility and popularity. They also opened his ministry to a far wider audience. As the crowds descended on the Strand in London to hear the gospel of free grace, some people came with less sanctified motives. Journalists, reporters, and sometimes even other preachers came in order to gather material to publish in articles that denigrated Spurgeon's ministry and, in some cases, openly attacked it.

1. *C. H. Spurgeon's Autobiography*, 2:52.
2. A fine summary and analysis of the criticisms of Spurgeon in both the popular and religious press of the day is found in Kruppa, *Charles Haddon Spurgeon: A Preacher's Progress*, 110–26.

The Nature of the Criticism

Though the criticisms were broad and diffuse, they seemed to hover around three main issues. The first category of criticism centered on doctrinal issues, particularly related to the centuries-old debates surrounding Calvinism and Arminianism. Chapter 8 of this book will discuss Spurgeon's theology and will include a consideration of his Calvinism. Suffice it to say for now, Spurgeon received criticism from people at both poles of this debate—those of a more hyper-Calvinist persuasion and those of a more Arminian bent.[3] The hyper-Calvinists criticized him because he offered Christ freely to the non-elect and taught the doctrine of duty-faith—namely, that it is a duty enjoined on all men and women to repent and believe the gospel.[4] They said of his preaching, "It's a second-hand ministry, deeply tainted with an Arminian Spirit."[5] Those who leaned in the direction of Arminianism criticized his Calvinistic doctrine, believing that his preaching of the doctrines of election and particular redemption diminished divine love and presented a God who was austere and removed.

A second focus of public censure was Spurgeon's manner, speech, and bearing in his preaching. Many regarded him as irreverent and vulgar and accused him of "a prostitution of the pulpit."[6] To them, he was unrestrained and impertinent, a kind of Victorian "shock jock" who was too ready to utilize humor, slang, and theatrics in order to win a following. They saw him as little more than an entertainer whose "trashy sermons" had the effect of sinking the pulpit ever

---

3. Pike, *Life and Works of Charles Haddon Spurgeon*, 1:148.

4. For a more thorough consideration of Spurgeon's conflict with hyper-Calvinism, see Iain Murray, *Spurgeon v. Hyper-Calvinism: The Battle for Gospel Preaching* (Edinburgh: Banner of Truth, 1995). Murray correctly notes that this was the first true controversy of Spurgeon's ministry. Though he was at the center of the controversy, it was largely prosecuted by his opponents among the Strict Baptists of London. See also Morden, *Communion with Christ and His People*, 63–66.

5. Pike, *Life and Works of Charles Haddon Spurgeon*, 1:169.

6. *C. H. Spurgeon's Autobiography*, 2:50.

lower as he impudently amused the basest members of society.[7] His sermons could be "highly gratifying," they said, only "to those who thirst after excitement as the drunkard thirsts after brandy or gin."[8]

The third category of criticism was related to Spurgeon's apparent pride and arrogance. To many, a man in his early twenties adopting such an air of authority, presuming to instruct the masses, and breaking so many social and religious conventions was simply unseemly. Who was this youth, this country yokel who supposed himself a prophet of the age? With what temerity and hubris did he assume such a high position in the religious arena of the greatest metropolitan center on earth? Surely he must be gripped by an overinflated ego and a smug sense of self-importance. Such were their suspicions.

There were papers that leveled other criticisms at Spurgeon, but these three types were the ones most often repeated. Each of the three can be seen in the examples below, which give a taste of the kind of censure and abuse Surgeon endured in his early years.

Samples of Criticism

The criticisms of Spurgeon were so severe and bitter that many people today may not believe such things were said of him without reading it for themselves. What follows is a sampling from the mountain of scurrilous articles and reports published in newspapers across the country. Most of what is included is drawn from Susannah Spurgeon's private collection of newspaper clippings about her husband, some of which was reproduced in Spurgeon's autobiography.

The hyper-Calvinists were among the first to level serious criticism at Spurgeon. In a January 1855 issue of the *Earthen Vessel*, a prominent hyper-Calvinist named James Wells published a scathing attack of Spurgeon under the pseudonym Job. Wells was a famous London preacher who was also a minister in the Southwark area of the city. He began his article by acknowledging Spurgeon's evident

---

7. *C. H. Spurgeon's Autobiography*, 2:55.

8. Carlile, *C. H. Spurgeon: An Interpretive Biography*, 116.

talents for oratory and public speech but then suggested that behind these public gifts lay a subtle deception: "We must then beware of words that are smoother than butter, and softer than oil.... It was by great, very great politeness that the serpent beguiled Eve; and, unhappily, her posterity love to have it so;—so true is it that Satan is not only a prince of darkness, but transformed also as 'an angel of light,' to deceive if it were possible, even the very elect."[9]

Having laid this foundation, even going as far as drawing a parallel between Spurgeon and the devil, Wells went on to make his meaning clearer:

> But I have—*most solemnly have*—*my doubts* as to the Divine reality of his conversion. I do not say—it is not for me to say—that he is not a regenerated man; but this I do know, that there are conversions which are not of God.... Concerning Mr. Spurgeon's ministry, I believe...that it is most awfully deceptive; that it passes by the essentials of the work of the Holy Ghost, and sets people by shoals down for Christians who are not Christians by the quickening and indwelling power of the Holy Ghost.... This is simply deceiving others with the deception wherewith he himself is deceived.[10]

A month later, the following comments appeared in the *Ipswich Express* on February 27, 1855:

> This youth is fluent, and the consequences are most distressing. As his own chapel is under repair, he preaches in Exeter Hall every Sunday, and the place is crammed to suffocation. All his discourses are redolent of bad taste, are vulgar and theatrical, and yet he is so run after that, unless you go half-an-hour before the time, you will not be able to get in at all. I am told, one leading minister of the Independent denomination, after hearing this precocious youth, said that the exhibition was "an insult to God and man."... The only impression, however, he seems to have produced upon the judicious few is one of

---

9. Quoted in *C. H. Spurgeon's Autobiography*, 2:38.
10. Quoted in *C. H. Spurgeon's Autobiography*, 2:38–39.

intense sorrow and regret that such things should be, and that such a man should draw.[11]

The *Essex Standard*, April 18, 1855, observed,

His style is that of the vulgar colloquial, varied by rant.... All the most solemn mysteries of our holy religion are by him rudely, roughly, and impiously handled. Mystery is vulgarised, sanctity profaned, common sense outraged, and decency disgusted.... His rantings are interspersed with coarse anecdotes that split the ears of the groundlings; and this is popularity! and this is the "religious *furor*" of London! and this young divine it is that throws Wesley, and Whitefield in the shade! and this is the preaching, and this is the theology, that five thousand persons from Sabbath to Sabbath hear, receive, and approve, and—profit by it![12]

The *Sheffield and Rotherham Independent*, April 28, 1855, had the following remarks:

Mr. Spurgeon preaches himself. He is nothing unless he is an actor,—unless exhibiting that matchless impudence which is his great characteristic, indulging in coarse familiarity with holy things, declaiming in a ranting and colloquial style, strutting up and down the platform as though he were at the Surrey Theatre, and boasting of his own intimacy with Heaven with nauseating frequency. His fluency, self-possession, oratorical tricks, and daring utterances, seem to fascinate his less thoughtful hearers, who love excitement more than devotion.... He glories in his position of lofty isolation, and is intoxicated by the draughts of popularity that have fired his feverish brain. He is a nine days' wonder,—a comet that has suddenly shot across the religious atmosphere. He has gone up like a rocket, and ere long will come down like a stick.[13]

---

11. Quoted in *C. H. Spurgeon's Autobiography*, 2:44.
12. Quoted in *C. H. Spurgeon's Autobiography*, 2:49.
13. Quoted in *C. H. Spurgeon's Autobiography*, 2:55.

Finally, the *Bristol Advertiser* of April 12, 1856, offered this analysis:

> Solemnly do we express our regret that insolence so unblush-ing, intellect so feeble, flippancy so ostentatious, and manners so rude should, in the name of religion, and in connection with the church, receive the acknowledgment of even a momentary popularity. To our minds, it speaks sad things as to the state of intelligence, and calm, respectful, and dignified piety among a mass of people who call themselves the disciples of Jesus. Where curiosity is stronger than faith, and astonishment easier to excite than reverence to edify, religious life must either be at a very low ebb, or associated with some other deleterious elements.[14]

Many more examples could be supplied to illustrate the kinds of vicious attacks the press leveled at Spurgeon, particularly at the dawn of his London ministry. In addition to these types of criticisms, some papers ran stories that included complete falsehoods and misinfor-mation. A few papers reported a story of Spurgeon sliding down the handrail of the pulpit stairs at New Park Street Chapel, a rumor that was not hard to refute, as the pulpit had no stairs.[15] Another espe-cially scandalous report was passed around and widely published suggesting that Spurgeon began one of his messages by publicly requesting that eligible young women in his audience cease sending private gifts to him in their efforts to court his affection.[16] The story was pure fiction, and it was eventually refuted and retracted, but by then it was too late. For some, the false report had already cemented in their minds the impression that Spurgeon was hopelessly preten-tious and conceited.

Many of the early criticisms of Spurgeon included prophecies that his popularity would soon come to an end. Several of his detrac-tors assumed his appeal was ephemeral and would simply run its course in a year or two. "Will his popularity last?" one paper asked.

---

14. Quoted in *C. H. Spurgeon's Autobiography*, 2:58.
15. Carlile, *C. H. Spurgeon: An Interpretive Biography*, 118.
16. *C. H. Spurgeon's Autobiography*, 2:60.

Spurgeon with his deacons in 1856

"We more than doubt it. It stands on no firm basis. Thousands who go now to hear him only go through curiosity.... The current will soon turn and leave him."[17] They viewed Spurgeon's preaching as the flavor of the month, a passing fascination among the masses that would ultimately prove transitory. That he would draw even larger crowds and keep them for nearly four decades would have been regarded as an impossibility by virtually all his opponents.

Reasons for the Criticism

Why was Spurgeon the victim of such an enormous tide of public hostility? It is hard for us today, with the limitations of more than a century and a half of historical and cultural distance, to fully comprehend all the factors behind these attacks. A few contextual factors can be identified, however, that help in explaining the opposition of many to Spurgeon's ministry.

First, Spurgeon was original in his preaching and showed little regard for religious tradition or convention. This is not to say he was original in his theology. Spurgeon often claimed that his theology was unoriginal and was broadly shared by the Puritans, the

17. Quoted in *C. H. Spurgeon's Autobiography*, 2:60–61.

Reformers, and the early church. He was always deeply suspicious of any novelty or originality in theology. But he did not show much regard or reverence for social and religious conventions, and it was this brand of originality that invited criticism. If the socially refined considered it uncouth for a preacher to shout in the pulpit, that meant essentially nothing to Spurgeon. If the educated elite expected sermons to contain little in the way of pathos, that did not affect him at all. If some thought that waving one's arms or walking back and forth across the platform was undignified for a preacher, Spurgeon hardly cared. He hated dead formalism. He had little regard for tradition for tradition's sake, and he felt no need to doff his hat for ceremony. He said, "As a general rule, I hate the fashions of society, and detest conventionalities, and if I conceived it best to put my foot through a law of etiquette, I should feel gratified in having it to do. No, we are men, not slaves, and are not to relinquish our manly freedom, to be the lacqueys of those who affect gentility or boast refinement."[18]

As the samples of criticism clearly demonstrate, this aspect of Spurgeon's ministry was one of the most odious to his detractors. He did not bow to the social expectations and religious formalities of his day, and this was severely off-putting to some. Thus, his originality in preaching invited the opprobrium of those who felt it their duty to guard the canons of polite convention.

A second and related contextual factor had to do with the state of preaching in London in the middle of the nineteenth century. Though Spurgeon was not wholly unique in his approach to preaching, it nonetheless seems to be generally true that few preachers in London in those days were marked by the same degree of earnestness and zeal in the pulpit. Many preachers in Victorian London, particularly in the Church of England, preached in a manner that was more removed and cerebral. Pathos and passion were in short supply. Spurgeon would often criticize preachers of his day, especially

---

18. Spurgeon, *Lectures to My Students*, 1:17.

those within the Church of England, for being too contrived, high-sounding, and grandiloquent in the pulpit.[19] He wanted preaching that spoke to the common man, who, he believed, had been completely forgotten by the contemporary religious establishment:

> The next thing we need in the ministry, now and in all time, is men of plain speech. The preacher's language must not be that of the classroom, but of all classes; not of the university, but of the universe. Men who have learned to speak from books are of small worth compared with those who learned from their mothers their mother tongue—the language spoken by men around the fireside, in the workshop, and in the parlor.... We must have plain preachers. Yet plain speech is not common in the pulpit. Judging from many printed sermons, we might conclude that many preachers have forgotten their mother tongue. The language of half our pulpits ought to be bound hand and foot, and with a millstone about its neck, cast into the sea: it is poisoning the "wells of English undefiled," and worse still, it is alienating the working classes from public worship.[20]

Spurgeon burst onto London's scene in the mid-1850s as a preacher who spoke directly to the average person on the street in plain English that anyone could understand. In doing so, he indicted his contemporaries, who, he believed, had failed the common people. His critics, for their part, responded by accusing him of irreverence, believing that his ministry tended to lower the dignity of the pulpit.

At least one more contextual factor is worth noting. Many people were troubled by Spurgeon's ministry because of what they perceived as his willingness to innovate in order to reach the masses. They were particularly critical of his readiness to rent large, public, secular venues for his services that were used for worldly purposes throughout the week. To some, this amounted to a kind of commercialization

---

19. David W. Bebbington, "Spurgeon and the Common Man," *Baptist Review of Theology* 5, no. 1 (Spring 1995): 70–71.

20. C. H. Spurgeon, "The Ministry Needed by the Churches, and Measures for Providing It," *Sword and the Trowel* (May 1871): 217–18.

of worship and a sacrilegious mixing of the sacred with the secular. Especially those in the Church of England, who were prohibited from conducting services outside their church buildings, found Spurgeon's practice an appalling experiment. When this tendency toward innovation was coupled with Spurgeon's relative youth and inexperience, it seemed impossible for some not to conclude that his unconventional methods were ostentatious and unbecoming.

Most of the criticisms of Spurgeon were truly shameful and unjust, and they appear even worse with the passage of time. Whatever their origin, it is plain the religious establishment of London was not prepared for this new force that had descended on the city. His opponents were knocked off balance and hardly knew how to respond to him except with derision and scorn.

The Criticism in Context

This recounting of Spurgeon's critics could give the impression that the public's attitude was universally hostile toward Spurgeon. But this would be a misrepresentation of the popular response to him. It must be remembered that while Spurgeon was being pilloried by some in the press, he was being gladly embraced by tens of thousands of ordinary people as a brilliant preacher and a kind of prophet of the age. Crowds flocked to hear him wherever he preached, and often as many people were turned away as were actually admitted. Furthermore, though he received his fair share of criticism, he also received a great deal of positive coverage in the press as well.[21] These more gracious and charitable treatments of his ministry more than rivaled the vituperative attacks of his critics.

Though there were scores of articles that positively reviewed Spurgeon's preaching, a couple of examples will suffice to illustrate the point. A fairly representative article in 1855 read,

---

21. In addition to the collection of negative articles on Spurgeon's ministry, Spurgeon's autobiography contains a substantial collection of positive articles that were also published in 1855 and 1856; see *C. H. Spurgeon's Autobiography*, 2:63–80.

God has wonderfully gifted this stripling; he has a powerful voice; an easy and abundant flow of matter. In fact, from the impression I was under, upon the whole, I could not help concluding that this young man is destined of the Lord to be a very useful and laborious servant of Christ. He speaks as one having authority, and not as the Scribes and Pharisees of our day. There are some of my friends who regard his youth as an obstacle to their well receiving him; but surely, God is able to work by means of a David or a Timothy as effectually as by more aged and experienced instruments; and a very few years' time will remove this objection.[22]

Numerous reports like this filled the papers all over London and throughout the nation. Though Spurgeon had his detractors, he also had many friends all over the country who were eager to publish glowing accounts of his preaching.

An especially memorable commendation came from one of the great actors and dramatists of the day, Sheridan Knowles. He was an early advocate of Spurgeon's preaching and was later to become a preacher himself. Knowles enthusiastically urged his acting students to attend the services of the new preacher from Cambridgeshire:

Go and hear him at once if you want to know how to preach. His name is Charles Spurgeon. He is only a boy, but he is the most wonderful preacher in the world.... He is simply perfect.... Why, boys, he can do anything he pleases with his audience! He can make them laugh, and cry, and laugh again, in five minutes. His power was never equaled. Now, mark my word, boys, that young man will live to be the greatest preacher of this or any other age. He will bring more souls to Christ than any man who ever proclaimed the gospel, not excepting the Apostle Paul. His name will be known everywhere, and his Sermons will be translated into many of the languages of the world.[23]

---

22. Pike, *Life and Works of Charles Haddon Spurgeon*, 1:149.
23. Quoted in *C. H. Spurgeon's Autobiography*, 1:354.

Knowles, who would die in 1862, would live to see the fulfillment of his prophecy.

Spurgeon's Response to Criticism

One might imagine that Spurgeon was undone by his critics, but nothing could be further from the truth. At times he seemed almost emboldened and invigorated by their attacks. Writing to his father in March 1855 he said, "For myself, I will rejoice; the devil is roused, the Church is awakening, and I am now counted worthy to suffer for Christ's sake."[24] In another letter he wrote, "I am usually careless of the notices of papers concerning myself,—referring all honor to my Master, and believing that dishonorable articles are but advertisements for me, and bring more under the sound of the gospel."[25] Speaking some years later to his students with the pedigree of long experience, Spurgeon said,

> Public men must expect public criticism, and as the public cannot be regarded as infallible, public men may expect to be criticised in a way which is neither fair nor pleasant. To all honest and just remarks we are bound to give due measure of heed, but to the bitter verdict of prejudice, the frivolous faultfinding of men of fashion, the stupid utterances of the ignorant, and the fierce denunciations of opponents, we may very safely turn a deaf ear.[26]

Though Spurgeon seemed to take these criticisms in stride, there were nonetheless indications that at times they drew blood. In one letter he said, "I am down in the valley, partly because of two desperate attacks in *The Sheffield Independent*, and *The Empire*.... Yet faith fails not. I know and believe the promise, and am not afraid to rest upon it. All the scars I receive, are scars of honour; so, faint heart, on to the battle."[27] In his sermons, Spurgeon at times even spoke of the

---

24. *C. H. Spurgeon's Autobiography*, 2:44.
25. *C. H. Spurgeon's Autobiography*, 2:52.
26. Spurgeon, *Lectures to My Students*, 2:173.
27. *C. H. Spurgeon's Autobiography*, 2:19.

pain caused by these attacks.[28] Though he was a man of extraordinary resilience, Spurgeon was not impenetrable. The constant waves of abuse made their mark and, at times, deeply discouraged him. He would be something less than human if they did not.

Nonetheless, though Spurgeon was at times disheartened by his critics, he reflected unusual fortitude in bearing up under their attacks. He was able to withstand the hostility of his opponents and to maintain a faith-filled outlook on his trials because of his understanding of the purposes of God in suffering. He knew that if he endured opposition for Christ's sake, he would be blessed and sanctified as a result. Spurgeon was helped to maintain this perspective by a gift his wife, Susannah (to be introduced in the next chapter), gave him. She, too, had read what she called the "heartless attacks" and "unjust and cruel words" written of her husband in the newspapers.[29] In the midst of a number of severe criticisms of him in the press, Susannah had printed and framed for her husband the text of Matthew 5:11–12: "Blessed are ye, when men shall revile you, and persecute you, and shall say all manner of evil against you falsely, for my sake. Rejoice, and be exceeding glad: for great is your reward in heaven: for so persecuted they the prophets which were before you." Susannah wrote, "The text was hung up in our own room, and was read over by the dear preacher every morning,—fulfilling its purpose most blessedly, for it strengthened his heart, and enabled him to buckle on the invisible armour, whereby he could calmly walk among men, unruffled by their calumnies, and concerned only for their best and highest interests."[30]

---

28. For examples, see C. H. Spurgeon, "Christ about His Father's Business," in *The New Park Street Pulpit: Containing Sermons Preached and Revised by the Rev. C. H. Spurgeon, Minister of the Chapel* (Grand Rapids: Baker Books, 2007), 3:61, 126.

29. *C. H. Spurgeon's Autobiography*, 2:61.

30. *C. H. Spurgeon's Autobiography*, 2:61.

God's Purposes in the Criticism

By 1857 the negative opinions of Spurgeon in the press began to shift. His opponents were fewer and less brazen. His friends and allies increased, and he began to enjoy a more vigorously positive reception throughout London. As time went on, many of the slanders against him proved false, and some of his critics warmed to him as they observed his faithfulness, devotion, and staying power. Many also changed their perspective on Spurgeon as they began to appreciate the lasting fruit in the lives of those who sat under his ministry. Spurgeon's church grew by the hundreds every year, and many other churches in the area were also enlarged and enriched by converts from Spurgeon's preaching. What some thought would be a ministry of passing interest proved to be more deeply rooted and genuinely fruitful. Though he would receive some measure of criticism his entire life, he would never again return to the experience of those early years when he endured such sustained abuse in the press.

Though the attacks on Spurgeon were bitter, one cannot help but discern something of God's hand in sanctifying him through these early trials. It would appear that God had a peculiar plan in exposing Spurgeon to such opposition, particularly at the outset of his ministry. It was as though the Lord were testing him and preparing him for a larger sphere of usefulness in the days ahead. To ascribe to God particular purposes in His mysterious providence, especially in the lives of others, necessarily involves some measure of speculation. Nonetheless, it appears that God's refining grace was at work in Spurgeon's life through the early attacks on his ministry. Criticism had a sanctifying influence on Spurgeon in at least three ways.

First, it humbled him. Spurgeon would struggle with pride all his life. As a young Christian, he referred to it as his "darling sin."[31] Considering his tremendous natural endowments, his prodigious public gifts, and the extraordinarily positive reception he received wherever he preached even as a teenager, it is hardly surprising to

---

31. *C. H. Spurgeon's Autobiography*, 1:146.

learn Spurgeon struggled with pride. One of the ways the Lord used criticism in Spurgeon's life was to guard him from becoming too puffed up with pride. Whatever the intentions of Spurgeon's critics, God used their criticisms for good. In the end, they performed a service for Spurgeon by helping him to remain humble and forcing him to learn at a young age that he was not immune to critique. The Lord did not permit Spurgeon to experience unmitigated adulation but rather peppered his experience with criticism so that his ministry would not become soured by ministerial pride and an overinflated ego. Spurgeon saw this as a kind of chastening from the Lord that was meant to guard him from vanity. He would observe to his ministerial students some years later,

> Pride is a deadly sin.... Forget expressions which feed your vanity, and if you find yourself relishing the unwholesome morsels, confess the sins with deep humiliation.... Knowing something myself of those secret whippings which our good Father administers to his servants when he sees them unduly exalted, I heartily add my own solemn warnings against your pampering the flesh by listening to the praises of the kindest friends you have. They are injudicious, and you must beware of them.[32]

Second, criticism softened him. Though we may marvel at the extraordinary maturity of his ministry even in his beginning years in London, he nonetheless had rough edges that needed to be smoothed over and aspects of his character that had to be refined. He also needed to go through trials and testing of various kinds in order to become a more effective and sympathetic pastor and preacher. One aspect of Spurgeon's sermons that has contributed greatly to their popularity is the evident sympathy he expresses for those who find themselves suffering in various ways. He was effective in his ability to encourage those who suffered, in large measure because of the extraordinary suffering he experienced. Had Spurgeon never

---

32. Spurgeon, *Lectures to My Students*, 2:174.

encountered any opposition or trial in his ministry, he would likely have been rougher, more cavalier, and more abrasive in his preaching. His sermons would have been more removed from the lives of his hearers, and he would not have expressed the same degree of gentleness, warmth, and care had he not endured some degree of trial and testing.

Spurgeon understood what it was like to be slandered and maligned for righteousness' sake. He knew what a bitter experience it was to be lied about and to be misrepresented. But Spurgeon also understood that God could use these trials to sanctify him, to soften him, and to refine him. The attacks on Spurgeon had the effect of making him a gentler and more tenderhearted pastor and better prepared him to sympathize with those who found themselves suffering for Christ's sake. He was already learning this lesson by 1858, when he said,

> There are none so tender as those who have been skinned themselves. Those who have been in the chamber of affliction know how to comfort those who are there. Do not believe that any man will become a physician unless he walks the hospitals; and I am sure that no one will become a divine, or become a comforter, unless he lies in the hospital as well as walks through it, and has to suffer himself.... Who shall speak to those whose hearts are broken, who shall bind up their wounds, but those whose hearts have been broken also, and whose wounds have long run with the sore of grief?[33]

Spurgeon was enabled to see God's purposes in the opposition he faced. God was working through his weakness and softening him in order that he might be more effective in his ministry to others.

Finally, criticism had the effect of focusing Spurgeon's attention and steeling his resolve to preach Christ freely and boldly to the needy people of London. Criticism and opposition have a way of

---

33. C. H. Spurgeon, "The Christian's Heaviness and Rejoicing," in *New York Street Pulpit*, 4:461.

provoking reconsideration of our course and direction. They cause us to look inward and to reevaluate our motives, our aims, and our path. As Spurgeon considered the course of his ministry in light of his opponents' attacks, he was confirmed in his belief that God had called him to the work of preaching the gospel and that it would demand nothing less than the best of him. This fresh resolve had the effect of exciting his zeal, increasing his boldness, and strengthening his determination to give his life in sacrificial service to Christ. With the assurance that God had called him, he would continue to preach the only way he knew how: as Christ's ambassador, earnestly offering grace to needy sinners who stood on the brink of eternity.

6

Love and Marriage

The years 1854 through 1856, though not without trials and challenges, were nonetheless a time of immense joy and happiness for Spurgeon. Despite the difficulties and criticisms he endured, he would regard this as one of the sweetest seasons of his life. It was during these years that he entered his life's calling to pastor the congregation of New Park Street Chapel. In the opening chapters of his ministry there, God allowed him to see extraordinary fruitfulness. Yet perhaps the greatest joy of all during these early years was that Spurgeon met and married the woman who would come to represent God's greatest earthly gift to him.

Susie

Susannah (Susie) Thompson was born in Old Kent Road, London, on January 15, 1832, a year and a half before Charles was born.[1] While Charles was raised a country boy, Susie grew up a city girl. She was reared by Christian parents in a solidly middle-class home. As such, she was granted access to many of the finest educational, social, and cultural opportunities that London afforded. Ray Rhodes notes, "Like most London girls, Susie was educated in music (she was a pianist), art, manners, etiquette, and homemaking."[2] Growing

---

1. The most significant treatment to date of Susannah Spurgeon's life is *Susie: The Life and Legacy of Susannah Spurgeon, Wife of Charles H. Spurgeon*, by Ray Rhodes Jr. (Chicago: Moody, 2018).
2. Rhodes, *Susie*, 32.

up in the culture of the city, she developed native good sense, keen intelligence, and a strong work ethic. In her adolescent years, she was well educated and was a pleasant and agreeable girl who loved to travel, enjoyed nature, and was comfortable in the society of friends and acquaintances. By the time she entered early adulthood, she had achieved many of the ideals of Victorian womanhood.

Susie came to faith in Christ in late 1852 at the age of twenty. Though she and her family often attended the services of New Park Street Chapel, she was converted while attending an evening service at Poultry Chapel, not far from St. Paul's Cathedral. That evening a minister named S. B. Bergne preached a sermon from Romans 10:8–9 that God used to draw Susie to Himself.[3] She would later testify, "From that service I date the dawning of the true light in my soul. The Lord said to me, through His servant, 'Give me thine heart,' and, constrained by His love, that night witnessed my solemn resolution of entire surrender to Himself."[4]

Though Susie had become a Christian, she nonetheless struggled with spiritual doubt and declension for the next year. Her first days as a Christian were not marked by the same kind of explosive joy and spiritual fervor that characterized Spurgeon's early Christian walk. She was spiritually timid and struggled as she sought to grow in her young faith. Though she was born again as a child of God, it was as though she possessed a kind of spiritual birth defect that impeded her from experiencing the fullness of fellowship with Christ that she so earnestly desired. Perhaps many young Christians can sympathize with Susie at precisely this point.

Susie Meets Charles

All of this began to change when Spurgeon first came to preach at New Park Street Chapel on December 18, 1853. Susie was not there that morning to hear his first sermon. After the morning message,

---

3. Rhodes, *Susie*, 46–47.
4. *C. H. Spurgeon's Autobiography*, 2:5–6.

however, many of the church's members spread the word throughout the community about the new preacher and invited their friends and family to come hear him preach again in the evening. Among those members was one of the church's leading deacons, Thomas Olney, who invited Susie to come and hear Charles preach that night. Susie had long been connected to the Olney family through her cousin who married Thomas's oldest son, William Olney. William would one day become a prominent deacon of the church as well. He and his father had been aware of Susie's spiritual struggles for some time.[5] The Olney family was eager for Susie to attend and hear Charles preach, hoping that he could be of some help to her.

Susie could not have been less impressed with Charles the night she first laid eyes on him. The sermon was largely lost on her, as she was too distracted by his shabby and inelegant appearance, observing his "huge black satin stock" and his "long, badly-trimmed hair, and the blue pocket-handkerchief with white spots." She was also put off by what she described as his "countrified manner and speech."[6] Rhodes writes, "She had been trained to appreciate societal propriety in speech, manner, and dress. Charles violated her preconceived notions of what was appropriate for a polite young man in Victorian times, and a preacher at that. Susie found Charles's hair, suit, mannerisms, and provocative preaching style offensive."[7] Some years later, Susie would reflect on her first impressions of Charles: "Ah! How little I then thought that my eyes looked on him who was to be my life's beloved; how little I dreamed of the honour God was preparing for me in the near future! It is a mercy that our lives are not left for us to plan, but that our Father chooses for us; else might we sometimes turn away from our best blessings, and put from us the choicest and loveliest gifts of His providence."[8]

---

5. Rhodes, *Susie*, 51.
6. *C. H. Spurgeon's Autobiography*, 2:8–9.
7. Rhodes, *Susie*, 47.
8. *C. H. Spurgeon's Autobiography*, 2:8.

Courtship

Despite her early misgivings about the new preacher from the country, Susie eventually began to attend New Park Street Chapel with more regularity. As she did, she started to profit more and more from Charles's preaching. What's more, she and Charles steadily began to cross paths outside the Sunday gatherings, often in the home of the Olneys. As Charles was getting to know Susie, he began to gain insight into her spiritual struggles. All indications are that his earliest interest in Susie was that of a pastor seeking to help one of the Lord's sheep. Their relationship was spiritual before it was romantic.

As Charles considered Susie's spiritual doubts and struggles, he gave her a special gift—an illustrated copy of John Bunyan's *Pilgrim's Progress*. In it he inscribed, "Miss Thompson, with desires for her progress in the blessed pilgrimage. From C. H. Spurgeon, April 20, 1854."[9] Bunyan's *Pilgrim's Progress* was exceedingly precious to Charles. "The allegory of the Pilgrim," notes Kruppa, "captured his imagination, and references to Christian's struggle toward the Celestial City appear frequently in the young Spurgeon's diary, sermons and letters."[10] Spurgeon professed to have read Bunyan's classic over one hundred times throughout his life and regarded it as the book he valued most besides

A photograph of Susannah Thompson, likely taken in the late 1850s

---

9. *C. H. Spurgeon's Autobiography*, 2:6–7.
10. Kruppa, *Charles Haddon Spurgeon: A Preacher's Progress*, 22.

the Bible.[11] With pastoral shrewdness, he selected it to suit Susie's spiritual need, as he believed it would direct her to the Bible and the precious promises of Scripture. Charles believed Bunyan possessed an extraordinary knowledge of the Bible and an unusual ability to infuse Scripture into his writing. He said of Bunyan,

> Read anything of his, and you will see that it is almost like read-ing the Bible itself. He had studied our Authorized Version.... He had read it till his whole being was saturated with Scrip-ture.... He cannot give us his *Pilgrim's Progress*—that sweetest of all prose poems,—without continually making us feel and say, "Why, this man is a living Bible!" Prick him anywhere; and you will find that his blood is Bibline, the very essence of the Bible flows from him. He cannot speak without quoting a text, for his soul is full of the Word of God.[12]

The book accomplished its intended purpose in Susie's life and became precious to her also as it spoke comfort to her aching heart. Bunyan's *Pilgrim's Progress*, coupled with Charles's Christ-centered preaching, had the effect of reviving Susie's faith and helping her make her way in her own spiritual pilgrimage.

As Charles and Susie continued to get to know one another, their friendship blossomed into romance. The date when this new chapter in their relationship began to be written was June 10, 1854. That day marked the reopening of the Crystal Palace, a massive architectural triumph constructed entirely out of iron and glass. The Crystal Pal-ace was first opened in Hyde Park for the Great Exhibition of 1851. For six months men and women came from all over the world to behold the technological, industrial, and cultural advances of the

---

11. C. H. Spurgeon, *Pictures from Pilgrim's Progress: A Commentary on Portions of John Bunyan's Immortal Allegory* (Pasadena, Tex.: Pilgrim Publications, 1992), 11. For Bunyan's influence on Spurgeon, see Morden, *Communion with Christ and His People*, 26–30.

12. *C. H. Spurgeon's Autobiography*, 4:268.

age. The Crystal Palace was then dismantled and reconstructed in South London near Sydenham Hill.[13]

Charles and Susie, along with a group of friends, attended the opening of the Crystal Palace in its new location. As they waited for the ceremony to begin, Charles quietly passed a book to Susie by Martin Tupper titled *Proverbial Philosophy*. As he gave it to her, he directed her attention to a chapter titled "On Marriage" and pointed to the following lines:

> Seek a good wife of thy God,
>   for she is the best gift of His providence;
> Yet ask not in bold confidence
>   that which He hath not promised:
> Thou knowest not His good will;
>   be thy prayer then submissive thereunto,
> And leave thy petition to His mercy,
>   assured that He will deal well with thee.
> If thou are to have a wife of thy youth,
>   she is now living on the earth;
> Therefore think of her, and pray for her weal;
>   yea, though thou has not seen her.[14]

Charles then whispered softly to Susie, "Do you pray for him who is to be your husband?"[15] She recalled,

> I do not remember that the question received any vocal answer; but my fast-beating heart, which sent a tell-tale flush to my cheeks, and my downcast eyes, which feared to reveal the light which at once dawned in them, may have spoken a language which love understood. From that moment, a very quiet and subdued little maiden sat by the young Pastor's side, and while the brilliant procession passed round the Palace, I do not think she took so much note of the glittering pageant defiling before

---

13. *C. H. Spurgeon's Autobiography*, 2:7.

14. M. F. Tupper, *The Poetical Works of Martin Tupper: Including Proverbial Philosophy, A Thousand Lines, Hactenus Geraldine, and Other Poems*, series 1 (New York: John Wilen, 1859), 156.

15. *C. H. Spurgeon's Autobiography*, 2:6–7.

her, as of the crowd of newly-awakened emotions which were palpitating within her heart.[16]

Once the festivities came to an end, Charles invited Susie to walk the palace grounds with him, and they spent the rest of the day together. Susie would later write, "During that walk, on that memorable day in June, I believe God Himself united our hearts in indissoluble bonds of true affection, and, though we knew it not, gave us to each other forever…. From that time our friendship grew apace, and quickly ripened into deepest love."[17]

Within two months Charles proposed to Susie on August 2, 1854, in her grandfather's garden. Susie recalled, "Was there ever quite such bliss on earth before?"[18] Indeed, the happiness and joy the two felt that day in one another's love was to continue for a lifetime, for God would give to Charles and Susie the happiest of marriages. Susie recorded in her diary that evening, "August 2, 1854.—It is impossible to write down all that occurred this morning. I can only adore in silence the mercy of my God, and praise Him for all His benefits."[19]

Marriage

Throughout the remainder of 1854 and all of 1855, Charles and Susie continued to spend time together as they anticipated their wedding day. During these months Charles's ministry was growing, as was criticism of him in the press. Susie proved herself to be a faithful encourager of Charles and a wonderful supporter of his ministry. She would always be a stabilizing force in his life and a seemingly endless source of wisdom, prayer, encouragement, and love.

The period leading up to the marriage was also sweetened by a number of happy events. On January 23, 1855, Susie shared her

---

16. *C. H. Spurgeon's Autobiography*, 2:8.
17. *C. H. Spurgeon's Autobiography*, 2:8.
18. *C. H. Spurgeon's Autobiography*, 2:8.
19. *C. H. Spurgeon's Autobiography*, 2:9.

testimony of saving faith before the congregation of New Park Street. Spurgeon could hardly contain his happiness, writing, "Oh! I could weep for joy (as I certainly am doing now) to think that my beloved can so well testify to a work of grace in her soul."[20] Charles enjoyed the added delight of getting to baptize his fiancé a week later on February 1.[21]

Over the course of the year 1855, the couple enjoyed a special and highly cherished experience as they embarked on a joint literary project that deeply enriched their relationship. One day Charles presented Susie with an old volume by the popular Puritan writer Thomas Brooks. He said to her, "I want you to go carefully through this volume, marking all those paragraphs and sentences that strike you as being particularly sweet, or quaint, or instructive; will you do this for me?"[22] Susie eagerly took up the project and pulled together a number of her favorite quotes from the book. The outcome was a small volume Charles published under the title *Smooth Stones Taken from Ancient Brooks*.[23]

The year was filled with romance and love between the couple and made for a sweet and memorable prelude to their wedding ceremony on January 8, 1856. The wedding was held at New Park Street Chapel, which was filled to overflowing. Over two thousand people had to be turned away, but that did not stop them from crowding the streets outside the chapel so they might catch a glimpse of the newly married couple.[24] The wedding was regarded as a major event all over the city, and a number of papers ran the story. Susie referred to the occasion as the day on which "I became the loved and loving wife of the best man on God's earth."[25] Charles knew that in a thousand

---

20. *C. H. Spurgeon's Autobiography*, 2:10.

21. Rhodes, *Susie*, 66.

22. *C. H. Spurgeon's Autobiography*, 2:19.

23. C. H. Spurgeon, *Smooth Stones Taken from Ancient Brooks* (London: W. H. Collingridge, 1859).

24. Rhodes, *Susie*, 66.

25. *C. H. Spurgeon's Autobiography*, 2:28.

lifetimes he could never find a more loving and supportive life companion. She would prove to be perfectly suited to walk alongside him in the extraordinary calling that God had given to him.

A Happy Home

After their honeymoon abroad in Paris, the Spurgeons moved into their first home on New Kent Road, London, not far from New Park Street Chapel, where they lived comfortably for a year and a half. The couple resided at three addresses over the course of their marriage. The second was a few miles farther south on Nightingale Lane, where they lived from 1857 to 1880 in a home they called Helensburgh House.[26] Their final home, which they called Westwood, was located farther south in Beulah Hill, not far from the Crystal Palace.

*The Spurgeons' second home,
called Helensburgh House, located in Clapham*

---

26. The home the Spurgeons first purchased on Nightingale Lane was torn down in 1869 and rebuilt. They lived there another decade until 1880.

It was in their first home on New Kent Road that the young couple welcomed their twin sons, Charles and Thomas, on September 20, 1856. Charles and Thomas, who would both go on to be ministers themselves, were a continual source of delight to their father and mother. The boys, for their part, regarded their parents throughout their lives with warmth and affection. In all the many recollections left behind by Charles and Thomas, they do not breathe even a word of disappointment or dissatisfaction with their father and mother but only exude the most earnest love and gratitude for their parents.

Spurgeon with his twin sons, Charles and Thomas, around 1858/59

Regrettably, some of the men who have been most celebrated throughout Christian history were not known for being especially good husbands and fathers. Some neglected their families as they pursued their ministry ambitions. Happily, this cannot be said of Charles Spurgeon, who shined brightly as a devoted husband and father even as he carried on an extraordinary ministry. His legacy is that of a man who led his family well, maintained the love and respect of his wife and children, and created a home environment marked by tenderness and joy. The Spurgeon family was immensely happy, and their home became "a warm and comfortable refuge."[27] As hundreds of visitors would attest over the years, the Spurgeon home was a harbor of hospitality, gladness, and generosity. Ray Rhodes writes, "Home was the base of their larger ministry and the starting point of all that was good in their service to others."[28] Spurgeon was the animating

27. Rhodes, *Yours, till Heaven*, 142.
28. Rhodes, *Yours, till Heaven*, 156.

force behind this domestic ethos, leading the family to serve one another and all who entered their door lovingly and cheerfully.

At the center of the Spurgeon home was their daily rhythm of family worship.[29] Spurgeon aligned himself with the views of one of the Puritan greats, saying, "I agree with Matthew Henry when he says, 'They that pray in the family do well; they that pray and read the Scriptures do better; but they that pray, and read, and sing do best of all.' There is a completeness in that kind of family worship which is much to be desired."[30] The Spurgeons enjoyed family worship in the morning and the evening, and it provided the spiritual pulse that gave life to everything they did. Spurgeon's approach to family worship was rather simple and unoriginal; it typically included prayer and Scripture reading followed by a few extemporaneous comments from Spurgeon and often the singing of a hymn. When toward the end of her life Susie recalled these small gatherings, what stood out to her most were her husband's prayers. She wrote, "After the meal was over, an adjournment was made to the study for family worship, and it was at these seasons that my beloved's prayers were remarkable for their tender childlikeness, their spiritual pathos, and their intense devotion. He seemed to come as near to God as a little child to a loving father, and we were often moved to tears as he talked thus face to face with his Lord."[31]

Spurgeon's friend and former student William Williams provided the following reminiscence from his visits to the Spurgeon home:

> One of the most helpful hours of my visits to Westwood was the hour of family prayer. At six o'clock all the household gathered into the study for worship. I was sometimes asked to pray, but usually, and happily, Mr. Spurgeon would take the exercises of reading and praying himself. The portion read was invariably accompanied with exposition. How amazingly helpful

29. Morden, *Communion with Christ and His People*, 140.
30. C. H. Spurgeon, "The Happy Duty of Daily Praise," in *Metropolitan Tabernacle Pulpit*, 32:289. See also Morden, *Communion with Christ and His People*, 147.
31. *C. H. Spurgeon's Autobiography*, 4:64.

those homely and gracious comments were!... How full, too, of tender pleading, of serene confidence in God, of world-embracing sympathy, were Mr. Spurgeon's prayers! With what gracious familiarity he could talk with his Divine Master! Yet what reverence ever marked his address to his Lord! His public prayers were an inspiration and benediction, but his prayers in the family were to me more wonderful still. The beauty of them was ever striking; figures, symbols, citations of choice Scriptural emblems, all given with a spontaneity and natural-ness that charmed the mind and moved the heart, and served to bring home the conviction that Mr. Spurgeon bowed before God in family prayer appeared a grander man even than when holding thousands spellbound by his oratory.[32]

Stories such as Williams's abound. The Spurgeon home emanated an aroma of love and worship that ministered not only to the family but to hundreds of guests over the years.

In Sickness and in Health

Though the Spurgeon residence was the happiest of homes, it was not without its sorrows and trials. Both Charles and Susie would endure severe tests of ill health throughout virtually the entirety of their adult lives. Chronic physical suffering would become one of the larger themes of both their marriage and their ministry. Many over the years have found comfort in the stories of Charles and Susannah Spurgeon precisely because of their familiarity with suffering of this kind.

Susie's health issues may have had a direct bearing on her abil-ity to bear children after the arrival of the twins. One may perhaps wonder why such a happy home was not populated with more chil-dren. Though it is possible Charles's demanding schedule influenced their decision to have only two children, it is more likely that this decision was related to a physical condition from which Susie suf-fered. Though no records of a clear diagnosis exist, we do know Susie underwent a fairly serious operation performed by one of England's

---

32. Williams, *Personal Reminiscences*, 83–85.

leading obstetricians in 1868.[33] Sir James Young Simpson was Queen Victoria's favorite doctor and a renowned surgeon. He was known for his breakthrough research in the study of gynecology.[34] Thus, that Spurgeon contracted Simpson for his wife's surgery provides at least one clue to Susie's condition. Some have speculated that she suffered from endometriosis, which can cause severe pain, chronic fatigue, and infertility, among other symptoms.[35] Nonetheless, a precise diagnosis has eluded historians.

Whatever her condition, Susie eventually became a functional invalid. She was largely confined to the home for much of the rest of her life. As we will see, however, this did not keep her from engaging in active service to Christ and His church. Though always restricted because of health issues, she nonetheless was an eager worker for Christ who invested her talents and labors for the kingdom of God. She also proved an extraordinary helper, lover, and companion to Charles, despite some of her physical limitations.

For his part, Charles suffered most of his adult life with rheumatic gout along with chronic kidney problems (later diagnosed as Bright's disease). By the time Spurgeon reached his forties, he had already begun to regularly experience protracted seasons of ill health that often laid him low for weeks on end, requiring him to be out of the pulpit, sometimes for months at a time.[36] During these seasons he would often seek retreat in a climate more conducive to rest and recuperation in the south of France in a town called Menton on the French Riviera. We will consider in a later chapter how these struggles sanctified Spurgeon and influenced his ministry.

Though their physical suffering introduced numerous challenges and sorrows to their family, Charles and Susie found that these trials brought them closer and enlarged their affection for one

---

33. Rhodes, *Susie*, 124–30.

34. Peter Masters, *Men of Destiny* (London: Wakeman Trust, 2008), 46.

35. Susan Valerie Baker, "'Susannah and the Lemon Tree': Mrs. C. H. Spurgeon's Book Fund," *Baptist Quarterly* 48, no. 4 (2017): 160n5.

36. Morden, *Communion with Christ and His People*, 259.

another. In a mysterious way, they even seemed to sweeten the home as Charles and Susie each served and supported the other amid the difficulties brought on by poor health. They experienced a kind of fellowship and intimacy born of suffering that deepened their love and enriched their marriage.

Tragedy Strikes

In 1856 the trials of ill health that the Spurgeons were to experience lay in the future. The domestic situation into which the twins were born in September of that year could not have been happier. The couple were still newlyweds, and Charles's ministry was thriving. By summer 1856, it was clear that the newly enlarged New Park Street Chapel would not be a sufficient venue for Spurgeon's congregation—certainly not as long as he was their pastor. On Monday evening, September 29, 1856, the congregation held a members' meeting in which they formally resolved to erect a new building that could serve as a permanent meeting space.[37] That night, the vision for what would become the Metropolitan Tabernacle was first set forth. At that point, however, no one fully comprehended the scale of the project they were about to undertake, nor did they anticipate the extraordinary things the Lord would do one day in their new building. Nonetheless, the work was formally begun as a result of that congregational meeting. In the meantime, the church would again search for a temporary venue that could accommodate the enormous crowds who came to hear their pastor preach week by week—a task that increasingly felt to them like trying to "put the sea into a tea-pot."[38]

This led Spurgeon and his deacons to consider the newly erected Surrey Gardens Music Hall as a suitable meeting place. Their options were severely limited, as they required a venue that held several thousand people, possessed good acoustics such that Spurgeon could be

---

37. *C. H. Spurgeon's Autobiography*, 2:311.
38. *C. H. Spurgeon's Autobiography*, 2:197.

The Surrey Gardens Music Hall

heard by all, and was not open on the Sabbath day for business. The Surrey Gardens Music Hall, which held up to twelve thousand people, met all these criteria.

Spurgeon knew the decision to rent the hall would be regarded as controversial by some. Not only would many in the press accuse him of hubris for renting so large a venue, but some also charged him with sacrilege for securing a hall that was used for secular purposes during the week, such as bear baiting, musical concerts, and firework displays. Nor was criticism limited only to the press. Some of New Park Street Chapel's members disapproved of the decision to rent the venue and made their complaints known to the church's officers.[39] But Spurgeon and the deacons forged ahead, confident that God would bless the services at the Surrey Gardens Music Hall and use them to bring many under the sound of the gospel.

The first service in the hall was scheduled for Sunday evening, October 19, 1856. Spurgeon thereafter spoke of that evening as "a

---

39. Morden, *C. H. Spurgeon: The People's Preacher*, 67–68; and *C. H. Spurgeon's Autobiography*, 2:199.

night which time will never erase from my memory."[40] Even as Spurgeon approached the building from a side street, where he used a private entrance, he "felt overweighted with a sense of responsibility, and filled with a mysterious premonition of some great trial shortly to befall me."[41] He later recounted, "Here I was to pass through the greatest ordeal of my life."[42]

Thousands of people poured into the hall until it was practically overrun, some fearing that too many had been allowed inside. Several thousand were still denied entry but nonetheless crowded shoulder to shoulder in the streets outside, hoping to get as near as they could to the momentous event. Inside was a scene of excited commotion and disorder as men and women pressed past one another to get as close as possible to the platform. The feeling in the air was electric. Anticipation mounted as they prepared to witness

Spurgeon preaching in the Surrey Gardens Music Hall in October 1856

40. C. H. Spurgeon, *The Saint and His Saviour, or the Progress of the Soul in the Knowledge of Jesus* (New York: Sheldon, Blakeman, 1857), 340.

41. *C. H. Spurgeon's Autobiography*, 2:199.

42. *C. H. Spurgeon's Autobiography*, 2:201.

what an observer described as "one of the most eventful nights that have descended upon our metropolis for generations."[43] Nothing like it had ever been seen in London. In one of the largest and most beautiful public venues in the heart of the city, London's premier preacher, a youth of only twenty-two, was to herald the gospel to over ten thousand souls.

Once he learned the room was full and the doors had been shut, Spurgeon decided to begin the service ten minutes early. As he took the platform, surrounded by an entourage of deacons, a reverential silence descended on the meeting, which seemed to consecrate the service. Spurgeon opened the meeting in prayer and then announced the hymn, which the assembly thunderously sang without any instrumental accompaniment. The whole building seemed to pulsate with the exalted sound of Christian worship that united the hearts of the thousands who had perhaps been strangers to one another until that night. Spurgeon then read a passage of Scripture, providing extemporaneous commentary as he made his way through the text. He then led the congregation once again in a moment of solemn prayer.

It was at this still moment, when the heads of all were bowed and their eyes closed, that a group of miscreants carried out what appeared to be a premeditated plot to disturb and disrupt the gathering. Multiple shouts of "Fire!" and "The galleries are giving way!" were heard throughout the building. Mass chaos ensued. There was no fire, but hundreds immediately began to rush toward the exits. In all the mayhem and disorder, a stairwell in one of the galleries collapsed, and numerous people were trampled underfoot. In the end, seven died and twenty-eight more were seriously injured.[44]

As many people looked around, trying to make sense of the commotion, Spurgeon did what he could to calm the gathering. Some encouraged him to move ahead with his sermon, and he even tried to preach, but to no avail. He quickly adjourned the meeting,

---

43. *C. H. Spurgeon's Autobiography*, 2:201.
44. *C. H. Spurgeon's Autobiography*, 2:212.

instructing the congregation to move in an orderly way to the exits. He then collapsed and had to be escorted out of the building. From there he was speedily ushered to the home of a friend to recover from the ordeal.

The Aftermath

Spurgeon was utterly undone by the disaster at the Surrey Gardens Music Hall. The event plunged him into the deepest depression of his life. Some close to him feared he might even be a danger to himself in the wake of the tragedy. Susie wrote, "My beloved's anguish was so deep and violent, that reason seemed to totter in her throne, and we sometimes feared that he would never preach again."[45] Spurgeon would later say, "Here my mind lay, like a wreck upon the sand, incapable of its usual motion." "My thoughts," he said, "were like pieces of broken glass, the piercing and cutting miseries of my pilgrimage."[46] He spoke of torturous nightmares, daily fits of uncontrollable weeping, and "a kind of stupor of grief [that] ministered a mournful medicine to me."[47]

The sad experience formed one of the definitive moments of Spurgeon's life. Historian Mark Hopkins goes so far as to suggest it was "an episode whose importance in Spurgeon's spiritual experience was second only to that of his conversion."[48] In truth, his life would never be the same again. The trauma of the event imposed such a severe toll on his body and mind that Susie later testified, "He carried the scars of that conflict to his dying day, and never afterwards had he the physical vigour and strength which he possessed before passing through the fierce trial."[49] His friend, William Williams, voiced what others perhaps thought—that the catastrophe at

45. *C. H. Spurgeon's Autobiography*, 2:192.
46. Spurgeon, *Saint and His Saviour*, 341.
47. Spurgeon, *Saint and His Saviour*, 340.
48. Hopkins, *Nonconformity's Romantic Generation*, 128.
49. *C. H. Spurgeon's Autobiography*, 2:193.

the Surrey Gardens Music Hall was one of the factors that contributed to Spurgeon's premature death at fifty-seven.[50]

It was not simply the trauma of the scene at the Surrey Gardens Music Hall that affected Spurgeon so intensely. He seemed to suffer also from a convoluted and irrational sense of guilt, a feeling that somehow his ministry precipitated this tragic episode and led to all the sorrow and bereavement that followed in its wake. Compounding Spurgeon's grief was that he was, as Fullerton put it, "traduced and slandered by almost the entire newspaper press."[51] The heinous and libelous accusations against Spurgeon that poured forth from the papers in the aftermath of the Surrey Gardens disaster were of a piece with the press's earlier treatment of him. Many of his opponents seemed to view the catastrophe as an opportunity to pounce. The whole affair was a living nightmare.

Many of Spurgeon's biographers have observed that one of the lingering effects of this episode in Spurgeon's life was that he suffered from a form of post-traumatic stress that manifested itself in what we would today call panic attacks.[52] "From this time on," Morden writes, "Spurgeon experienced mood swings which could be violent and sudden with ecstasy giving way to weeping and despair."[53] Spurgeon could be preaching in another church, enjoying a vacation, or simply sitting in his back garden when, unbeckoned, the memories of that fateful evening would all of a sudden flood his mind and overwhelm his psyche, impressing on him the misery of that night as though it were occurring all over again.

Spurgeon already tended to become nervous in crowds. The disaster at the Surrey Gardens Music Hall greatly magnified this

---

50. Williams, *Personal Reminiscences*, 46.

51. Fullerton, *C. H. Spurgeon: A Biography*, 92.

52. Kruppa, *Charles Haddon Spurgeon: A Preacher's Progress*, 92–94; Morden, *C. H. Spurgeon: The People's Preacher*, 71; and Robert Shindler, *From the Usher's Desk to the Tabernacle Pulpit: Pastor C. H. Spurgeon, His Life and Work* (London: Passmore and Alabaster, 1892), 96–97.

53. Morden, *Communion with Christ and His People*, 261.

struggle. For a man who hardly preached anywhere without attracting massive audiences, this became an almost weekly battle for him. "Persons he feared not at all," noted Fullerton; "a multitude of people made him tremble."[54] When Spurgeon found himself preaching in an unfamiliar chapel or hall, he would often inspect the building beforehand, especially if it had galleries, to make sure the venue was in reliable structural condition.

Recovery, Renewal, and Resolve

For several days after the event, Spurgeon's mind was in tatters, his heart broken, and his voice silenced. He could not envision ever preaching again and was not even able to bring himself to read the Scriptures. He said, "Even the sight of the Bible, brought me a flood of tears."[55] But as God rescued David from the miry clay, He rescued Spurgeon from his despair and did so by a sudden deliverance. As Spurgeon described it,

> On a sudden, like a flash of lightning from the sky, my soul returned unto me. The burning lava of my brain cooled in an instant.... I was free, the iron fetter was broken in pieces, my prison door was opened and I leaped for joy of heart. On wings of a dove, my spirit mounted to the stars,—yea, beyond them. Whither did it wing its flight, and where did it sing its song of gratitude? It was at the feet of Jesus, whose Name had charmed its fears, and placed an end to its mourning. The Name—the precious Name of Jesus, was like Ithuriel's spear, bringing back my soul to its own right and happy state. I was a man again, and what is more, a believer.... Never since the day of my conversion had I known so much of His infinite excellence, never had my spirit leaped with such unutterable delight.[56]

We may wish for more details regarding this extraordinary experience. What exactly should we make of Spurgeon's account of it? His

---

54. Fullerton, *C. H. Spurgeon: A Biography*, 123.
55. *C. H. Spurgeon's Autobiography*, 2:207.
56. Spurgeon, *Saint and His Saviour*, 342–43.

description seems almost mystical. Whatever the nature of this experience, Spurgeon felt himself revived, refreshed, and recommissioned for gospel service. He would not descend endlessly into despair but would recover and once again preach the gospel to needy sinners.

On November 2, 1856, Spurgeon took to the pulpit of New Park Street Chapel just two weeks after the tragedy that had threatened to end his ministry. He spoke haltingly and solemnly for a few moments about the "terrible catastrophe" that "well-nigh prostrated me before." He then said with mounting confidence, "God will overrule it, doubtless.... It shall not stop us, however; we are not in the least degree daunted by it. I shall preach there again yet; aye, and God will give us souls there, and Satan's empire shall tremble more than ever. God is with us; who is he that shall be against us?"[57]

Spurgeon may have walked with an emotional and psychological limp after the Surrey Gardens Music Hall disaster, but even this trial would prove to deepen his spiritual experience and enlarge his sense of God's love and grace. He would continue to preach and would do so now with greater earnestness, sympathy, and resolve.

---

57. C. H. Spurgeon, "The Exaltation of Christ," in *New Park Street Pulpit*, 2:377.

The Metropolitan Tabernacle

The disaster at the Surrey Gardens Music Hall would not be the last word on Spurgeon's ministry—nor even the last word on his preaching in that venue. Spurgeon led his congregation to return to the Surrey Gardens on November 23, 1856, determined to preach Christ there to the thousands who thronged to hear him. He would hold services there on Sunday mornings for three consecutive years, until December 11, 1859. These were years of extraordinary fruitfulness for Spurgeon and his congregation. Not only did the church experience explosive growth in its membership during this time, but many outside the church who otherwise would not be found in a place of worship came to hear Spurgeon while he ministered at the Surrey Gardens Music Hall. Furthermore, many other churches in London subsequently grew in their membership as men and women were converted through Spurgeon's preaching. When Spurgeon recounted these years, what stood out to him most was the unusual blessing of God that attended the congregation's time there:

> God was with us. Conversions were numerous, and some of them were of a very striking kind; they were mainly from that stratum of society which is not touched by ordinary religious services.... All along through the years in which we worshipped in it, there were continual additions to the church, perpetual discoveries of fresh workers, and constant initiations of new enterprises. The College, Orphanage, Colportage, Evangelists, College Missions and our various branch mission-stations, have all benefited through the advance made by the

church during those services. We have seen good brought out of evil; and in our case we have been made to say with the psalmist, "Thou hast caused men to ride over our heads: we went through fire and through water; but Thou broughtest us out into a wealthy place."[1]

As blessed as these years were in the Surrey Gardens Music Hall, however, Spurgeon knew the church could not remain there forever, nor could they continue endlessly to rent enormous venues throughout the city. He knew they must seek a more permanent location in order to facilitate the long-term health, stability, and effectiveness of the church's ministry in London. Thus, the church initiated one of the most ambitious building projects in the history of Nonconformity in England.

Plans Are Laid
Spurgeon faced a serious pastoral dilemma, as he saw it. Thousands wished to hear him preach, and many of those converted under his preaching wished to join the church as proper members in order to come under the formal care and ministry of the church. But there was no room at New Park Street Chapel to accommodate such crowds. One of Spurgeon's close friends and a prominent member of the church, Morton Peto, stated the problem this way:

> Every week has borne testimony to the saving influence of the gospel, as it has been proclaimed in the Music Hall to an assembly of 5,000 persons. Still, with so large a congregation, and so small a chapel, the inconvenience of a temporary meeting-place becomes more and more grievously felt. There is, and has been for the past two years, as fair an average of that large congregation, who are devout persons, and regular attendants, as in any sanctuary in London. Yet not one-third of them can find a place under the same ministry for more than one service during the week. The church-members far exceed the extent of

---

1. *C. H. Spurgeon's Autobiography*, 2:223.

accommodation in our own chapel to provide all of them with sittings. It is only by having two distinct services that we can admit our communicants to the table of the Lord.[2]

Faced with this pressure, Spurgeon felt compelled either to build a building large enough to accommodate the growing membership of the church or to leave off being a pastor altogether and instead become a traveling evangelist.[3] If he were to be a true pastor, he could not tolerate holding numerous services in the same building where the body could never truly gather as one church. Nor could he allow a situation in which the members were forced to go without adequate pastoral care and accountability and the experience of meaningful congregational life. As important as preaching was to Spurgeon, he always felt there was more to the ministry of the church than preaching. The church is fundamentally a gathering of God's people who live together as one body, worshiping God, mutually loving and serving one another, observing the ordinances of baptism and the Lord's Supper, and working together to fulfill the Great Commission. If the congregation could not gather together and function as a true New Testament congregation, the church was effectively handicapped. Thus, it was principally pastoral instincts that fueled Spurgeon's ambition to erect a building that could house the whole of his church's burgeoning membership.[4]

On September 29, 1856, the New Park Street Chapel voted to build a new building that would accomplish this purpose. A building committee had been appointed a few months earlier to consider the matter and present a practical proposal to the congregation regarding what kind of building should be built and at what cost. The initial plan was to erect a facility that would seat five thousand people and would cost roughly twelve to fifteen thousand pounds. The final

2. *C. H. Spurgeon's Autobiography*, 2:322–23.
3. Chang, *Spurgeon the Pastor*, 6–7, 89.
4. *C. H. Spurgeon's Autobiography*, 2:313, 322–23.

structure would have room for nearly sixty-five hundred people and cost over thirty-one thousand pounds.[5]

Literally hundreds of architects bid for the project, but the one who ultimately secured the contract was William Higgs, who, as it turned out, was one of Spurgeon's early converts. He would later become one of the church's deacons and a lifelong friend to Spurgeon. He would also go on to supervise the construction of a number of other buildings connected to the church's ministry.[6]

The building would be called the Metropolitan Tabernacle. It was *metropolitan* because it was a church built *by* the city *for* the city. The project would be supported by literally thousands of contributors both inside and outside the church. People across the city of London from among every denomination were invested in the success of Spurgeon's church, and thus it was seen as a truly metropolitan enterprise. It was called a *tabernacle* because Spurgeon saw the church's building as only a temporary dwelling place for the congregation as they made their way to heaven. He wanted his people to be confronted with the reality that this building, as august and grand as it may appear, was not their final home. They, along with all God's people throughout the ages, looked finally to the Celestial City that awaited them. Until then, the Metropolitan Tabernacle would draw people from all over the city to come hear the preaching of the gospel, that they might be prepared for the world to come.

Building a New Home

The prospect of erecting a new and permanent building for the church seemed to marshal the congregation to fresh exertions of service and sacrifice. The weekly worship gatherings of the church began to be marked by an increased focus and energy. Prayer meetings took on new life. It seemed that the whole congregation

---

5. *C. H. Spurgeon's Autobiography*, 2:311, 333.

6. Eric W. Hayden, *A History of Spurgeon's Tabernacle* (Pasadena, Tex.: Pilgrim Publications, 1971), 61. After Higgs's death, his firm would rebuild the Metropolitan Tabernacle after it burned down in 1898.

experienced renewed zeal in the pursuit of this shared goal. The members banded together to give, to pray, and to prepare for what lay ahead.

A new building would mean new possibilities and new opportunities for the church. It would effectively provide them with a geographical locus from which to carry on a thriving ministry of word and deed in the heart of the largest city in the world. From the beginning, the vision for the Metropolitan Tabernacle was for a building that could function as both a highly visible and easily accessible preaching center as well as a central hub for the church's growing network of benevolent ministries.

For Spurgeon, this vision for a city-center church was immensely strategic from the viewpoint of God's kingdom. Such a ministry would be uniquely situated in the metropolis to witness to the saving power of the gospel and to evidence that power through compelling ministries of mercy. The church understood that the building project represented more than just a larger space to accommodate the crowds. It embodied a strategic kingdom outpost, a spiritual bulwark against the forces of hell, an altogether unique and unprecedented opportunity to reach the city and influence it for eternal good.

The proposed plan was not without its risks. It was wondered whether building so large a space was too ambitious and might even be perceived as ostentatious. Could it really be expected that a hall with a capacity of nearly sixty-five hundred people would actually be filled week by week? Spurgeon was an exceedingly popular preacher, but what if that popularity faded over the years? What about after Spurgeon's tenure as pastor? Could his successor keep the church together and continue to fill the building?

These were real objections and concerns that had to be seriously considered if the building campaign was to be pursued. In the end, however, the congregation judged it to be a risk worth taking. Spurgeon often addressed crowds far larger than sixty-five hundred. In fact, Spurgeon once preached to an assembly numbering 23,654 people at the Crystal Palace on October 7, 1857. On that occasion,

Spurgeon was invited to address the massive gathering on what was a day of national mourning in response to a violent mutiny that had taken place in India against the British East India Company.[7] Though this was an especially enormous gathering, it was still not unusual for Spurgeon to preach to congregations numbering over ten thousand. Furthermore, it must be remembered that Spurgeon was only twenty-two years old when the plan to build the Metropolitan Tabernacle was first proposed. He was twenty-six when the building was completed. Undoubtedly, the congregation was justified in their expectation that Spurgeon would be there for a long time. They were not disappointed in their expectation, as he would be their pastor for another three decades. The immense size of the project, though at times debated and discussed, did not finally present an insurmountable hurdle to the erection of the new building.

A further concern was the sheer expense of the whole endeavor. The initial estimate of twelve to fifteen thousand pounds, which proved to be less than half the actual cost, was daunting enough, even

*Spurgeon preaching in the Crystal Palace to a crowd
of approximately 23,654 on October 7, 1857*

7. *C. H. Spurgeon's Autobiography*, 2:239–40; and C. H. Spurgeon, "Fast-Day Service," in *New Park Street Pulpit*, 3:373–88.

for so large a congregation. What's more, Spurgeon had an extreme aversion to debt going back to his childhood.[8] If the Tabernacle were to be built at all, it would be built on cash, not credit. This made the final cost of over thirty-one thousand pounds seem that much more insurmountable. How could they hope to raise such a large amount of money? And even if such funds could be raised, could they not be better spent elsewhere?

On this point it appears Spurgeon and other leaders of the church were soundly convinced that the potential good coming from such an effort more than justified such an expenditure. Spurgeon seemed to never stray from his confidence that the winds of God's sovereign purposes were at his back and divine blessing rested on the work. As he believed it was God's will for them to erect the new building, Spurgeon encouraged his congregation to trust God to supply all the means necessary to complete the endeavor. "The Tabernacle is to be built," he would say, "and it will be built, and God will fill it with His presence and glory."[9] If funds were needed, God would surely provide them.

The church recognized that Spurgeon's ministry had been of enormous public benefit to people across the city. Already by 1856 hundreds had been converted through Spurgeon's preaching, and the whole religious world of London seemed to be newly awakened. Thus, the church felt certain that a building campaign would be met with the vigorous financial support of hundreds of willing friends beyond the New Park Street membership. The night the church approved plans to build the Tabernacle, they entered into the minute books a church resolution that stated, "[The building committee members] earnestly solicit the hearty co-operation of the Christian public in this undertaking. Their chief object in this movement is the welfare of the masses, who hitherto have been neglectful of their souls. Steady, earnest assistance is required, that the building may

---

8. *C. H. Spurgeon's Autobiography*, 1:39–40; 2:360–61.
9. *C. H. Spurgeon's Autobiography*, 2:327.

be erected. It would be gratifying to the Committee if every church in the kingdom had a brick or a beam in the new Tabernacle."[10] In the end, contributions would come from literally thousands of people across London—and indeed the entire nation—to support the new building.

Nonetheless, despite the assistance of many helpers, Spurgeon knew the heaviest stone would be his to lift and that if the funds were to be raised, he would have to put his hand to the plow himself in order to secure the needed amount. Thus, the church freed Spurgeon to commence a grueling preaching tour across the country in order to raise funds for the Tabernacle. For three years, from 1858 through 1860, Spurgeon had preaching engagements almost every day.[11] Though he would rarely be away from his church on Sunday, he often preached during the week in cities, towns, and villages across the nation and as far away as Scotland and Ireland. At these weekday meetings, he would preach a sermon and invite a collection of funds as part of each service, half of which went to support the Tabernacle and the other half to support the work of the gospel in that particular town or village. By this means, roughly half the needed funds for the erection of the Metropolitan Tabernacle were raised.[12]

Breaking Ground

A landmark day in the campaign arrived on August 16, 1859, as the first stone was laid in the building of the Metropolitan Tabernacle.[13] On that clear Tuesday afternoon, three thousand people gathered in the neighborhood of Newington Butts in South London, just across the street from the Elephant and Castle station. This new location was about four miles northeast of New Park Street Chapel, placing

10. *C. H. Spurgeon's Autobiography*, 2:311–12.

11. Morden, *Communion with Christ and His People*, 193; and *C. H. Spurgeon's Autobiography*, 2:335–52.

12. *C. H. Spurgeon's Autobiography*, 2:327, 335–52.

13. *C. H. Spurgeon's Autobiography*, 2:322.

the church closer to the heart of London and in a much more accessible district.

The meeting commenced with the singing of the Old Hundredth, a well-known versification of Psalm 100, the third stanza of which reads,

> O enter then His gates with praise,
> Approach with joy His courts unto;
> Praise, laud, and bless His name always,
> For it is seemly so to do.[14]

The hymn was followed by a short statement prepared by the deacons on the church's extraordinary recent history from 1854 through 1859 under Spurgeon's ministry. Then Spurgeon addressed the gathering. He had with him a large bottle that was to be buried under the foundation stone of the Tabernacle. In it he placed five items. The first was the King James Version of the Bible. Spurgeon said, "The Bible, the Word of God, we put that as the foundation of our church." He next placed a copy of the Second London Baptist Confession of Faith, "which," he reminded the audience, "was signed in the olden times by Benjamin Keach, one of my eminent predecessors." Spurgeon then deposited a copy of the deacons' statement that had just been read to the gathering, as well as a copy of John Rippon's hymn book. The last item was simply a record of the day's proceedings.[15]

Spurgeon went on to announce that the building they would erect would be deliberately constructed in what he called the Grecian style, as opposed to the Gothic style, which characterized the architecture of much of the rest of the neighborhood:

> It is to me a matter of congratulation that we shall succeed in building in this city a Grecian place of worship.... The standard of our faith is Greek; and this place is to be Grecian.... We

---

14. William Kethe, "Psalm 100," in *"Our Own Hymn-Book": A Collection of Psalms and Hymns for Public, Social, and Private Worship*, ed. C. H. Spurgeon (London: Passmore and Alabaster, 1866), no. 100.

15. *C. H. Spurgeon's Autobiography*, 2:323.

have a great part of our Scriptures in the Grecian language, and this shall be a Grecian place of worship; and God give us the power and life of that master of the Grecian tongue, the apostle Paul, that here like wonders may be done by the preaching of the Word as were wrought by his ministry![16]

Spurgeon then articulated what he regarded as the heart of the church's theology. He freely acknowledged the church's Calvinistic and Baptistic distinctives, but deliberately subordinated them to the broader gospel unity the church shared with the larger Christian family. In doing so, Spurgeon signaled that the church would not be marked by tribalism and division but by glad-hearted fellowship with all those who love the preaching of the cross:

As for our faith, as a church, you have heard about that already. We believe in the five great points commonly known as Calvinistic; but we do not regard those five points as being barbed shafts which we are to thrust between the ribs of our fellow-Christians. We look upon them as being five great lamps which help to irradiate the cross; or, rather, five bright emanations springing from the glorious covenant of our Triune God, and illustrating the great doctrine of Jesus crucified.... I love those five points as being the angles of the gospel, but then I love the centre between the angles better still. Moreover, we are Baptists, and we cannot swerve from this matter of discipline, nor can we make our church half-and-half in that matter. The witness of our church must be one and indivisible. We must have one Lord, one faith, and one baptism. And yet dear to our hearts is that great article of the Apostles' Creed, "I believe in the communion of saints." I believe not in the communion of Episcopalians alone; I do not believe in the communion of Baptists only, I dare not sit with them exclusively.... Whosoever loves the Lord Jesus Christ in verity and truth hath a hearty welcome, and is not only permitted, but invited to communion with the Church of Christ.... However sternly a man may hold the right of private judgment, he yet can give his

16. *C. H. Spurgeon's Autobiography*, 2:327–28.

right hand with as tight a grip to everyone who loves the Lord Jesus Christ.[17]

The day proved to be a memorable one for Spurgeon and the large crowd of witnesses. Many of those assembled had the sense that an extraordinary new work had been inaugurated and that something truly historic was taking place. An aura of reverential joy and expectation hung over the whole event. Spurgeon added the following entry to the church's minute books that day: "As a record of the laying of the first stone, the accompanying report is inserted. We were highly favored with the smile of our Heavenly Father, and desire to raise a joyful Ebenezer in remembrance of the happy event. May God speed the work, and permit us to meet for His service within the walls of the spacious edifice thus joyously commenced!"[18]

When the foundation stone was laid, Spurgeon was in the midst of the busiest preaching tour of his life. The fruit of this season of itinerant gospel ministry would be impossible to quantify. Hundreds of individuals across the country attributed their conversion to Spurgeon's preaching during this season. Small villages in the Cotswolds, Yorkshire, and Essex, as well as in large cities such as Bristol, Manchester, and Liverpool were graced with the preaching of the gospel from the famed Prince of Preachers. Whenever Spurgeon visited a new community, the local population bustled with commotion and excitement as thousands clamored to hear him preach the message of the cross and the good news of the grace and mercy found in Jesus.

Back in London, as Christmas approached, Spurgeon once again sought a temporary home for his church while they awaited the completion of the Metropolitan Tabernacle. The last service held at the Surrey Gardens Music Hall was on December 11, 1859. Spurgeon led the church to vacate the hall when the directors of the venue began to make it available on Sunday afternoons for secular events, which Spurgeon regarded as profaning the Sabbath day. From December

17. *C. H. Spurgeon's Autobiography*, 2:328.
18. *C. H. Spurgeon's Autobiography*, 2:330.

18, 1859, to March 31, 1861, the church would once again hold services in Exeter Hall until the Tabernacle was finished.[19]

The Opening of the Metropolitan Tabernacle

"In the providence of God, we, as a church and people, have had to wander often.... In each of our movings we have had reason to see the hand of God.... And now we journey to the house which God has in so special a manner given to us."[20] Spurgeon uttered these words during the last service at Exeter Hall before the congregation moved into their new facility. From 1854 through 1861, the congregation outgrew and then enlarged their chapel (to little effect), spent three years meeting in the Surrey Gardens Music Hall, and sojourned in Exeter Hall three different times. The day had finally come for the congregation to move into their new home, where they would reside for over a century and a half all the way to the present.

The Metropolitan Tabernacle

19. Pike, *Life and Works of Charles Haddon Spurgeon*, 1:326–27.
20. *C. H. Spurgeon's Autobiography*, 3:2–3.

At the start of 1861, a remaining four thousand pounds was needed to open the Metropolitan Tabernacle debt free. Spurgeon, ever confident this goal would be met, set a target date of March 31, 1861, for the first Sunday service in the Tabernacle. Sure enough, the sum was raised with the final contributions coming in no more than five days before Sunday, March 31. As Spurgeon had promised, the Tabernacle would be open free of debt.

The Metropolitan Tabernacle was a massive structure with three levels of seating, including main-floor seating and two balconies that wrapped all the way around the sanctuary. The room was designed in the shape of an oval, with all eyes being naturally directed toward the platform at the front, which was surrounded by a short wooden rail. The main platform had two levels: an upper level elevated above the main-floor seating that contained Spurgeon's preaching desk as well as room for several chairs where the deacons would sit, and a lower level that contained the baptistry, which was reached by two staircases on either side of the upper level.

The acoustics of the room were exceptionally good and perfectly suited the purposes for which the building had been erected. Visitors often commented that Spurgeon could be heard with ease from any seat in the sanctuary, and most listeners could catch even his most subtle vocal inflections. The a cappella singing of the thousands who attended the Tabernacle services became famous throughout the English-speaking world. Future American president James A. Garfield wrote of the Tabernacle singing in 1867, "The whole building was filled and overflowed with the strong volume of song. The music made itself felt as a living, throbbing presence, that entered your nerves, brain, heart, and filled and swept you away in its resistless current."[21] Spurgeon said, "Concerning this vast chapel, I believe it is the most perfect triumph of acoustics that has ever been achieved."[22]

---

21. H. L. Wayland, *Charles H. Spurgeon: His Faith and Work* (Philadelphia: American Baptist Publication Society, 1892), 57.

22. *C. H. Spurgeon's Autobiography*, 2:355.

Beyond the sanctuary, there were numerous other rooms throughout the building that were used for many purposes. Behind the sanctuary's upper platform was Spurgeon's vestry as well as the deacons' room and the elders' room, where both bodies held regular meetings. Underneath the sanctuary was a large lecture hall that could seat roughly fifteen hundred and was used for various purposes, including many of the church's prayer meetings and congregational members' meetings. In addition, the basement of the Tabernacle held numerous classrooms that were employed for Sunday schools, along with other rooms that housed all kinds of ministries and meetings.

Annexed to the building was a series of almshouses for poor widows, eventually totaling seventeen. This ministry, originally founded by Spurgeon's predecessor John Rippon in New Park Street, was designed to serve needy widows in the congregation who lacked the means to support themselves.[23] With the church now relocated in a new neighborhood, Spurgeon made provisions to substantially

A view of the interior of the Metropolitan Tabernacle from the back of the sanctuary

---

23. *C. H. Spurgeon's Autobiography*, 2:313–14.

expand this ministry.[24] The Tabernacle Almshouses, as they came to be known, would always occupy a special place in his heart. In Victorian London, widows were especially vulnerable and faced high economic and social hurdles. Spurgeon was thus eager to provide for their relief and protection, and he took on their burdens as his own. Peter Morden writes, "For some years he met the women's basic expenses, for example the costs of heating and lighting, from his own pocket. Spurgeon was not just the people's preacher—he was a man who helped ordinary people in practical ways."[25]

"To Teach and Preach Jesus Christ"

Though the first Sunday worship service would be held on March 31, 1861, the first sermon Spurgeon preached in the new building was actually on the afternoon of the preceding Monday, March 25, at a special gathering of the church to commemorate the opening of the Tabernacle. The occasion was truly momentous. Spurgeon knew he was embarking on a historic ministry in a historic venue at a historic period. His congregation had just completed the erection of the largest Protestant church building in Christendom. What's more, by 1861 Nonconformity in England was at the apex of its influence, and Spurgeon knew his church represented the very "forefront of Nonconformity."[26] He thus found himself at the helm of one of the most prominent churches in the Christian world as it made its celebrated new beginning in South London. What would Spurgeon preach on such a historic occasion?

He chose as his text Acts 5:42, "And daily in the temple, and in every house, they ceased not to teach and preach Jesus Christ." Spurgeon deliberately selected this text as a kind of mission statement for

---

24. C. H. Spurgeon, *The Metropolitan Tabernacle: Its History and Work, Mr. Spurgeon's Jubilee Sermons, A Memorial Volume* (London: Passmore and Alabaster, 1876), 52–53, 93–95; Hayden, *History of Spurgeon's Tabernacle*, 20–21; and Nicholls, *C. H. Spurgeon: The Pastor Evangelist*, 56–57.

25. Morden, *C. H. Spurgeon: The People's Preacher*, 153.

26. *C. H. Spurgeon's Autobiography*, 2:360.

the church. He began his message saying, "I do not know whether there are any persons here present who can contrive to put themselves into my present position, and to feel my present feelings.... I declare that I feel totally unable to preach." The occasion seemed to almost overwhelm Spurgeon. He took a few moments to highlight what he regarded as the defining feature of the teaching of the apostles—namely, their emphasis on the person and work of Jesus Christ. To them, He was "the central point." But Spurgeon quickly turned his mind from the primitive church to his own congregation, which sat before him in rapt attention. He then made a statement that would prove definitive for his ministry and for that of the Metropolitan Tabernacle over the next three decades:

> I would propose that the subject of the ministry of this house, as long as this platform shall stand, and as long as this house shall be frequented by worshippers, shall be the person of Jesus Christ. I am never ashamed to avow myself a Calvinist.... I do not hesitate to take the name of Baptist...but if I am asked to say what is my creed, I think I must reply—"It is Jesus Christ." My venerable predecessor, Dr. Gill, has left a body of divinity, admirable and excellent in its way; but the body of divinity to which I would pin and bind myself forever, God helping me, is not his system of divinity or any other human treatise, but Christ Jesus, who is the sum and substance of the gospel; who is in himself all theology, the incarnation of every precious truth, the all-glorious personal embodiment of the way, the truth, and the life.[27]

More than a century before the adjective *gospel-centered* began to make its way into the evangelical lexicon, Spurgeon announced that the ministry of the Metropolitan Tabernacle would indeed be centered on the gospel and would proclaim the person and work of Christ above all else. He closed this historic sermon with a characteristic appeal to prayer:

---

27. C. H. Spurgeon, "The First Sermon in the Tabernacle," in *Metropolitan Tabernacle Pulpit*, 7:169.

May I entreat in closing, your earnest prayer, each one of you, that in this house as well as in all the places of worship round about, Christ may evermore be preached.... Let me have your incessant prayers. May God speed every minister of Christ. But where there is so large a field of labor may I claim your earnest and constant intercessions, that where Christ is lifted up, men may be drawn to hear, and afterwards drawn to believe, that they may find Christ the Saviour of our soul.[28]

With the opening of the Metropolitan Tabernacle, a new day had dawned in London, and a new chapter was opened in Spurgeon's extraordinary ministry. By the time the Tabernacle opened its doors, many had already identified Spurgeon as the leading preacher of the age. Hundreds, and perhaps thousands, had been converted under his preaching. Tens of thousands among the common people of London had been brought under the preaching of the gospel for the first time. His church had grown to roughly two thousand members with a weekly attendance of three times that number at the regular worship gatherings of the church. Yet for all that, Spurgeon's most fruitful days of ministry still lay ahead of him.

Spurgeon seemed to possess an inward sense that greater things were before him. At the first Sunday evening service in the Metropolitan Tabernacle in 1861, Spurgeon concluded his message by inviting God to send the fires of revival among them and to do extraordinary things in their midst. Certainly, in hindsight, these words appear to be not only a prayer but a kind of prophecy. Perhaps Spurgeon knew, perhaps not, that he prophesied in truth:

Let God send the fire of his Spirit here, and the minister will be more and more lost in his Master. You will come to think less of the speaker and more of the truth spoken; the individual will be swamped; the words spoken will rise above everything; when you have the cloud, the man is forgotten; when you have the fire, the man is lost, and you only see his Master.

---

28. Spurgeon, "First Sermon in the Tabernacle," in *Metropolitan Tabernacle Pulpit*, 7:176.

Suppose the fire should come here, and the Master be seen more than the minister—what then? Why, this Church will become two, or three, or four thousand strong! It is easy enough in God to double our numbers, vast though they be. We shall have the lecture-hall beneath this platform crowded at each prayer-meeting, and we shall see in this place young men devoting themselves to God; we shall find young ministers raised up, and trained, and sent forth to carry the fire to other parts. Japan, China, and Hindostan shall have heralds of the cross, who have here had their tongues touched with the flame. The whole earth shall receive benedictions; if God shall bless us, he will make us a blessing unto all. Let but God send down the fire, and the biggest sinners in the neighbourhood will be converted; those who live in the dens of infamy will be changed. The drunkard will forsake his cups, the swearer will repent his blasphemy, the debauched will leave their lusts;

> "Dry bones be raised and clothed afresh
> And hearts of stone be turned to flesh."[29]

---

29. Spurgeon, "Temple Glories," in *Metropolitan Tabernacle Pulpit*, 7:223.

8

The Prince of Preachers

This chapter offers a brief pause in the chronological narrative of the extraordinary life and ministry of Charles Spurgeon to consider his preaching. What would it have been like to hear Spurgeon preach? How was he able to draw so many people to listen to him week by week—and not only to draw them but to keep them for nearly four decades? What were the qualities of his preaching that contributed most to its peculiar force and power? This chapter will attempt to answer these questions and will also outline something of the scope and content of Spurgeon's sermons as well as some of the foremost characteristics of his preaching. The aim is to provide the reader with a sense of what truly made Spurgeon the Prince of Preachers.

The Sermons and Their Reach

It is important to first note the extraordinary volume and reach of Spurgeon's sermons. Preaching was the prevailing activity of his life. He began to preach shortly after his conversion in early 1850 and continued to do so at an almost breathless pace until his death over forty years later. By the time he arrived in London in early 1854 at the age of nineteen, Spurgeon had already preached over six hundred sermons, mostly in chapels, cottages, and fields across the Cambridgeshire countryside.[1] When he was well, he never preached

1. Hayden, "Did You Know?," 2.

fewer than three sermons a week, often preached seven sermons a week, and occasionally preached more than ten sermons a week.[2]

The primary outlets for Spurgeon's preaching were the three standing sermons he preached weekly to his congregation at the Metropolitan Tabernacle. This included two sermons on Sundays, both morning and evening, as well as an additional sermon preached at the regular Thursday night service. Beyond these regularly scheduled sermons, Spurgeon accepted numerous invitations for midweek preaching in various churches and halls across London and all over the country. Spurgeon was constantly preaching.

He typically prepared his Sunday morning sermons on Saturday nights. The largest part of his preparation was taken up with selecting a text that gripped his mind and heart. Once the text was in hand, Spurgeon would study it intently, sometimes with the assistance of commentaries, always with the help of prayer. The last step in the process was to organize his thoughts into the form of a useful and memorable outline that suited his congregation. When it came time to preach the sermon, he usually brought nothing more into the pulpit with him than a small notecard with his main headings written on it.[3]

Today, the principal collections of his sermons span roughly seventy published volumes, amounting to literally tens of thousands of pages.[4] Beyond these volumes he published roughly seventy-five other books on a broad array of Christian subjects. This vast corpus earned Spurgeon the distinction of publishing more words in the English language than any other Christian author in history.

The reach of his preaching ministry was expanded profoundly by the decision to publish a weekly sermon for mass distribution.

---

2. Eric W. Hayden, *Highlights in the Life of C. H. Spurgeon* (Pasadena, Tex.: Pilgrim Publications, 1990), 12; and Fullerton, *C. H. Spurgeon: A Biography*, 112–13.

3. For more on Spurgeon's sermon preparation process, see Chang, *Spurgeon the Pastor*, 21–27.

4. These sermons are contained in three primary collections: *New Park Street Pulpit*; *Metropolitan Tabernacle Pulpit*; and *Lost Sermons of C. H. Spurgeon*.

In 1855, with the help of his publishers, Joseph Passmore and James Alabaster, Spurgeon undertook what would become one of the most extraordinary publishing enterprises in the history of Christianity. It became the work of a lifetime, and the effort continued beyond Spurgeon's life until 1917, when World War I brought on a national paper shortage, abruptly ending the endeavor. One may wonder how Spurgeon's publishers were

Spurgeon with one of his publishers and dear friends Joseph Passmore

able to continue publishing weekly sermons for so many years after his death, but it must be remembered that Spurgeon published only one sermon per week during his life. This left a massive backlog of material from the numerous other sermons he preached throughout the week.

Spurgeon saw the weekly publication of his sermons as one of the most important ventures of his life, and he gave himself to the work with singular devotion and care. "The labour has been far greater than some supposed," he said, "and has usually occupied the best hours of Monday, and involved the burning of no inconsiderable portion of midnight oil. Feeling that I had a constituency well deserving of my best efforts, I have never grudged the hours, though often the brain has been wearied, and the pleasure has hardened into a task."[5] Peter Morden provides a summary of the weekly process by which the sermons were brought to the masses:

> Each week someone sat in the Tabernacle congregation and took down Spurgeon's message, word for word, in longhand.

---

5. Spurgeon, "Twenty Years," *Sword and the Trowel* (January 1875): 5.

The many people who have enjoyed reading Spurgeon's sermons down the years owe them a significant debt. The preacher would be given these longhand notes on the Monday. These he would proceed to edit, usually quite lightly. The edited notes would then be typeset by his publishers.... The next phase involved returning the draft printed pages to Spurgeon. Spurgeon would work from these galley proofs, doing any further editing he thought was required. It was the corrected galley proof that was the basis of the final published message.... The process by which the preached sermon became the printed text was so well honed that Sunday's sermon could be available to buy and read before the week was out.[6]

Rather than use a written-out manuscript, Spurgeon chose to depend largely on the Spirit of God and his extraordinary mental powers of concentration, assemblage, and recall.[7] Thus, his published sermons represent not what Spurgeon had written down, but are instead word-for-word transcriptions of what was actually said, with only minor edits afterward.

The reach of the sermons was simply enormous and probably impossible to accurately quantify. The published sermons eventually achieved a weekly readership of twenty-five thousand.[8] Some have estimated that by the opening decades of the twentieth century, they had sold well over one hundred million copies, though the true total (likely much higher) will never be fully known.[9] The sermons were translated into forty different languages during Spurgeon's lifetime, including Arabic, Chinese, German, Syriac, and Russian.[10] The collections translated into Russian were published under the imprimatur of the Russian Orthodox Church, and Russian ministers were strongly encouraged to read Spurgeon sermons

6. Morden, *C. H. Spurgeon: The People's Preacher*, 112.

7. Morden, *Communion with Christ and His People*, 127.

8. C. H. Spurgeon, "To You," *Sword and the Trowel* (January 1871): 1–3.

9. Fullerton, *C. H. Spurgeon: A Biography*, 213; and Carlile, *C. H. Spurgeon: An Interpretive Biography*, 233.

10. *C. H. Spurgeon's Autobiography*, 4:291.

to their congregations at least once a year.[11] Christian George notes that Spurgeon's sermons "were found in the hands of fishermen in the Mediterranean, coffee farmers in Sri Lanka, sailors in San Francisco, and even Catholics on pilgrimage."[12] The famous revivalist preacher and Spurgeon's dear friend D. L. Moody said, "It is a sight in Colorado on Sunday to see the miners come out of the bowels of the hills and gather in the schoolhouses or under the trees while some old English miner stands up and reads one of Charles Spurgeon's sermons."[13]

Spurgeon was intensely aware that his audience each week extended far beyond the walls of the Metropolitan Tabernacle. Though he knew he was chiefly accountable for the sheep of his own flock, he also felt the weight of his larger ministry, which he knew traveled land and sea, reaching countless men and women all over the world whom he would never meet. He felt a profound sense of privilege and solemn responsibility knowing that his sermons enjoyed so wide a hearing. Many were the testimonies of salvation through the instrumentation of his sermons. He once wrote, "Seldom does a day pass, and certainly never a week, for some years past, without letters from all sorts of places, even at the utmost ends of the earth, declaring the salvation of souls by the means of one or other of the sermons."[14] All this had the effect of giving his preaching an added sense of spiritual intensity and sacred moment.

For Spurgeon, nothing he did in his life was more important to him than preaching not only because of the extraordinary reach of his own sermons but because of what he understood preaching to be theologically. To preach was to proclaim the oracles of God (1 Peter 4:11). It was to stand in Christ's stead and to plead with sinners to look to Jesus as He shines forth in the gospel and in the pages

---

11. Fullerton, *C. H. Spurgeon: A Biography*, 276.

12. Christian T. George, "A Man of His Time," in *Lost Sermons*, 1:14.

13. William R. Moody, *The Life of Dwight L. Moody* (New York: Fleming H. Revell, 1900), 456.

14. Spurgeon, "Twenty Years," *Sword and the Trowel* (January 1875): 6.

of Scripture. It was to herald the word of the living God. Preaching was thus the most hallowed and momentous work of his life. Reflecting on his ministry in 1875, twenty years after he commenced the weekly publication of his sermons, he said,

> Chief of all is the responsibility which the preaching of the Word involves; I do not wish to feel this less heavily, rather would I fain feel it more, but it enters largely into the account of a minister's life-work, and tells upon him more than any other part of his mission. Let those preach lightly who dare do so, to me it is the burden of the Lord…. However let no man mistake me, I would sooner have my work to do than any other under the sun. Preaching Jesus Christ is sweet work, joyful work, heavenly work…. It is a bath in the waters of Paradise to preach with the Holy Ghost sent down from heaven. Scarcely is it possible for a man, this side the grave, to be nearer heaven than is a preacher when his Master's presence bears him right away from every care and thought, save the one business in hand, and that the greatest that ever occupied a creature's mind and heart.[15]

The incredible popularity of Spurgeon's sermons raises the question, What made his preaching so extraordinary? Why was he so highly sought after as a preacher? What was it that touched the hearts of so many and gave Spurgeon such universal appeal? The answers to these questions must begin with the content of the message he preached.

A Doctrinal Preacher

To date, no comprehensive treatment of Spurgeon's theology exists.[16] This biography will not attempt such a mammoth task. But we can briefly sketch the theological traditions and major doctrines that shaped his thought and contributed to the success of his preaching.

---

15. Spurgeon, "Twenty Years," *Sword and the Trowel* (January 1875): 7.
16. The best general treatments of Spurgeon's theology are found in Hopkins, *Nonconformity's Romantic Generation*, 132–66; and Morden, *Communion with Christ and His People*, 39–45.

Spurgeon's theology was Protestant, Puritan, Calvinist, Baptist, and evangelical. He gladly subscribed to the main doctrines associated with these movements. Each one contributed in some way to the character of his theology, giving it its peculiar shape and life.

Protestant

Spurgeon's Protestantism and reformational theology was mediated chiefly through figures like Martin Luther and John Calvin, the great Reformers whose portraits hung outside his study. Spurgeon gloried in the Protestant Reformation and viewed it as a period of extraordinary revival in which the gospel itself was recovered. He embraced and preached what are known today as the five *solas* of the Reformation; he believed in the sole authority of Scripture alone (*sola scriptura*), which taught salvation by grace alone (*sola gratia*) through faith alone (*sola fide*), in Christ alone (*solus Christus*), to the glory of God alone (*soli Deo gloria*). The doctrine of justification by faith alone, which was at the heart of Luther's Reformation breakthrough, was especially dear to Spurgeon and utterly foundational to his understanding of the gospel.

Puritan

Spurgeon first met the Puritans in his grandfather's study as he pored over the large folio volumes of writers such as John Bunyan, Richard Baxter, and Thomas Brooks. Thereafter, the Puritans would become his favorite authors, and he would return to them repeatedly throughout his life for instruction, edification, and comfort. He would eventually amass the largest Puritan library in England and was constantly passing along Puritan volumes to younger men in the ministry. So strong was Spurgeon's Puritanism that the English prime minister, William Gladstone, famously referred to him as the "last of the Puritans."[17]

---

17. George, "A Man Behind His Time," in Spurgeon, *Lost Sermons*, 1:18.

Though Puritan theology was never uniform (the Puritan movement was quite broad and diffuse), many regard the Westminster Confession of Faith (1646) to be the purest distillation of Puritan doctrine and thought. Baptists in London in the seventeenth century prepared their own version of the Westminster Confession that came to be known as the Second London Baptist Confession, published in 1689 (often referred to today simply as "the 1689"). This confession maintained the Puritan theology of Westminster but altered it in a few places primarily to accommodate Baptist distinctives (the Westminster Confession taught a presbyterian view of church government and the sacraments).

In 1855 Spurgeon republished the Second London Baptist Confession with his own introduction. "This ancient document," he wrote, "is the most excellent epitome of the things most surely believed among us."[18] Though Spurgeon never required strict subscription to the confession for his officers or members, he nonetheless viewed it as an excellent summary of the church's basic theology and the message he preached. The 1689 had largely been forgotten and abandoned by the time Spurgeon arrived in London, as English Baptists had become increasingly Arminian. Yet Spurgeon stood in his generation as a champion for the old Puritanism of England. The major features of his Puritan theology were its emphasis on the absolute authority of the Bible, the sovereignty and glory of God, the priority of holiness and experiential godliness, the importance of communion with God in Christ, a decidedly Reformed view of salvation, and a broadly Puritan understanding of covenant theology, which emphasized the unity of God's gracious covenant with His elect throughout all ages.

---

18. *Thirty-Two Articles of Christian Faith and Practice; or; Baptist Confession of Faith, with Scripture Proofs, Adopted by the Ministers and Messengers of the General Assembly, Which Met in London in 1689, with a Preface by the Rev. C. H. Spurgeon* (London: Passmore and Alabaster, 1855), n.p.

Calvinist

Spurgeon loved the doctrines of grace and was perhaps the nine-teenth century's foremost defender of evangelical Calvinism. He said, "The old truth that Calvin preached, that Augustine preached, that Paul preached, is the truth that I must preach today, or else be false to my conscience and my God."[19] He had learned these great doctrines first from his grandfather, then from his Puritan heroes, and finally from the cook at Newmarket, Mary King (see chapter 2).

When Spurgeon first arrived in London, Calvinistic preaching was at a low ebb. Spurgeon found himself caught between the errors of Arminianism and hyper-Calvinism on either side. His solution was the clear evangelical preaching of the doctrines of grace that honored both God's absolute sovereignty in salvation and man's responsibil-ity to respond to the gospel call in repentance and faith. At the heart of Calvinism was the assertion that salvation from beginning to end is entirely a work of God's grace. He believed that people are utterly hopeless and unable to come to faith in Christ apart from God's gra-cious initiatives. God's sovereign grace alone could change the human heart and effectually draw a sinner to Christ in saving faith.

Yet for Spurgeon, there existed no contradiction between the Calvinistic doctrine of the sovereignty of God in salvation and the free offer of the gospel. Spurgeon believed the Bible provided the warrant for him to offer Christ freely and universally to every soul under heaven. He earnestly invited all to come to Christ, know-ing that God would use the preaching of the gospel to draw His elect to Himself. Thus, the doctrine of divine election, far from being a hindrance to evangelism, actually became an incentive. Spurgeon understood it to be the preacher's work to offer the gospel of grace to all. God's work was to sovereignly draw all those whom He had predestined to eternal life. This combination of a high view of God's sovereignty wedded to the free and sincere offer of the gospel had

---

19. *C. H. Spurgeon's Autobiography*, 1:167.

a compelling appeal among a population unaccustomed to finding these truths united in the same ministry.[20]

Baptist

Though baptized as an infant and raised a Congregationalist (a denomination that held to infant baptism), Spurgeon embraced Baptistic convictions before he even embraced faith in Christ. While still a boy in school, he came to believe the Baptist position on baptism through his own study of the Bible. From that point on, he never looked back.

Spurgeon was vocal about his Baptist convictions throughout his years of ministry in London. In his early days, he gladly partnered with various Baptist groups and associations, such as the Baptist Union and the London Baptist Association, though these relationships would eventually be strained (and even severed) as Baptists generally drifted leftward theologically in the latter part of the nineteenth century. Spurgeon endeavored to plant Baptist churches all over England and became known as a staunch advocate for Baptistic principles. His Baptist beliefs extended to his view not only of baptism but also of the church. He believed the local church's membership should be regenerate and that the members of the congregation had a sacred responsibility to exercise care for one another through a robust every-member ministry. From the addition and removal of members to formal church discipline, to the approval of church officers, the members of the church were meant to be fully engaged in congregational life under the oversight of the pastors of the church.

Spurgeon's Baptist convictions influenced his preaching in two primary ways. First, they intensified his belief in the necessity of personal regeneration. Second, they elevated his sense of his own responsibility to equip the saints for the work of ministry. As a Baptist, he had the highest expectations for his members and their function in congregational life, which meant that as their pastor, he

---

20. For more on this subject, see Murray, *Spurgeon v. Hyper-Calvinism.*

had a greater responsibility to prepare and train them for their work through his preaching.

Evangelical

In our own day, the meaning of the word *evangelical* can be somewhat ambiguous, and at times it is disputed. But historically the term has been used to refer to the eighteenth-century movement of God that brought extraordinary spiritual awakening and revival on both sides of the Atlantic through the widespread preaching of the gospel. At the center of the movement were great preachers of revival, such as George Whitefield and John Wesley. Of these men Spurgeon said, "If there were wanted two apostles to be added to the number of the twelve, I do not believe that there could be found two men more fit to be so added than George Whitefield and John Wesley."[21] Throughout his lifetime, Spurgeon was frequently compared to George Whitefield in particular.[22] In fact, the first biography of Spurgeon, published in 1856 when he was only twenty-one years old, was titled *The Modern Whitfield*. Spurgeon himself said he regarded Whitefield as "my own model."[23]

The evangelical movement was marked by a pronounced emphasis on the doctrine of the new birth and the need for personal experiential regeneration by the Holy Spirit. Evangelicals also emphasized the earnest preaching of the biblical gospel, which had, at its center, the substitutionary death of Jesus on the cross. The atonement, they taught, was the pulsating center of the Christian message. In 1886 Spurgeon expressed this same evangelical impulse when he said, "The heart of the gospel is redemption, and the essence of redemption is the substitutionary sacrifice of Christ. They who preach this truth preach the gospel in whatever else they may be mistaken; but they who preach not the atonement, whatever

---

21. *C. H. Spurgeon's Autobiography*, 1:176.
22. *C. H. Spurgeon's Autobiography*, 2:47, 66, 104–5.
23. *C. H. Spurgeon's Autobiography*, 2:66.

else they declare, have missed the soul and substance of the divine message."[24] This message of redemption by the blood of Jesus was the grand theme of Spurgeon's preaching.

Spurgeon's basic evangelical commitments lay at the heart of his theology and rose above everything else in terms of importance to him. Though Spurgeon was never shy about his Calvinism or his Baptist convictions, he was nonetheless an evangelical first and foremost. What mattered most to him was the message of new birth and the simple gospel of the blood of Jesus.

The Appeal of Doctrine

Spurgeon's friend W. P. Lockhart said, "His Pauline Calvinism, his sturdy Puritanism, his old-fashioned apostolic gospel remained unchanged to the end."[25] This potent mix of theological convictions shaped Spurgeon's preaching and gave vitality to his message. His belief in the lofty and muscular doctrines of the Reformers and Puritans, fused with his warm and lively exposition of the evangelical gospel of the cross, produced a kind of preaching that was exceptionally compelling. Spurgeon presented his hearers with an exalted view of God, a humble view of man, and a captivating view of grace. It was powerfully convicting, stirring, and inviting at the same time. It arrested listeners and demanded their attention. It pierced their hearts with the pronouncement of humanity's sin and guilt before a just and holy God and then applied the healing balm of the promise of mercy and forgiveness found in the blood of Christ. Such serious, sobering, and sweet doctrine gave a richness and depth to Spurgeon's sermons. To those who had never heard such preaching, it could be positively mesmeric in its effect. There was simply nothing like it in all of Victorian London.

---

24. C. H. Spurgeon, "The Heart of the Gospel," in *Metropolitan Tabernacle Pulpit*, 32:385.

25. Fullerton, *C. H. Spurgeon: A Biography*, 84.

The Character of Spurgeon's Preaching

Undoubtedly, the depth of Spurgeon's doctrine and the content of his message contributed to the unusual power and appeal of his preaching. He heralded the great and glorious doctrines that lay at the heart of the Bible—the sovereignty and majesty of Almighty God, humanity's utter depravity and sin, the justice and mercy of God revealed in Christ, the substitutionary death of Jesus on behalf of ruined humanity, and the gospel call to repentance and faith. These mighty doctrines, proclaimed without adjustment or apology, lent strength and power to Spurgeon's preaching. But this alone cannot account for the unique attraction of his preaching, for Spurgeon was not the only preacher in history to preach these doctrines and not even the only preacher in his own generation to do so. The doctrinal content of his preaching was essential, but some further explanation must be offered.

Having read hundreds of Spurgeon's sermons and numerous accounts from those who heard him preach in person, I would suggest three other qualities that contributed to his extraordinary appeal and made him what he was as a preacher. These three distinguishing characteristics of Spurgeon's preaching gave his sermons their peculiar charm and superlative brilliance.

Christ-Centeredness

The first distinguishing feature of Spurgeon's preaching was its Christ-centeredness. Spurgeon's sermons consistently foregrounded the person and work of Jesus, especially in His love for needy sinners displayed on the cross. Christ was the keynote of every sermon Spurgeon ever preached. He urged younger ministers likewise to "make Christ the diamond setting of every sermon."[26] "The Christian ministry," he said, "should preach all the truths which cluster around the person and work of the Lord Jesus."[27]

---

26. Williams, *Personal Reminiscences*, 175.
27. Spurgeon, *Lectures to My Students*, 2:181.

Spurgeon knew that the most urgent need of every soul that came under his preaching was to know the good news "that Christ Jesus came into the world to save sinners" (1 Tim. 1:15). He knew and felt in the inmost part of his being that Christ was the only solution to humanity's sinfulness and all in his audience were united in their great need of salvation by Jesus's blood. Thus, he made Christ and His work on the cross the central theme in his preaching and labored to proclaim the gospel in all of his sermons. Speaking of Spurgeon's preaching, the Methodist preacher Hugh Price Hughes said, "I have always believed that the chief secret of his attractiveness was the fact that, in every sermon, no matter what the text or the occasion, he explained the way of salvation in simple terms. There are thousands of people everywhere who, beneath their superficial indifference or apparent opposition, long in their hearts to know what they must do to be saved."[28] An Anglican clergyman said, "No one, we may safely say, has set forth the claims of Christ to men's love and service with such winning sweetness, and such melting pathos, with such eloquence of the inmost soul, as Charles Spurgeon."[29] The *British and Foreign Evangelical Review* recorded that

> the chief desire amongst Christians is to gain an assurance of God's Love, and to the subject Mr. Spurgeon constantly recurs, not discussing it with a wave of the hand, but taking it up fully and elaborately. Many excellent sermons act merely as mental stimulus: they instruct, and even to some extent excite, but they do not meet the deep needs of the soul. It is, we believe, one of Mr. Spurgeon's chief sources of power that he devotes himself almost entirely to the great concern. It is this that has made his writings so dearly prized by the dying. There is no more enviable popularity than the popularity this eminent minister has amongst those who are in the presence of the profoundest

---

28. *The Methodist Times*, Feb. 4, 1892, quoted in Fullerton, *C. H. Spurgeon: A Biography*, 276.

29. *Christian World*, Feb. 4, 1892, quoted in Fullerton, *C. H. Spurgeon: A Biography*, 208.

realities. When cleverness and eloquence have lost their charms, the dying often listen hungrily to Mr. Spurgeon's writings, when nothing else, save the Word of God, has any charm or power.[30]

Spurgeon was Christ-centered not merely because he emphasized the person and work of Jesus in the content of his messages. He was also Christ-centered in the sense that he himself embodied a Christlike disposition toward his hearers as he preached. In his tone, his manner, and his whole bearing he brought to his audience something of the nature and posture of the Lord Jesus. As he took to his lips Christ's promises of grace and forgiveness, he exuded the Lord's warmth and tenderness toward sinners. As he intoned Christ's invitations to the hungry, the thirsty, the weary, and the heavy laden, Spurgeon's very countenance and demeanor seemed to woo sinners to the Savior. Spurgeon did not just teach the truth about Christ; he also represented Christ to his hearers by the character, mood, and temper of his preaching. He was committed to being a Christ-*centered* preacher, and this made him a Christ*like* preacher.

Perhaps there is something especially instructive here for preachers today. Ministers must not only preach Christ faithfully; they must also embody something of His heart in their public ministries. Christ's undershepherds are called to be like the Chief Shepherd (1 Peter 5:1–4). It is to some degree unavoidable that people will associate what Jesus is like with those who claim to be His ministers. How many children have had their view of Jesus shaped in large measure by their childhood pastor? How many men and women instinctively identify Jesus with the person who preaches to them about the Lord most often? It is only natural that people will associate what Christ is like with the one who regularly represents Him to them. Spurgeon understood this, and thus he endeavored

---

30. W. R. Nicoll, "Extempore Preachers: Beecher, Parker, Spurgeon, and Talmage," in *The British and Foreign Evangelical Review*, ed. J. S. Candlish (London: James Nisbet, 1877), 326.

always to embody the person of Jesus to needy sinners in all His tender love, His eagerness to forgive, and His readiness to receive those who come to Him in repentance and faith.

Though a reading of a Spurgeon sermon cannot possibly carry the full effect of what it must have been like to sit under Spurgeon's live preaching, his heart for needy sinners nonetheless comes through even on the printed page. The following passage, from one of Spurgeon's most well-known sermons titled "Compel Them to Come In" (Luke 14:23), serves as a fitting example. In the sermon Spurgeon pleaded earnestly with sinners to believe on the Lord Jesus Christ:

> It makes my heart rejoice to think that I should have such good news to tell you.... Permit me to tell you what the King has done for you. He knew your guilt, he foresaw that you would ruin yourself. He knew that his justice would demand your blood, and in order that this difficulty might be escaped, that his justice might have its full due, and that you might yet be saved, *Jesus Christ hath died*. Will you just for a moment glance at this picture. You see that man there on his knees in the garden of Gethsemane, sweating drops of blood. You see this next: you see that miserable sufferer tied to a pillar and lashed with terrible scourges, till the shoulder bones are seen like white islands in the midst of a sea of blood. Again you see this third picture; it is the same man hanging on the cross with hands extended, and with feet nailed fast, dying, groaning, bleeding; methought the picture spoke and said, "It is finished." Now all this hath Jesus Christ of Nazareth done, in order that God might consistently with his justice pardon sin; and the message to you this morning is this—"Believe on the Lord Jesus Christ and thou shalt be saved." That is trust him, renounce thy works, and thy ways, and set thine heart alone on this man, who gave himself for sinners....
>
> Come, I beseech you, on Calvary's mount, and see the cross. Behold the Son of God, he who made the heavens and the earth, dying for your sins. Look to him, is there not power in him to save? Look at his face so full of pity. Is there not love

in his heart to prove him *willing* to save? Sure sinner, the sight of Christ will help thee to believe.[31]

Earnestness

The second distinctive characteristic that defined Spurgeon's preaching has been variously described as conviction, zeal, urgency, unction, and passion. Perhaps a word that brings all of these ideas together is *earnestness*. Indeed, hundreds employed this term in their efforts to describe what distinguished Spurgeon's preaching. Spurgeon himself seemed to favor the word and even delivered a famous lecture on the importance of earnestness in preaching titled "Earnestness: Its Marring and Maintenance."[32]

This quality of Spurgeon's preaching, perhaps more than any other, is impossible to fully appreciate on the written page (though even there Spurgeon's sincere and intense conviction may still be felt to some degree). Those who heard Spurgeon preach invariably noted the unmistakable quality of earnestness that permeated his preaching. One of his contemporaries went so far as to suggest that his earnestness in preaching was for Spurgeon like Samson's hair (Judg. 16:17).[33] The following account in the *Examiner*, written in the year of Spurgeon's death, captures something of this particular quality in his preaching:

> In person Mr. Spurgeon was of medium height and stout build. He had a massive head and large features of the heavy English type. In repose his face, while strong, might have been called phlegmatic if not dull in expression. But when he spoke it glowed with animation of thought, quick flashes of humour, benignity, and earnestness and every phase of the emotion that stirred within him.... No one from merely reading his sermons, can form any idea of their effect when delivered....

---

31. C. H. Spurgeon, "Compel Them to Come In," in *New Park Street Pulpit*, 5:17–24.

32. Spurgeon, *Lectures to My Students*, 2:145–62.

33. *C. H. Spurgeon's Autobiography*, 2:79.

In listening to Mr. Spurgeon, one recognized that the chief element of his commanding force in the pulpit was his profound and burning conviction. The message he gave had for him supreme importance. All his soul went with its utterance. The fire of his zeal was consuming, intense, resistless.[34]

Spurgeon's earnestness stemmed from his unflagging confidence in the truth of his message as well as his belief in what preaching itself ought to be. He believed that in faithful preaching, God condescended to have real and personal dealings with people. He believed the gospel to be the power of God unto salvation (Rom. 1:16), that faith comes by hearing (Rom. 10:17), and that the call of the minister is to preach the word (2 Tim. 4:2). The preacher's task is to herald the gospel in the hope that God, by His Spirit, would awaken faith in the hearts of those who hear the word preached. The preacher himself stands as a kind of ambassador for Christ, appointed by the risen Lord Jesus to proclaim His message of salvation to sinners. Thus, preaching had the grandest possible associations for Spurgeon. He believed that God, Satan, angels, demons, and a whole host of spiritual powers gazed on the affair and had an eternal interest in the outcome. He believed the never-dying souls of men and women hung in the balance and that the preaching event was where spiritual warfare took place. As he saw it, the gravity of the moment, the nature of his message, and the imminence of eternity made demands on him as the preacher; he dared not be anything less than earnest.

Spurgeon's earnestness in preaching was conveyed first in his words, then in his voice, then in his eyes, and finally in his entire body. Every facet of his personality was awake and alive as he preached the message. One who heard many of his sermons said, "Spurgeon was dramatic to his finger-tips. He not only uttered the words, he acted them. He made the simple things live; every

---

34. *The Examiner* (New York), Feb. 4, 1892, quoted in *Spurgeon on the Christian Life: Alive in Christ*, by Michael Reeves (Wheaton, Ill.: Crossway, 2018), 25.

movement contributed so that when he preached, the whole man was engaged in conveying the message."[35]

This quality of earnestness and conviction in Spurgeon's preaching could produce the most singular effect on his hearers. Many individuals testified to feeling as though Spurgeon was speaking directly to them as he preached, though the Tabernacle might be filled to overflowing. One young man, after visiting the church, wrote to his mother, "They say there were six thousand present in the Tabernacle, but to me it was as though I were alone, and he was speaking to me."[36] Another wrote, "There is not one in the whole of that great mass of human beings (in the Tabernacle) who does not feel that Mr. Spurgeon's discourse is absolutely addressed to him as much as if it were given to him alone."[37]

Popularity

To Spurgeon's Christ-centeredness and earnestness can be added a third distinctive feature of his preaching: his popular, warm, and accessible style. Spurgeon was eminently a preacher for the masses. He spoke to the common people of England in language they could understand. His sermons were filled with popular applications, colorful illustrations, and powerful word pictures. Spurgeon's manner of speaking seemed to appeal to all classes. He possessed the exceptional ability to reach both high and low in the same address; none were excluded by his style of preaching. His language was so simple and accessible that even the humblest listener heard him with profit and yet was so elevated and eloquent that those of high birth and refined sensibilities found him profoundly captivating. Spurgeon read poetry often and could quote long passages of Shakespeare from memory. He was well-versed in classical and contemporary

---

35. Carlile, *C. H. Spurgeon: An Interpretive Biography*, 110.

36. *Vanity Fair*, Dec. 10, 1870, quoted in Fullerton, *C. H. Spurgeon: A Biography*, 275.

37. *The Daily Telegraph*, Dec. 24, 1880, quoted in Fullerton, *C. H. Spurgeon: A Biography*, 275.

literature. He demonstrated a compelling mastery of the English language and seemed to marshal his words with effortless command. The result was preaching that can properly be called beautiful. One observer wrote,

> To hear him preach, especially in his own Tabernacle, was to feel his marvelous power, even though it was difficult to understand or explain it. There was the perfect ease of manner, the voice of such remarkable clearness, compass, flexibility and volume; the directness of the address, the tremendous force of conviction that throbbed in each sentence, the purpose that from the beginning to the end of the service was kept well in view, the pure, homely, Saxon style and apt illustration, the earnest and pathetic [i.e., emotional] appeal. And withal there was a strong magnetic force which riveted the attention of his audience and kept them spellbound.[38]

In this regard, Spurgeon stood apart from the rest of London's preachers. A contemporary observer wrote, "Mr. Spurgeon is preeminently the preacher of the people. The scholarly will drop in to hear Dr. Vaughn or Dr. Dykes; the intellectual gather about the pulpits of Liddon or Stanley; the lovers of oratory follow Punshon; but the crowd goes to the Tabernacle."[39] Another said, "Mr. Spurgeon is 'extraordinary' because he is one of the people and preaches to the people. The people follow him—the people love him—and he is made useful in the salvation of the souls of the people."[40]

To thousands of forgotten Londoners, Spurgeon became like an old, familiar friend. They felt him to be sincere, relatable, and accessible, and thus they listened to him. But it wasn't just that he was easy to listen to; the masses felt Spurgeon understood them, and,

---

38. *Christian World*, Feb. 4, 1892, quoted in Fullerton, *C. H. Spurgeon: A Biography*, 268.

39. An unnamed observer, quoted in *Victorian Pulpit: Spoken and Written Sermons in Nineteenth-Century Britain*, by Robert H. Ellison (London: Associated University Press, 1998), 62.

40. A reporter from the *Daily Press*, quoted in Drummond, *Spurgeon: Prince of Preachers*, 297.

what's more, he loved them. They could sense in him a genuine interest in their practical and spiritual welfare. An unmistakable quality of authenticity pervaded Spurgeon's sermons, which disarmed his audience and readied them to receive the word from him. Where perhaps others had left them behind, Spurgeon warmly invited them in and engaged them with loving familiarity and candor. As one observer wrote,

> As soon as he begins to talk he begins to act; and that not as if declaiming on the stage, but as if conversing with you in the street. He seems to shake hands with you all round and put every one at his ease. His colours are taken from the earth and sky of common human experience and aspirations. He dips his pencil, so to speak, in the veins of the nearest spectator, and makes his work a part of every man's nature. He does not narrate occurrences, he describes them with a rough graphic force and faithfulness. He does not reason out his doctrines, but announces, explains, and applies them.[41]

The Prince of Preachers

This chapter has provided readers with a better understanding of the scope, content, and defining characteristics of Spurgeon's storied preaching ministry. Spurgeon has often been called the Prince of Preachers because he seems to stand apart in a class of his own. Thus, it seems appropriate to close with an especially poignant and moving description of Spurgeon's preaching that suggests something of its uniqueness in church history. This account comes from his contemporary and friend, the Congregationalist minister R. W. Dale, and was published shortly after Spurgeon's death. Speaking of those who sat under Spurgeon's ministry, Dale wrote,

> While they were worshipping with him, the glory of the Lord shone round about them, and this has never been to the same extent their experience in listening to any other man. Never

---

41. An undated report from the *Evening Star*, quoted in Fullerton, *C. H. Spurgeon: A Biography*, 97–98.

again will they listen to a preacher at whose word God will become so near, so great, so terrible, so gracious; Christ so tender and so strong; the Divine Spirit so mighty and so merciful; the Gospel so free; the promises of God so firm; the troubles of the Christian man so light; his inheritance in Christ so glorious and so real. Never again.[42]

42. *Irish Times*, Feb. 16, 1892, quoted in Fullerton, *C. H. Spurgeon: A Biography*, 158.

9

The Pastors' College

"This is my life's work, to which I believe God has called me."[1] Spurgeon said this not of his preaching ministry, his publishing ministry, or his pastoral ministry among his congregation. Rather, he said this of a ministry that eventually came to be known as the Pastors' College. Of the many institutions and ministries he would go on to establish, none was more precious to him than the Pastors' College.[2] After his church, it received most of his attention and his best efforts. His friend William Williams wrote, "The Pastors' College was the first philanthropic institution Mr. Spurgeon founded, and to the last it was dearer to his heart than any other."[3] Mike Nicholls writes, "The College was his most cherished creation. Its idea, formulation and support were his chief concern."[4]

Training men for ministry would become one of the most significant callings of Spurgeon's life. He felt there was hardly anything he could do that would be of greater strategic benefit to the kingdom of God than to equip pastors for preaching the gospel and building

1. Fullerton, *C. H. Spurgeon: A Biography*, 227.

2. The best studies of the Pastors' College are Ian Randall, *A School of the Prophets: 150 Years of Spurgeon's College* (London: Spurgeon's College, 2005); Mike Nicholls, *Lights to the World: A History of Spurgeon's College, 1856–1992* (Harpenden, UK: Nuprint, 1994); and David W. Bebbington, "Spurgeon and British Evangelical Theological Education," in *Theological Education in the Evangelical Tradition*, ed. D. G. Hart and R. A. Mohler Jr. (Grand Rapids: Baker, 1996), 217–34.

3. Williams, *Personal Reminiscences*, 131.

4. Nicholls, *Lights to the World*, 45.

up healthy churches. In an 1871 article he wrote, "It appears to us that the maintenance of a truly spiritual College is probably the readiest way in which to bless the churches. Granting the possibility of planting such an institution, you are no longer in doubt as to the simplest mode of influencing for good the church and the world."[5] A few years later in 1875 he said, "Our assured conviction is that there is no better, holier, more useful or more necessary Christian service than assisting to educate young ministers."[6]

It may be assumed that because Spurgeon did not attend college himself, he thought education was unimportant. To the contrary—though God's sovereign plan led Spurgeon to forego formal college training, he thought such instruction was nonetheless tremendously valuable. He received an excellent education throughout his childhood and teenage years and became a spectacular autodidact in adulthood. Few preachers of his generation read as much as Spurgeon, and he accumulated a massive library of over twelve thousand volumes, which he mastered. He believed it was important for pastors to be educated in every major subject, to know Greek and Hebrew, and to read widely in both sacred and secular literature. Though many of the predilections and prejudices of the upper classes at times repulsed him, and though he never put much stock in advanced academic degrees, he nonetheless believed in the ideal of an educated ministry, which constantly informed and shaped his vision for the Pastors' College.

The Work Begins

Amid all the hustle and bustle of Spurgeon's early ministry in the 1850s, a significant new venture was beginning to take shape almost as a kind of side project. Though the Pastors' College was formally established in 1857, its origins date back to 1855, when a

---

5. C. H. Spurgeon, "The Ministry Needed by the Churches, and Measures for Providing It," *Sword and the Trowel* (May 1871): 215.

6. C. H. Spurgeon, "A Plea for the Pastors' College," *Sword and the Trowel* (June 1875): 252.

man named T. W. Medhurst was converted under Spurgeon's preaching. Medhurst immediately attached himself to Spurgeon's ministry and regarded Spurgeon as a kind of mentor. As Spurgeon continued to get to know his new convert, it became clear to him that Medhurst was a deeply pious man who possessed an evident ability to preach.[7] Medhurst had no means of pursuing any kind of formal theological training, however. Spurgeon thus

T. W. Medhurst, the first student of the Pastors' College

developed a plan to personally support Medhurst if he would agree to pursue a program of pastoral training under a friend of Spurgeon, the Reverend C. H. Hosken. Medhurst agreed to the arrangement, and Spurgeon was faithful to his end of the bargain, though at times this was difficult for him. He wrote, "With a limited income, it was no easy thing for a young minister to guarantee £50 a year."[8] The arrangement continued after Spurgeon married Susannah in 1856. Susie would recall, "My dear husband earnestly longed to help young men to preach the gospel, and from our slender resources we had to contribute somewhat largely to the support and education of T. W. Medhurst.... Together, we planned and pinched in order to carry out the purpose of his loving heart."[9]

From its inception, the college was designed to provide free pastoral training to qualifying students. Spurgeon said, "We determined

---

7. *C. H. Spurgeon's Autobiography*, 2:142–47.
8. *C. H. Spurgeon's Autobiography*, 2:148.
9. *C. H. Spurgeon's Autobiography*, 2:183.

never to refuse a man on account of absolute poverty, but rather to provide him with needful lodging, board, and raiment, that he might not be hindered on that account."[10] As college president, Spurgeon was utterly devoted to maintaining this policy, not only providing free education, room, and board but other benefits without cost, such as books, healthcare, and occasionally even spending money.[11] He was committed to eliminating as many obstacles as possible for qualified men wishing to give themselves to a focused season of training for ministry. If he believed a man was truly called and gifted by God, Spurgeon would not permit economic and educational disadvantages to hinder him from being trained. He wrote,

> We had before us but one object, and that was, the glory of God by the preaching of the gospel. To preach with acceptance, men, lacking in education, need to be instructed; and therefore our Institution set itself further to instruct those whom God had evidently called to preach the gospel, but who laboured under early disadvantages.... We proceeded to sweep away every hindrance to the admission of fit men. We determined never to refuse a man on account of absolute poverty, but rather to provide him with needful lodging, board, and raiment, that he might not be hindered on that account. We also placed the literary qualifications of admission so low that even brethren who could not read have been able to enter and have been among the most useful of our students in after days. A man of real ability as a speaker, of deep piety, and genuine faith, may be by force of birth and circumstances, deprived of educational advantages, and yet, when helped a little, he may develop into a mighty worker for Christ.[12]

Spurgeon possessed a strong, inborn aversion to elitism and

10. *C. H. Spurgeon's Autobiography*, 2:149.

11. Spurgeon, "Ministry Needed," *Sword and the Trowel* (May 1871): 224; and Dallimore, *Spurgeon: A New Biography*, 105.

12. *C. H. Spurgeon's Autobiography*, 2:148–49.

credentialism in all its forms.[13] His rearing in rural Essex and his religious heritage as a Nonconformist and later a Baptist conditioned him to be unimpressed by the world's applause and accolades. They also inclined him to find promise in surprising places. Concerned with neither prestige nor pedigree, Spurgeon made character, churchmanship, and spiritual gifting the main prerequisites for the training he would offer.

Medhurst would not remain the only student for long. A growing number of men gravitated to Spurgeon for training, and by 1857 the Pastors' College was formally established. That same year Spurgeon invited George Rogers, a Congregationalist minister, to serve as the college's first principal.[14] Under Rogers's leadership, the school began to grow rapidly as dozens of students were continually added. The work prospered, and it seemed as though things would carry on unabated.

The Work Is Threatened

For the first few years of the college's existence, Spurgeon shouldered the school's financial burden on his own.[15] He was able to do this largely through the fantastic sales of his published sermons in America, which provided him with a significant revenue stream. Spurgeon was so popular in America that his sermons were published regularly in the *New York Times*. With the funds he gained from his sermon sales overseas, along with occasional supplementing from his personal savings, Spurgeon was able to cover the entire six to eight hundred pounds that were needed annually to provide for the college.[16] The stream was soon to dry up suddenly and unexpectedly, however, bringing the college to a point of near crisis.

---

13. Bebbington, "Spurgeon and the Common Man," 63–75; and Bebbington, "Spurgeon and British Evangelical Theological Education," 219.

14. *C. H. Spurgeon's Autobiography*, 2:148.

15. Nicholls, *Lights to the World*, 33.

16. *C. H. Spurgeon's Autobiography*, 3:138.

In the late 1850s, on the eve of the American Civil War, the slavery issue had reached a fever pitch in the United States. By that time the slave trade had already been outlawed in England for a half century largely because of the efforts of William Wilberforce and his intimate network of colleagues and friends. In the American South, however, slavery was alive and well. It would take a civil war and over six hundred thousand American lives to rid the country of what had neatly been termed its "peculiar institution." Spurgeon, for his part, was vigorously opposed to slavery and was unsparing in his denunciations of it. Few vices drew more intense ire from him. He referred to slavery as the "crime of crimes, a soul destroying sin, and an iniquity which cries aloud for vengeance."[17] On one occasion he said, "I do from my inmost soul detest slavery anywhere and everywhere, and though I commune at the Lord's Table with men of all creeds, yet with a slave-holder I have no fellowship of any sort or kind. Whenever one has called upon me, I have considered it my duty to express my detestation of his wickedness, and I would as soon think of receiving a murderer into my Church or into any sort of fellowship, as a man-stealer."[18]

At a special Thursday evening service in December 1859, Spurgeon invited a fugitive slave named John Andrew Jackson to take the pulpit at New Park Street Chapel to share about his experiences of slavery in America. After Jackson shared a heartrending account of his life as a slave, Spurgeon could not resist taking to the platform again and speaking his mind:

> Slavery is the foulest blot which ever stained a national escutcheon, and may have to be washed out with blood. America is in many respects a glorious country, but it may be necessary to teach her some wholesome lessons at the point of a bayonet— to carve freedom into her with a bowie knife or send it home to her heart with a revolver. Better far should it come to this issue,

---

17. Carlile, *C. H. Spurgeon: An Interpretive Biography*, 160.

18. Carlile, *C. H. Spurgeon: An Interpretive Biography*, 160–61.

that North and South should be rent asunder, and the States of the Union shivered into a thousand fragments, than that slavery should be suffered to continue. Some American divines seem to regard it, indeed, with wonderful complacency. They have so accustomed themselves to wrap it up in soft phrases that they lose sight of its real character. They call it a "peculiar institution," until they forget in what its peculiarity consists. It is indeed a peculiar institution, just as the Devil is a peculiar angel, and hell is a peculiarly hot place. For my part, I hold such miserable tamperings with sin in abhorrence, and can hold no communion of any sort with those who are guilty of it.[19]

As a result of these and other remarks, Spurgeon's publishers in the American South began to edit out all references to slavery in his sermons. As soon as Spurgeon became aware of this, he insisted his publishers include his comments on slavery or cease publishing his sermons altogether. Moreover, Spurgeon began to publish his thoughts on slavery in several newspapers in New England and in other areas of the country. As a result, his American publishers ended all publication of his sermons in the South.[20] Furthermore, many towns across the South actually held community book burnings where people were invited to come and burn their copies of Spurgeon's sermons.[21] In North Carolina efforts were made to outlaw the reading of Spurgeon sermons altogether. In Virginia thousands of copies were confiscated and banned. Spurgeon's sermons, so full of Christ and His grace toward needy sinners, had become contraband.

Newspapers across the South viciously lambasted Spurgeon. One read, "Last Saturday, we devoted to the flames a large number of copies of Spurgeon's Sermons.... We trust that the works

---

19. Carlile, *C. H. Spurgeon: An Interpretive Biography*, 159–60.

20. The best treatment of the controversy surrounding Spurgeon and the slavery issue is Thomas Kidd, "'John Brown Is Immortal': Charles Spurgeon, the American Press, and the Ordeal of Slavery," *American Nineteenth Century History* (October 2023): 1–17.

21. Christian T. George, editor's preface to *Lost Sermons of C. H. Spurgeon*, 1:xvii–xx.

of the greasy cockney vocif-
erator may receive the same
treatment throughout the
South." The article went on to
say, "If the Pharisaical author
should ever show himself in
these parts, we trust that a
stout cord may speedily find
its way around his eloquent
throat."[22] The intense backlash
against Spurgeon, aroused by
his remarks regarding slavery,
proved to be but desperate
cries in defense of a failing
institution. A Boston corre-
spondent hinted at this when

*Spurgeon, likely in his
mid- to late thirties*

he wrote to London, "Our Baptist papers are overflowing with
indignation and call on all publishers and booksellers to banish
[Spurgeon's books] from their counters.... The poor slave holders
are at their wits' end and know not what to do to save their doomed
system."[23] Slavery would at last be defeated through the passing
of the Thirteenth Amendment to the US Constitution on January
31, 1865.

As the sale of his sermons was brought to an abrupt end in 1860
in the American South, Spurgeon was forced to find funding for
the college elsewhere.[24] At first he sought to make up the difference
entirely from his own savings. He also considered selling some of
his possessions to close the gap, even proposing the sale of his horse
and carriage. Susie ultimately dissuaded him from this rash move, as

---

22. "Mr. Spurgeon's Sermons Burned by American Slaveowners," *The Southern Reporter and Daily Commercial Courier*, April 10, 1860, quoted in George, editor's preface to *Lost Sermons*, 1:xviii.

23. Carlile, *C. H. Spurgeon: An Interpretive Biography*, 161.

24. *C. H. Spurgeon's Autobiography*, 3:138.

his carriage was indispensable to his frequent itinerating throughout the week.[25]

Ultimately, Spurgeon addressed the financial shortfall by beginning to raise funds for the college, which he did for the rest of his life. Additionally, the Metropolitan Tabernacle eventually adopted the Pastors' College as one of its official ministries in 1861, and the church supported the work from its central budget thereafter.[26] Though it had been briefly threatened, the college would continue into the future and would thrive.

Requirements for Admission

The Pastors' College would be wholly unique among England's leading theological colleges and ministerial training institutions. In the formation of the school, Spurgeon was not concerned primarily with academic or intellectual achievement or satisfying the expectations of the social and educated elite. Rather, he wanted all the men to receive a thoroughly practical course of study that emphasized piety, preaching, knowledge of the Bible, and committed churchmanship. These priorities were reflected not only in the college's curriculum but in its admission standards.

In order to enter the college, three main prerequisites had to be met. First, Spurgeon required that all incoming students exhibit vigorous personal godliness and a high degree of experimental piety.[27] He believed that in pastoral ministry personal devotion and spiritual discipline, along with Christlike virtue and character, were utterly imperative. What a man is in his heart before God is the greatest indicator of his usefulness to Christ's kingdom. Spurgeon refused to admit students who reflected "a low state of piety, a want of

---

25. *C. H. Spurgeon's Autobiography*, 3:138.
26. *C. H. Spurgeon's Autobiography*, 3:139.
27. Spurgeon, "Ministry Needed," *Sword and the Trowel* (May 1871): 225; see also Spurgeon's lecture "The Minister's Self-Watch," in Spurgeon, *Lectures to My Students*, 1:1–17. For more on the spirituality of the students at the Pastors' College, see Randall, *School of the Prophets*, 44–57.

enthusiasm, a failure in private devotion, a lack of consecration."[28] He always believed vital communion with God and a near walk with Christ needed to be the pulsating center of a pastor's ministry.

Second, Spurgeon required all prospective students to possess no less than two years of preaching experience before being accepted.[29] He insisted on receiving only men into the college who possessed significant ministry experience before their admission. He said, "We never tried to make a minister, and should fail if we did; we receive none into the College but those who profess to be ministers already."[30] Moreover, Spurgeon expected that such experience should be accompanied with the fruit of conversion, at least in some degree.[31] This was not because he thought preachers could manufacture conversions, but rather he believed God ordinarily provided a kind of seal and anointing on a man's ministry by converting souls through his preaching.

Finally, Spurgeon expected all incoming students to demonstrate a devoted commitment to real churchmanship. He required all eligible students to possess a proven track record as active members in their churches, engaging in some level of substantive church work. He believed vigorous churchmanship, not professional "ministerialism," was the pathway to pastoral ministry. He said, "We want soldiers, not fops, earnest labourers, not genteel loiterers. Men who have done nothing up to their time of application to the college, are told to earn their spurs before they are publicly dubbed as knights."[32]

These three requirements steered the institution's vision and set its strategic course. Spurgeon personally undertook to ensure fidelity

---

28. C. H. Spurgeon, "Annual Paper Concerning the Lord's Work in Connection with the Pastors' College, Newington, London, 1888–89," *Sword and the Trowel* (June 1889): 311.

29. Nicholls, *Lights to the World*, 62–64.

30. Spurgeon, *Lectures to My Students*, 1:33.

31. *C. H. Spurgeon's Autobiography*, 2:148; Spurgeon, *Lectures to My Students*, 1:23–30; and Bebbington, "Spurgeon and British Evangelical Theological Education," 223–24.

32. Spurgeon, *Lectures to My Students*, 1:34.

to these principles by conducting rigorous personal interviews with all the applicants.[33] If the established standards were not met, he did not hesitate to reject a prospective student and often did so.[34] He insisted, "The selection of candidates for admission is principally determined by evidences of eminent piety, of adaptation for public teaching, of great zeal for the salvation of souls, and of instances of actual usefulness."[35]

Though Spurgeon assiduously maintained these high expectations for incoming students, he also set the bar quite low in other respects. As already indicated, Spurgeon did not permit financial and educational disadvantages to present an obstacle to admission. He was eager to invite students to train for the ministry regardless of class or social status. In fact, he may even have preferred to draw men from the working classes, as he believed such men were often best positioned to reach the common people with the gospel. He said, "Let the church, when the Lord sends her a man of rough but great natural ability, and of much grace, meet him all the way, take him up where he is, and help him even to the end."[36]

Many of the men who applied to the college were severely limited from an educational standpoint, and some of them could barely read. Spurgeon made special accommodation for such men by arranging to provide them with remedial education via free evening classes during the week.[37] These classes were open to the community at large and offered instruction in subjects such as mathematics, science, and grammar. They attracted hundreds of students at any given time and benefited working-class people of all stripes and

---

33. Nicholls, *Lights to the World*, 64–65.

34. Spurgeon, *Lectures to My Students*, 1:33.

35. C. H. Spurgeon, "Work of the Metropolitan Tabernacle," *Sword and the Trowel* (March 1866): 135.

36. Spurgeon, "Ministry Needed," *Sword and the Trowel* (May 1871): 224.

37. Nicholls, *Lights to the World*, 78–81; Randall, *School of the Prophets*, 76–78; and Bebbington, "Spurgeon and British Evangelical Theological Education," 227–28.

backgrounds.[38] Many students at the Pastors' College profited from these classes in addition to their regular regimen of coursework.

Because of the relaxed requirements regarding educational prerequisites and the subsidization of all expenses, the Pastors' College opened up ministerial training to men who otherwise could have never hoped to enjoy such an opportunity. This was at a time when educational standards among Baptist colleges in England were rising, with most colleges requiring men to achieve at least their baccalaureate prior to admission.[39] Men of real gift, character, and piety from the lower classes were enabled to receive the equipping they needed for ministry and were helped to reach their full potential through the education the Pastors' College afforded them. The Pastors' College was designed to train men from among the masses who could in turn reach the masses with the gospel.

Preachers for the Masses

Spurgeon once said in reference to the work of the college, "By that I multiply myself."[40] Spurgeon's aim through the Pastors' College was to multiply preachers who embodied his particular vision for pastoral ministry. He was not interested in training ivory tower theologians and, still less, pastors who were unable to engage effectively with ordinary people. He wanted to raise up preachers for the masses, drawn from among them, who possessed the needed experience and competence to move the common man. He was after men who were earnest, godly, and devout, who could enter into the lives of ordinary men and women with sincerity and sympathy. He wrote,

> It seems to me that many of our churches need a class of ministers who will not aim at lofty scholarship, but at the winning of souls;—men of the people, feeling, sympathizing, fraternizing

38. Randall, *School of the Prophets*, 77; and C. H. Spurgeon, "The College Report for 1876–7," *Sword and the Trowel* (May 1877): 214.

39. Briggs, *English Baptists of the Nineteenth Century*, 88–90; and Bebbington, "Spurgeon and British Evangelical Theological Education," 218–19.

40. Carlile, *C. H. Spurgeon: An Interpretive Biography*, 169.

with the masses of working men;—men who can speak the common language, the plain blunt Saxon of the crowd;—men ready to visit the sick and the poor, and able to make them understand the reality of the comforts of religion. There are many such men among the humbler ranks of society, who might become master-workmen in the Lord's Church if they could get an education to pare away their roughness, and give them more extended information.... Why should not such men have help? Why should they be compelled to enter our ministry without a competent knowledge of Scripture and Biblical literature? Superior in some respects already, let them be educated, and they will be inferior to none. It was the primary aim of this Institution to help such men, and this is still its chief end and design.... Whether the student be rich or poor, the object is the same,—not scholarship, but preaching the gospel,—not the production of fine gentlemen, but of hard-working men.[41]

Regarding training popular preachers who could embrace the masses and speak directly to the lives and circumstances of common, every-day people, Spurgeon said, "Our men seek no Collegiate degrees, or classical honors,—though many of them could readily attain them; but to preach efficiently, to get to the heart of the masses, to evangelize the poor,—this is the College ambition, this and nothing else."[42]

One of the ways that Spurgeon prepared his students to reach the masses was by instructing them in the manner of their address, their use of language, and their bearing in the pulpit. He cautioned his students to "avoid everything which is stilted, official, fussy, and pretentious"[43] and implored them instead to "speak plainly."[44] He often complained that most of the preaching in London in his day

---

41. *C. H. Spurgeon's Autobiography*, 3:129.

42. *C. H. Spurgeon's Autobiography*, 2:149.

43. Spurgeon, *Lectures to My Students*, 1:180.

44. Spurgeon, *Lectures to My Students*, 1:141; C. H. Spurgeon, "Report of the Pastors' College," *Sword and the Trowel* (May 1882): 260; and C. H. Spurgeon, "Fields White for Harvest," in *Metropolitan Tabernacle Pulpit*, 12:460.

was stuffy, pedantic, and inaccessible to ordinary people and was more suited for Oxford or Cambridge than for the local church. He wanted his students to aim for a kind of blessed simplicity in preaching. He was after simplicity, not in the sense of childishness or shallowness but in terms of clarity and directness. The great Anglican evangelical J. C. Ryle famously wrote a treatise titled *Simplicity in Preaching*, which is still widely read today. In it Ryle commended Spurgeon as a shining exemplar of the kind of simplicity in preaching that should mark every minister:

> Mr. Spurgeon can preach most ably, and he proves it by keeping his enormous congregation together.... Now when you read Mr. Spurgeon's sermons, note how clearly and perspicuously he divides a sermon, and fills each division with beautiful and simple ideas. How easily you grasp his meaning! How thoroughly he brings before you certain great truths that hang to you like hooks of steel, and which, once planted in your memory, you never forget![45]

For Spurgeon, as well as for Ryle, the importance of simplicity and clarity in preaching was an urgent necessity. The masses of English people needed to hear preaching that was earnest, direct, and plain and went straight to their hearts.

Because Spurgeon wished to raise up preachers who could reach the common man on the street, the curriculum at the college took on a highly practical character.[46] Mike Nicholls notes, "This curriculum was designed to give men the education of which many were deprived in childhood and to enable them to proclaim the gospel with interest and relevance."[47] "Its training was to be practical rather than literary," Bebbington writes, "a down-to-earth affair rather than an imitation of Oxford or Cambridge. There would be no attempt

---

45. John Charles Ryle, *Simplicity in Preaching: A Few Short Hints on a Great Subject* (London: William Hunt, 1882), 20–21.
46. Nicholls, *Lights to the World*, 67–78.
47. Nicholls, *Lights to the World*, 69.

to compete for scholarly distinctions or to turn theology from a vocational into an academic subject."[48] As Spurgeon declared to his students, "We are not called to proclaim philosophy and metaphysics, but the simple gospel."[49]

In Spurgeon's efforts to train ministers who could reach ordinary people, he labored to develop men who possessed true sympathy for the masses. Simply put, he believed pastoral ministry was people ministry. The pastor was not to be a kind of detached theologian-in-residence but was to be an eager shepherd of the sheep who humbly lived and worked among them for their good. Pastors should know their people and be intimately involved with the affairs of their souls. He believed members of the congregation should feel loved and understood by their pastor. They needed to have the confidence that their pastor knew how to enter lovingly and sympathetically into their experience. Spurgeon was convinced that if the ordinary people of London were to be reached, it would be by men who understood them and sincerely cared about them. He said, "The more our hearts beat in unison with the masses, the more likely will they be to receive the gospel kindly from our lips."[50] This is why Spurgeon preferred to draw students for the college from among the working classes. Such men were specially conditioned, he believed, to reach the people:

> We require men of popular sympathies; men of the people, who feel with them…. Unless a man is a lover of the people in his inmost soul he will never be greatly useful to them. The people do not require more of those gentlemen who condescend to instruct the lower orders…. London's millions spurn the foppery of caste, they yearn for great hearts to sympathize with their sorrows; such may rebuke their sins and lead their minds, but no others may lecture them. The working classes of

---

48. Bebbington, "Spurgeon and British Evangelical Theological Education," 219–20.

49. Spurgeon, *Lectures to My Students*, 1:83.

50. Spurgeon, "Ministry Needed," *Sword and the Trowel* (May 1871): 220.

England are made of redeemable material after all; those who
believe in them can lead them.[51]

Over the years, the Pastors' College graduated hundreds of these
types of men who were unusually effective at reaching ordinary
working-class people with the gospel. The great social reformer and
Spurgeon's dear friend Lord Shaftesbury said of the men of the college, "They had a singular faculty for addressing the population, and
going to the very heart of the people."[52]

By the grace of God, Spurgeon raised up a generation of pastors
who were uniquely successful at reaching the last, the lost, and the
least of needy London and the nation as a whole. "That was the hall-
mark of Spurgeon's training project," Bebbington writes, "to ensure
that all the pastors remained men of the people."[53] Under Spurgeon's
leadership, the Pastors' College developed a legacy for training
ministers who were enabled to take the gospel to the masses with
unmatched sincerity, earnestness, and love.

A Noble Life-Work

Through the sovereign blessing of God, the Pastors' College was
spectacularly fruitful under Spurgeon's leadership. From its inception in 1857 to Spurgeon's death in 1892, the college trained and
graduated 863 men.[54] During that span, the Pastors' College contributed more to the growth of the Baptist ministry in England and
Wales than any other college by far. By 1871, roughly fifteen years
after the college was founded, its graduates accounted for 10 percent
of all Baptist ministers in England and Wales. By the year of Spurgeon's death, that number was over 20 percent.[55]

---

51. Spurgeon, "Ministry Needed," *Sword and the Trowel* (May 1871): 219–20.
52. Spurgeon, *Metropolitan Tabernacle: Its History and Work*, 101.
53. Bebbington, "Spurgeon and the Common Man," 74.
54. Bebbington, "Spurgeon and British Evangelical Theological Education," 221.
55. Brown, *Social History of the Nonconformist Ministry*, 33, 98. See also Briggs,
English Baptists of the Nineteenth Century, 3:88–90.

Many of Spurgeon's men pastored in rural villages and in fairly obscure churches, but several of his graduates pastored some of the most historic and eminent Baptist churches in Britain. The men occupied "some of the pulpits of the denomination most valuable and illustrious in past generations," including T. G. Tarn of St. Andrew's Street Baptist Church, Cambridge (the church where Spurgeon, as a teenager, was a member while living in Cambridge), and E. G. Gange of Broadmead Chapel, Bristol.[56] Some of the men from the college also planted new churches that became some of the largest Baptist churches in the country, such as Archibald G. Brown of the East London Tabernacle and William Cuff of the Shoreditch Tabernacle.[57]

The Pastors' College tried to track basic statistics, such as baptisms and membership in the churches pastored by alumni. In 1892, the year of Spurgeon's death, the college reported that in the churches pastored by its graduates, nearly one hundred thousand people had been baptized. After adjustments were made for standard deductions, such as death and transfers of membership, the net increase in the membership of the churches was roughly eighty thousand. The true figures were likely higher, as numbers of churches neglected to report their statistics. The editors of Spurgeon's autobiography wrote, "Truly, if Mr. Spurgeon had done nothing beyond founding and carrying on the Pastors' College, it would have been a noble life-work; yet that was only one of his many forms of labour for the Lord."[58]

---

56. C. H. Spurgeon, "Concerning College Work as We See It," *Sword and the Trowel* (May 1883): 276.

57. Spurgeon, "Concerning College Work," 276.

58. *C. H. Spurgeon's Autobiography*, 4:330.

10

Wielding the Sword

The 1860s were years of extraordinary fruitfulness for Spurgeon and a period of exceptional growth, progress, and maturation in his ministry. It was during these years that Spurgeon set in place some of the last major enterprises that would define his life's work. As he entered the 1860s, his preaching ministry, with the massive and intricate publishing efforts that extended its reach, was well established. His pastoral ministry was thriving, as well as his work in the Pastors' College. These formed some of the major pillars of his overall ministry. Throughout the 1860s he would add to these efforts several new ministries, agencies, and institutions that would become integral to his long-term efforts at promoting the cause of the gospel in London and beyond. After 1869 Spurgeon's ministry would become much more about maintaining and growing what had been started rather than creating something new. But the 1860s were focused on breaking new ground.

Growth, Progress, and Maturity

This decade was marked by three major developments in Spurgeon's life and ministry that illustrate the importance of these vital years. The first had to do with the extraordinary growth of his congregation. Spurgeon's church, now with a new name and a new building, reached a point of significant maturity, in terms of both the growth of its membership and the establishment of an accompanying church structure that facilitated the church's long-term stability. For years the large majority of people among Spurgeon's congregations were not actually members of his church. This began to change in the 1860s as the church settled into a permanent location and many of the regular attenders began to formally join the church's membership. Shortly before the congregation first entered their new building in 1861, the membership sat at roughly fifteen hundred.[1] By the end of the decade, that figure had risen to just over four thousand.[2] The congregation would continue to see tremendous growth in its membership throughout the 1870s, finally leveling off in the 1880s. Yet it was in the 1860s that the church could first claim the title of the largest Protestant church in the world.

This growth in the membership was also attended by a solidifying of the church's ecclesiastical structure. In 1859 Spurgeon led the church, which had long benefited from the ministry of faithful deacons, to also recognize and affirm the biblical office of elder.[3] This office, he taught, was given by Christ for the regular oversight, leadership, and care of the church body.[4] Near the close of the decade in 1868, the church also approved a long-term associate pastor, Spurgeon's brother James Archer Spurgeon, who came alongside his brother to help lead and care for the church (see chapter 11).[5] Thus, as the membership grew, so did the pastoral oversight of the church and so did the accountability of the individual members. Arrangements were made to meticulously track the church's membership and to ensure that members were cared for, were actively engaged in

---

1. *C. H. Spurgeon's Autobiography*, 2:331.

2. See membership additions and losses as reported in "The Militant Ecclesiology and Church Polity of Charles Haddon Spurgeon," by Geoffrey Chang (PhD diss., Midwestern Baptist Theological Seminary, 2020), 312–13.

3. Most Baptist churches in Spurgeon's day did not use a plurality of elders, and typically referred to the sole elder as *the* pastor.

4. *C. H. Spurgeon's Autobiography*, 3:22–23; and Chang, *Spurgeon the Pastor*, 146–50.

5. *C. H. Spurgeon's Autobiography*, 3:30–35; and Chang, *Spurgeon the Pastor*, 156–57.

the life of the church, and were present for church gatherings.[6] The convenience of a comfortable building, with space enough to accommodate the church's entire membership, allowed the congregation to gather as one body on a regular basis for congregational members' meetings. These meetings were typically held after the Monday night prayer meeting or the Thursday night midweek service. They were held to discuss the regular affairs of the church and included hearing testimonies, adding and removing members, nominating and electing church officers, considering matters related to the church's finances, and hearing reports on various church ministries. Throughout the 1860s, the church held an average of sixty-seven congregational members' meetings annually![7]

The second important development in Spurgeon's ministry during these years was the establishment of a number of ministries, institutions, and publications that became major hallmarks of his ministry throughout the rest of his life. This chapter will consider a number of them, including the inauguration of Spurgeon's monthly magazine, the *Sword and the Trowel*, which continued in regular circulation from 1865 until after his death. The *Sword and the Trowel* would eventually become the most significant organ of public communication for Spurgeon outside his regular preaching ministry. These years also saw the founding and expanding of several significant ministries that were dear to Spurgeon's heart, including the Stockwell Orphanage, the Colportage Association, and numerous Sunday schools, Bible classes, and street missions. During the 1860s there was also an extraordinary boom in Spurgeon's efforts in church planting.

The third important development during this crucial decade of Spurgeon's life had to do with his personal growth and maturation as a man, a minister, and a public Christian figure. It was during these years that Spurgeon made the successful transition from the

---

6. Chang, *Spurgeon the Pastor*, 133–34.
7. Chang, "Militant Ecclesiology and Church Polity," 317.

boy preacher of New Park Street Chapel and Exeter Hall to the seasoned pastor of the Metropolitan Tabernacle. In the 1850s many saw Spurgeon as the youthful and sprightly preaching sensation of London, moving from hall to hall throughout the metropolis as thousands followed his ever-rising star. But the 1860s marshaled in a gradual and graceful change in Spurgeon, one that saw him mature into something of a spiritual mentor and father to younger men as well as a kind of evangelical statesman in the Christian world of his day. Throughout the sixties, a growing number of budding ministerial aspirants came under his spiritual leadership and training. At the same time, more of his fellow ministers across the city began to look to him as a reliable model for faithful ministry. Little by little, Spurgeon began to assume a larger public role in the wider evangelical world, lending his voice to public debates and discussions that affected the church in the United Kingdom and beyond. During these years Spurgeon became the most visible Christian pastor in the English-speaking world, a position he never wanted but one from which he did not retreat.

Confronting Error

Spurgeon's growing visibility was an important factor in what would become one of the greatest controversies of his life. From his earliest days as a young Christian, Spurgeon maintained serious concerns about the established church in England. Some of the underlying tensions between Anglicans and Nonconformists were briefly sketched in chapter 1. Though the painful and at times bloody conflicts of the sixteenth and seventeenth centuries lay in the past, the Anglican Church still enjoyed numerous advantages and rights that were not extended to the Nonconformist churches of England, even by late into the nineteenth century. These advantages included the exclusive right to education at Oxford and Cambridge, the use of national tax revenue for erecting and maintaining Anglican church buildings, and the right to burial in public graveyards. It had been only since 1828 that Nonconformists were even permitted to serve in

Parliament. By the 1860s, their representation had not yet caught up with that of their more privileged counterparts in the state church, who enjoyed a three-hundred-year head start.

Throughout his life, Spurgeon was a vigorous advocate for the disestablishment of the state church. He believed an established church threatened religious freedom and violated liberty of conscience. Moreover, it effectively created a class system in England that was prejudiced against Baptists, Congregationalists, and other Nonconformists, who were guilty only of practicing and worshiping according to what they sincerely believed the Bible to teach. To Spurgeon, the problems with the establishment were legion.

His most serious criticisms of the Church of England were not political but doctrinal. Like many of his Puritan heroes, Spurgeon objected to a number of doctrines and practices prevalent within Anglicanism. In his day, Spurgeon was especially concerned about what was known as the Oxford Movement, sometimes referred to as Tractarianism or Puseyism.[8] The Oxford Movement represented a current within Anglicanism in the mid-nineteenth century that sought to introduce and revive various Roman Catholic doctrines and practices within the Church of England. It also aimed to strengthen the ties of fellowship between Catholicism and Anglicanism. John Henry Newman, who eventually converted to Roman Catholicism, was the foremost leader of the Oxford Movement, along with men such as E. B. Pusey and John Keble.

Spurgeon loathed the Oxford Movement and feared that the Anglicanism of his generation was slipping steadily toward Rome in both its doctrine and liturgical practices. Spurgeon's utter disdain for Roman Catholicism in every form and vestige was long-standing and deeply felt.[9] A few months before his conversion at the age

---

8. Steward J. Brown, Peter B. Nockles, and James Pereiro, eds., *The Oxford Handbook of the Oxford Movement* (Oxford: Oxford University Press, 2017); and Owen Chadwick, *The Victorian Church*, part 1, *1829–1859* (London: SCM Press, 1971), 167–231.

9. Morden, *Communion with Christ and His People*, 24–25, 90–92.

of fifteen, Spurgeon won a prize for an essay spanning 295 hand-written pages titled *Against Anti-Christ and Her Brood; or, Popery Unmasked.*[10] That he would live to see the resurgence of numerous Catholic traditions and practices in the Church of England in his day filled him with abhorrence. Spurgeon warned, "It is a most fearful fact, that in no age since the Reformation has Popery made such fearful strides in England as in the last few years."[11] He viewed the established church as the epicenter for this renewal of Roman Catholic belief and practice in England and became convinced that it must be confronted head on.

The Baptismal Regeneration Controversy

To Spurgeon's mind, this slide toward Rome was aided and abetted by the language of the Anglican Book of Common Prayer—namely, its teaching on baptismal regeneration. Spurgeon interpreted the prayer book to teach that in baptism, regeneration was conferred on the individual being baptized (usually an infant). Not only did Spurgeon understand this view to represent a dangerous departure from the clear biblical teaching on baptism, but it also jeopardized other doctrines such as salvation by grace and justification by faith alone.

Spurgeon's concerns over Anglicanism's drift toward Rome grew steadily in the early years of the 1860s, climaxing in a sermon he preached on June 5, 1864, simply titled "Baptismal Regeneration." It would be the most widely distributed sermon he ever preached, selling over 350,000 copies within a year of its publication. It would also precipitate one of the most intense controversies of his life, often referred to as the Baptismal Regeneration Controversy.[12]

Spurgeon had prayerfully anticipated preaching this message several weeks in advance. He had invited his close friends to pray

---

10. *C. H. Spurgeon's Autobiography*, 1:57–66.

11. C. H. Spurgeon, "Baptismal Regeneration," in *Metropolitan Tabernacle Pulpit*, 10:322.

12. Kruppa, *Charles Haddon Spurgeon: A Preacher's Progress*, 254–81; and Morden, *Communion with Christ and His People*, 90–93.

for him, as he knew this message would represent a major public stand and would likely invite conflict. When June 5 came, he stood before his congregation and announced that he preached out of "an awful and overwhelming sense of duty."[13] In this sermon, and in the controversy that followed, Spurgeon acted not only as the pastor of the Metropolitan Tabernacle but as a kind of spokesman for Nonconformity, wielding his enormous public influence to combat a theological error that he feared was misleading tens of thousands of people and ushering the church in his day further and further away from evangelical Christianity.

In the sermon, Spurgeon not only warned against the errors of the doctrine of baptismal regeneration but indicted evangelical clergy within Anglicanism for remaining within an established church that taught such error. He believed this element within the prayer book violated evangelical doctrine, and thus evangelical clergymen could only stay within the Anglican communion at the cost of their integrity. He was unsparing in his denunciations of such men and accused them of rank duplicity and hypocrisy:

> For clergymen to swear or say that they give their solemn assent and consent to what they do not believe is one of the grossest pieces of immorality perpetrated in England, and is most pestilential in its influence, since it directly teaches men to lie whenever it seems necessary to do so in order to get a living or increase their supposed usefulness: it is in fact an open testimony from priestly lips that at least in ecclesiastical matters falsehood may express truth, and truth itself is a mere unimportant nonentity.... It is time that there should be an end put to the flirtations of honest men with those who believe one way and swear another. If men believe baptism works regeneration, let them say so; but if they do not so believe it in their hearts and yet subscribe, and yet more, get their livings by subscribing

---

13. Spurgeon, "Baptismal Regeneration," in *Metropolitan Tabernacle Pulpit*, 10:314.

to words asserting it, let them find congenial associates among men who can equivocate and shuffle, for honest men will neither ask nor accept their friendship.[14]

In light of the vehemence of Spurgeon's protest, it is hardly surprising that a bitter controversy ensued. Numerous sectors of the religious world accused Spurgeon of a tribal spirit and of misrepresenting the Anglican Church and its ministers. Many evangelical clergymen within the Church of England, some of whom were cobelligerents with Spurgeon in the fight against the Oxford Movement, felt betrayed by him. What's more, Spurgeon had been for some years a happy member of the Evangelical Alliance, an interdenominational fellowship of evangelical churches (including a number of evangelical Anglican churches) that were organized to advocate for religious liberty and to promote the evangelical faith. On account of his sermon on baptismal regeneration, however, the Evangelical Alliance required Spurgeon to withdraw, viewing his public posture as out of step with the alliance's principles. Yet Spurgeon was undeterred by the backlash and even preached follow-up sermons that sustained and intensified many of his objections to what he saw as gross error within the established church. Over the coming years, Spurgeon would continue to state publicly his serious criticisms and concerns regarding the present and future state of Anglicanism. Despite intense opposition, he never relented from his public protest. Indeed, many of his ongoing concerns would be given voice in a new enterprise that would become part of the bedrock of Spurgeon's public ministry from the mid-1860s until the end of his life.

The Sword and the Trowel

Though Spurgeon's published sermons enjoyed an ever-expanding reach at this time, he nonetheless desired another mechanism for

---

14. Spurgeon, "Baptismal Regeneration," in *Metropolitan Tabernacle Pulpit*, 10:316–17.

reaching the public and promoting the cause of truth in the world. He wanted to see more work being done for Jesus and longed for the opportunity to champion kingdom efforts that he regarded as practically valuable and strategically important. Thus, in 1865 Spurgeon founded a monthly magazine that would become the primary coordinating publication for a growing roll of ministries, agencies, and institutions that were dear to his heart.

The name of the periodical, *The Sword and the Trowel*, was based on Nehemiah 4:17–18, which speaks of God's people simultaneously building up the walls of Jerusalem with one hand while armed with their swords in the other, ready at all times to do battle as the need arose. In the magazine's opening issue in January 1865, Spurgeon described the publication's mission this way:

> Our magazine is intended to report the efforts of those Churches and Associations, which are more or less intimately connected with the Lord's work at the Metropolitan Tabernacle, and to advocate those views of doctrine and Church order which are most certainly received among us. It will address itself to those faithful friends scattered everywhere, who are our well-wishers and supporters in our work of faith and labor of love. We feel the want of some organ of communication in which our many plans for God's glory may be brought before believers, and commended to their aid.... Our monthly message will be a supplement to our weekly sermon and will enable us to say many things which would be out of place in a discourse. It will inform the general Christian public of our movements, and show our sympathy with all that is good throughout the entire Church of God. It will give us an opportunity of urging the claims of Christ's cause, of advocating the revival of godliness, of denouncing error, of bearing witness for truth, and of encouraging the laborers in the Lord's vineyard.... We shall supply interesting reading upon general topics, but our chief aim will be to arouse believers to action, and to suggest to them plans by which the kingdom of Jesus may be extended. To widen the bounds of Zion and gather

together the outcasts of Israel is our heart's desire. We would
sound the trumpet, and lead our comrades to the fight.[15]

For over twenty-five years, Spurgeon was true to this mission for
the *Sword and the Trowel*. The magazine's monthly issues contained
a broad mix of content, including printed sermons; articles on practical, theological, and popular subjects; reports on various agencies
and ministries connected to the Metropolitan Tabernacle; cartoons;
solicitations for funds; book reviews; and a host of other material.
This offering of diverse content appealed to a wide range of readers.
By 1871 the magazine achieved a regular circulation of fifteen thousand.[16] Spurgeon served as editor in chief and personally contributed
an enormous amount of material to the magazine's monthly issues.
He also enlisted the help of a large number of regular contributors,
most of whom occupied various positions in the larger Spurgeon network. The magazine was issued on a monthly basis, but at the end
of every year its various monthly installments were bound and published together, providing readers with the entire year's content in one
volume. A typical annual volume ran about six hundred pages.

The *Sword and the Trowel* provides an extraordinary and intimate window into Spurgeon's life and thought. He once referred to
it as "in some sense our autobiography."[17] He was often at his most
candid in its pages and frequently spoke to subjects of practical,
social, and national interest that he never would have addressed in
his sermons, choosing to preserve the pulpit for the preaching of
the word of God. The *Sword and the Trowel* provided Spurgeon with
a strategic channel for communicating his vision for pastoral leadership, church ministry, Christian faithfulness, public engagement,
and social activism to the wider Christian public. It remains an
invaluable resource for those who wish to comprehend Spurgeon's
thought more broadly.

---

15. Spurgeon, "To You," *Sword and the Trowel* (January 1871): 1–2.

16. Spurgeon, "To You," *Sword and the Trowel* (January 1871): 3.

17. C. H. Spurgeon, "Notice of Books," *Sword and the Trowel* (January 1885): 35.

Church Planting

One of the primary reasons Spurgeon founded the *Sword and the Trowel* was to promote the work of numerous daughter congregations that were springing up from the Metropolitan Tabernacle. The 1860s saw the beginning of one of the most successful and extraordinary programs of church planting perhaps ever achieved by a single congregation. Over the course of his ministry in London, Spurgeon planted 187 churches in Britain alone.[18] Between 1865 and 1887, he and his students founded over half of the new Baptist congregations in England.[19] Moreover, between 1865 and 1876, Spurgeon planted fifty-three of the sixty-two new Baptist churches in London.[20] Mike Nicholls records that the result of all these efforts in church planting was that by Spurgeon's death in 1892, "nearly half the Baptist membership in London was found in Spurgeon churches."[21]

The beginning of this extraordinary movement of church planting can be traced to the end of the 1850s. At the laying of the foundation stone of the Metropolitan Tabernacle on August 16, 1859, Spurgeon shared something of his vision for church planting with the assembled congregation:

> I look on the Tabernacle as only the beginning; within the last six months, we have started two churches,—one in Wandsworth and the other in Greenwich,—and the Lord has prospered them; the pool of baptism has often been stirred with converts. And what we have done in two places, I am about to do in a third, and we will do it, not for the third or the fourth, but for the hundredth time, God being our Helper. I am sure I may make the strongest appeal to my brethren, because we do

18. Nicholls, *C. H. Spurgeon: The Pastor Evangelist*, 175–77. It should be noted that beyond the churches he had a direct hand in planting, Spurgeon supported and resourced dozens of other new churches in a variety of ways, from financial support to sending members from the Tabernacle or students from the Pastors' College.

19. Morden, *C. H. Spurgeon: The People's Preacher*, 151.

20. Nicholls, *C. H. Spurgeon: The Pastor Evangelist*, 98.

21. Nicholls, *C. H. Spurgeon: The Pastor Evangelist*, 99.

not mean to build this Tabernacle as our nest, and then to be idle. We must go from strength to strength, and be a missionary church, and never rest until, not only this neighborhood, but our country, of which it is said some parts are as dark as India, shall have been enlightened with the Gospel.[22]

Spurgeon believed the church ought to be vigorous and proactive in its efforts in evangelism, missions, and church planting. The glory of God and the urgency of eternity demanded it. In an April 1865 article in the *Sword and the Trowel*, he said,

The Christian church was designed from the first to be aggressive. It was not intended to remain stationary at any period, but to advance onward until its boundaries became commensurate with those of the world. It was to spread from Jerusalem to all Judaea, from Judaea to Samaria, and from Samaria unto the uttermost part of the earth. It was not intended to radiate from one central point only, but to form numerous centers from which its influence might spread to the surrounding parts.[23]

Spurgeon did not limit himself to only one method of church planting, but adopted a variety of approaches to starting new churches.[24] Many of his church plants arose out of evangelistic mission stations that were carried on in various districts of the city. These "street missions," as they were called, were typically led by members of the Tabernacle or men from the Pastors' College and usually involved evangelistic preaching, targeted ministry to children, and various mercy ministries among the community. Some new churches grew out of Sunday schools and Bible classes that were carried on in particular neighborhoods in London. In the case of some church plants, it was not uncommon for Spurgeon to gather

---

22. *C. H. Spurgeon's Autobiography*, 2:329.

23. C. H. Spurgeon, "Metropolitan Tabernacle Statistics," *Sword and the Trowel* (April 1865): 174.

24. Geoff Chang provides a helpful outline of Spurgeon's church planting process; see *Spurgeon the Pastor*, 240–44.

together a small core team of members and send them along with a minister from the Pastors' College for the express purpose of starting a new church in a needy area.[25] Spurgeon explained,

> We have never sought to hinder the uprising of other churches from our midst or in our neighborhood. It is with cheerfulness that we dismiss our twelves, our twenties, our fifties, to form other churches. We encourage our members to leave us to found other churches; nay, we seek to persuade them to do it. We ask them to scatter throughout the land to become the goodly seed which God shall bless. I believe that so long as we do this we shall prosper.[26]

All throughout the 1860s and into the decades that followed, Spurgeon organized new churches in precisely this fashion, sometimes as many as eight or nine in a given year. In this decade of tremendous ministry expansion, church planting became an integral part of Spurgeon's growing national influence. His zeal for souls and commitment to reach men and women with the gospel led him to launch one of the most ambitious programs of church planting ever seen in the English-speaking world. Yet there was still more to do in these pivotal years.

The Colportage Association

From his earliest days as a Christian and even before he was converted, Spurgeon appreciated the importance of good Christian literature. As a boy, he devoured Christian books and tracts that shaped his view of the gospel, the Christian life, and biblical doctrine. In his beginning days as a new believer in Cambridgeshire, Spurgeon devoted

---

25. Dallimore, *Spurgeon: A New Biography*, 157; Dallimore noted, "At [Spurgeon's] suggestion two hundred and fifty members left the Tabernacle to begin a new church at Peckam" (172).

26. C. H. Spurgeon, "The Waterer Watered," in *Metropolitan Tabernacle Pulpit*, 11:238. See also C. H. Spurgeon, *Trumpet Calls to Christian Energy: A Collection of Sermons Preached on Sunday and Thursday Evenings at the Metropolitan Tabernacle* (London: Passmore and Alabaster, 1875), 134–35.

himself to passing out scores of tracts in some of the local districts in Newmarket. He longed to see good books and resources in the hands of ordinary people to help them understand the gospel and the Christian faith.

The inventory of the Colportage Association

It was this concern that moved Spurgeon to write an article in the *Sword and the Trowel* in August 1866 about the need for Christians to promote the publication and mass distribution of good Christian literature among the common people of England.[27] In this article, titled "The Holy War of the Present Hour," he made his appeal in the context of his growing concerns surrounding the rise of Anglo-Catholicism in the Church of England. He feared the average person on the street was liable to embrace falsehood under the guise of truth, and therefore he believed evangelical orthodoxy needed to go on the offensive. What was needed was the widespread proliferation of truth to combat error. Spurgeon wrote, "We should like to see the country flooded, and even the walls placarded with bold exposures of error and plain expositions of truth. We will take our own share in the effort if any friends should be moved to work *with us*."[28] This was the beginning of what came to be known as the Colportage Association, which was established a few months later on November 1, 1866.

---

27. C. H. Spurgeon, "The Holy War of the Present Hour," *Sword and the Trowel* (August 1866): 339–45.

28. Spurgeon, "Holy War of the Present Hour," *Sword and the Trowel* (August 1866): 343.

The Colportage Association was essentially a coalition of traveling salesmen, known as *colporteurs*, who itinerated from door to door distributing solid Christian literature at heavily discounted prices. These colporteurs would travel all across the United Kingdom, selling literature in cities, towns, and villages in practically every corner of the country. Within a decade of its founding, there were nearly a hundred colporteurs serving part- or full-time in the association.[29] They carried all kinds of literature, from Spurgeon's sermons to Puritan classics. By this means Spurgeon was able to place tens of thousands of books and tracts with sound theology and gospel teaching into the hands of ordinary English people all across the nation.

Spurgeon constantly promoted the work of the Colportage Association in the pages of the *Sword and the Trowel* and viewed it as a strategically important work among the growing network of agencies and institutions associated with his ministry. He made rooms available at the Tabernacle to house the association's inventory and often funded individual colporteurs out of his own pocket. The ministry was spectacularly fruitful, and by 1892, the year of Spurgeon's death, the Colportage Association had sold 153,784 pounds' worth of literature and paid nearly twelve million home visits.[30]

The Stockwell Orphanage

Though Spurgeon is most often remembered today as a preacher, he was known almost as much in his own day as a philanthropist.[31] Beyond the Metropolitan Tabernacle and the Pastors' College, no institution was more closely associated with his name than the Stockwell Orphanage, which he founded in 1867 and led for the next twenty-five years.[32] The orphanage would eventually become famous throughout the United Kingdom and America as an exemplary

---

29. Morden, *C. H. Spurgeon: The People's Preacher*, 152.
30. Fullerton, *C. H. Spurgeon: A Biography*, 288.
31. DiPrima, *Spurgeon and the Poor*.
32. DiPrima, *Spurgeon and the Poor*, 129–36.

A drawing of the Stockwell Orphanage grounds

charitable enterprise and would greatly contribute to Spurgeon's reputation as a leading evangelical philanthropist of his day.

The orphanage had its origin in three conspicuous events, all occurring in late summer 1866 as Spurgeon's ministry was rapidly growing. The first came in the form of an article Spurgeon published in the *Sword and the Trowel* in August of that year, the same article that gave life to the Colportage Association. In the article he argued for the founding of Christian schools and institutions that would have as part of their mission the religious instruction of children, with the particular aim of teaching them the gospel at an early age.[33] He regarded such institutions as vital, in part, because there was no system of public education in England at that time and no widespread public mechanism for the education of children in religious subjects.

The second key event occurred at one of the Tabernacle's regular Monday evening prayer meetings in August 1866. At the opening

---

33. Spurgeon, "Holy War of the Present Hour," *Sword and the Trowel* (August 1866): 339–45; and *C. H. Spurgeon's Autobiography*, 3:167.

of the meeting, Spurgeon addressed his congregation, saying, "Dear friends, we are a huge church, and should be doing more for the Lord in this great city. I want us, tonight, to ask Him to send us some new work; and if we need money to carry it on, let us pray that the means may also be sent."[34]

The final occurrence was the most singular and extraordinary. A few days after the aforementioned prayer meeting, Spurgeon received a letter from a woman he had never met. Her name was Anne Hillyard, and she introduced herself as the widow of an Anglican priest. She had inherited a large estate from a deceased relative and wished to commit twenty thousand pounds in service to the kingdom of God. It was while contemplating how best to use these funds that she came across Spurgeon's article in the *Sword and the Trowel* on the need for children to have a Christian education. She determined she would use the funds to found an orphanage where needy boys could not only be cared for and educated in basic subjects like reading, writing, and arithmetic but also taught the things of God and the gospel of Jesus Christ. She felt certain Spurgeon was the best man to lead such an enterprise and wrote to him to suggest they partner together for the purpose of establishing the orphanage. Though Spurgeon, in an expression of sincere modesty, suggested Mrs. Hillyard might find a better use for the funds, she would not be refused. When Spurgeon realized how determined she was, he concluded God's providential hand was in it and that the church's prayers of the previous Monday evening prayer meeting had been answered. "Here was the new work," Spurgeon said, "and the money with which to begin it."[35] Thus began a monumental effort that would rescue over fifteen hundred children over the course of Spurgeon's life, and thousands more beyond it.[36]

---

34. *C. H. Spurgeon's Autobiography*, 3:168.

35. *C. H. Spurgeon's Autobiography*, 3:168–69.

36. C. H. Spurgeon, "Annual Report of the Stockwell Orphanage, 1890–91," *Sword and the Trowel* (August 1891): 486. The Stockwell Orphanage continues today as Spurgeon's Children's Charity and serves thousands of children in need each year

The orphanage began as an institution for orphan boys only, but a girls' wing would be added in 1879. Though they were regarded as orphans, in most cases the children had lost only their fathers, and their mothers were still living. In Victorian England, a society without an expansive system of social welfare, the economic challenges facing a mother without a husband were immense and often insurmountable. Thus, fatherless children with surviving mothers were regarded as primary candidates for support. The typical child in the Stockwell Orphanage was one whose father had died and whose mother could not adequately provide for her children. In this way, the orphanage was designed to serve both the fatherless and the widow not only by providing for orphans but by relieving their widowed mothers who were in distress. Spurgeon said, "Often sickly themselves, altogether without business capacity, grieving for the loss of their husbands, and having half-a-dozen or more children tugging at their skirts, they are true objects of Christian sympathy.... The relief afforded by our taking one child has often inspired a poor woman with hope, given her a little breathing-space, and enabled her to accomplish the difficult task which still remained."[37]

Creating a New Family

The orphanage grounds were designed to accommodate what was called the "family system," which aimed at creating as comfortable a setting as possible for the children. The orphanage was set up as a massive rectangular campus, with several houses connected to one another facing inward on a lovely green courtyard adorned with lush flowers and bushes. Spurgeon did not want the orphans to be forced to live together in one great hall or common room but instead arranged for them to be organized into "families" of about a dozen

---

through a variety of different services. See Spurgeon's Children's Charity, accessed on April 22, 2023, https://www.spurgeons.org.

37. C. H. Spurgeon, "Annual Report of the Stockwell Orphanage, 1882–83," *Sword and the Trowel* (July 1883): 403–4.

orphans. Each family would occupy one house under the supervision of one "house mother" per family.[38]

In his efforts to create as normal and comfortable an atmosphere as possible for the orphans, Spurgeon insisted that the children not be required to wear the standard uniforms that were customary in such institutions. He said, "Orphanhood is a child's misfortune, and he should not be treated as though it were his fault. In a garb which is a symbol of dependence, it is difficult, if not impossible for an orphan to preserve a feeling of self-respect."[39]

After the girls' wing was erected, the Stockwell Orphanage had accommodation for five hundred orphans at any given time. Spurgeon visited the orphanage regularly and spent most of his Christmas mornings there. Time spent at the orphanage was one of his greatest delights. He was always at home around children. He took an eager interest in their lives, their concerns, their games, their curiosities, and, most of all, their souls. Spurgeon was perhaps never more himself than when offering Christ to children. It was certainly the goal of the orphanage to provide material care and adequate education for the children, but its primary aim was to introduce them to the Savior.

As for the orphans themselves, they regarded Spurgeon as their champion. He was to them like a devoted uncle or, in later years, a beloved grandfather who always came with charms and gifts and loved to lead the children in all sorts of playful games. Whenever he visited the orphanage, he was met with an eruption of loud shouts and cheers as the children surrounded him and showered him with expressions of love and affection. He was the grand old man, their rescuer, and their intimate friend. An 1880 article in the

---

38. Richard E. Day, *The Shadow of the Broad Brim: The Life Story of Charles Haddon Spurgeon, Heir of the Puritans* (Philadelphia: Judson, 1934), 124. This method of organization was not uncommon in other orphanages in the Victorian era; see Kathleen Heasman, *Evangelicals in Action: An Appraisal of Their Social Work in the Victorian Era* (London: Geoffrey Bles, 1962), 98–99.

39. C. H. Spurgeon, "Annual Report of the Stockwell Orphanage, 1884–85," *Sword and the Trowel* (August 1885): 460.

Daily Telegraph described one of his visits to the orphanage: "As to the happiness of the orphans, there is no doubt about it. When Mr. Spurgeon opened the door there was a shout of delight at the appearance of their friend. It was like a welcome to an old school fellow, and was repeated in every house we entered. Not the kind of cheer that requires a lead, but one that sprang up on the instant when it was known that Mr. Spurgeon was at the orphanage."[40]

The Spurgeon memorial at the Stockwell Orphanage

Spurgeon believed the cause of the Stockwell Orphanage and institutions like it should be of universal interest to Christian people. With James 1:27 in mind, Spurgeon said, "The work of caring for the widow and the fatherless is specially mentioned by the Holy Spirit as one of the most acceptable modes of giving outward expression to pure religion and undefiled before God and the Father, and therefore the Lord's people will not question that they should help in carrying it out."[41] Therefore, Spurgeon did not shy away from making regular appeals for the orphanage's support, particularly in the *Sword and*

---

40. Fullerton, *C. H. Spurgeon: A New Biography*, 245.
41. C. H. Spurgeon, "Annual Report of the Stockwell Orphanage, 1880–81," *Sword and the Trowel* (August 1881): 440.

the Trowel. He said, "The duty of each Christian to the mass of destitute orphanhood is clear enough, and if pure minds are stirred up by way of remembrance there will be no lack in the larder, no want in the wardrobe, no failing in the funds of our Orphan House."[42]

Spurgeon was indeed a great evangelical philanthropist, filled with compassion for the needy and the afflicted. This compassion would flow into practical action. When confronted by the extraordinary needs that surrounded him on all sides in London, he rolled up his sleeves and got to work:

> The objects of our care are not far to seek, there they are at our gates—widows worn down with labour, often pale, emaciated, delicate, and even consumptive—boys half-famished, growing up neglected, surrounded with temptation! Can you look at them without pity? We cannot. We will work for them, through our Orphanage, as long as our brain can think, and our pen can write, and our heart can love; neither sickness nor weariness shall tempt us to flag in this sacred enterprise.[43]

A Greater and Grander Man

Spurgeon is well known today as the great Prince of Preachers. Spurgeon the philanthropist is lesser known. But we must hold the two together in order to appreciate what his ministry truly was—what one biographer described as "the perfect blending of evangelistic fervency and deep social concern."[44] His was a ministry in word *and* deed.

An anecdote from Spurgeon's friend, the famous American temperance activist John B. Gough, illustrates well Spurgeon's devotion to ministries of mercy and benevolence. In 1879 Gough visited England, eager to attend the Tabernacle to hear Spurgeon preach and

---

42. Spurgeon, "Annual Report of the Stockwell Orphanage, 1880–81," *Sword and the Trowel* (August 1881): 432.

43. C. H. Spurgeon, "Annual Report of the Stockwell Orphanage, 1878–79," *Sword and the Trowel* (December 1879): appendix, 13.

44. Drummond, *Spurgeon: Prince of Preachers*, 398.

to visit the Stockwell Orphanage, which he had also heard so much about. Spurgeon was delighted to give Gough a tour of the orphanage, which, by that time, had been in operation for a decade. As they were walking the grounds, however, Spurgeon was called to the infirmary to the bedside of a dying orphan boy. Immediately Spurgeon went to visit the child and invited Gough to accompany him. Gough's account of the episode gives us a view into Spurgeon's fervent compassion for the poor, the least, and the forgotten members of society.

Gough recorded that as the great preacher sat at the boy's bedside, Spurgeon took the child's hand in his and said to him, "Jesus loves you. He bought you with His precious blood, and He knows what is best for you. It seems hard for you to lie here and listen to the shouts of the healthy boys outside at play. But soon Jesus will take you home, and then He will tell you the reason, and you will be so glad."[45] Spurgeon then prayed softly over the boy, "O Jesus, Master, this dear child is reaching out his thin hand to find thine. Touch him, dear Saviour, with thy loving, warm clasp. Lift him as he passes the cold river, that his feet be not chilled by the water of death; take him home in thine own good time. Comfort and cherish him till that good time comes. Show him thyself as he lies here, and let him see thee and know thee more and more as his loving Saviour."[46] He then said after a moment's pause, "Now, dear, is there anything you would like? Would you like a little canary in a cage to hear him sing in the morning? Nurse, see that he has a canary tomorrow morning. Goodbye, my dear; you will see the Saviour perhaps before I shall."[47]

Gough had sat there in silence all the while, observing this solemn and precious scene. He later recorded the impression it made on him, writing, "I had seen Mr. Spurgeon holding by his power sixty-five hundred persons in a breathless interest; I knew him as a great

---

45. John B. Gough, *Sunlight and Shadow; or, Gleanings from My Life Work* (Hartford, Conn.: A. D. Worthington, 1881), 407–8.

46. Gough, *Sunlight and Shadow*, 408.

47. Gough, *Sunlight and Shadow*, 408.

man universally esteemed and beloved; but as he sat by the bedside of a dying pauper child, whom his beneficence had rescued, he was to me a greater and grander man than when swaying the mighty multitude at his will."[48]

---

48. Gough, *Sunlight and Shadow*, 408.

11

Finding Strength amid Weakness

Charles Spurgeon died when he was fifty-seven years old. His father died when he was ninety-one, and his grandfather when he was eighty-eight. Had Spurgeon lived as long as his forebears, he likely would have been ministering in London during World War I and into the 1920s. It is possible that he and Winston Churchill might have met one another, and a young Martyn Lloyd-Jones might have heard him preach. Spurgeon also would have lived during the modernist/fundamentalist controversies of the early decades of the twentieth century and likely would have been a formidable champion on the side of conservative orthodoxy in those historic conflicts that convulsed the evangelical world on both sides of the Atlantic.

But this was not to be since, sadly, Spurgeon died at a relatively young age. Part of the reason for Spurgeon's premature death was his immense workload as well as his attitude toward it. He once declared, "People said to me years ago, 'You will break your constitution down with preaching ten times a week,' and the like. Well, if I have done so, I am glad of it. I would do the same again. If I had fifty constitutions I would rejoice to break them down in the service of the Lord Jesus Christ."[1] Spurgeon would die overworked, and his physical appearance in his fifties and even his forties bears witness to this. In pictures taken toward the end of his life, Spurgeon looked like a man who was decades older than he actually was.

---

1. C. H. Spurgeon, "For the Sick and Afflicted," in *Metropolitan Tabernacle Pulpit*, 22:45.

Overwork, however, was not the only factor contributing to Spurgeon's early death. Even while still a young man, Spurgeon developed some significant health issues that greatly troubled him for most of his adult life. From 1867 on, he was seldom well physically and rarely got through a year without having to spend significant time away from the pulpit because of sickness and poor health.[2]

Bodily Suffering

In the autumn of 1867, at the age of thirty-three, Spurgeon suffered a serious illness rendering him unable to preach for several weeks. This was the beginning of his struggles with chronic kidney issues that went undiagnosed for years but would eventually be diagnosed near the end of his life as Bright's disease.[3] Today, Bright's disease is referred to as nephritis and involves inflammation of the kidneys. The disease plagued Spurgeon for the rest of his life and would be the leading cause of his death in 1892.

Spurgeon's health was also greatly compromised by a second condition that was diagnosed in 1869. He developed rheumatic gout, a form of arthritis that causes severe attacks of pain in the joints as well as significant swelling, often developing most acutely in the feet. This condition would also bedevil Spurgeon for the rest of his life and would regularly cause him excruciating physical agony. Attempting to describe the difference between ordinary rheumatism and rheumatic gout, Spurgeon said to a friend, "Put your foot in a vice, and turn the screw as tight as you can—that is rheumatism; give it an extra turn, and that is rheumatic gout."[4] In an 1886 sermon he said, "When I am suffering very greatly from gout, if anybody walks heavily and noisily across the room, it gives me pain."[5]

In some of Spurgeon's letters to friends, he included affecting accounts of sudden attacks of gout that would throw him to the floor

---

2. Morden, *Communion with Christ and His People*, 130.
3. Morden, *Communion with Christ and His People*, 195.
4. Fullerton, *C. H. Spurgeon: A Biography*, 164–65.
5. C. H. Spurgeon, "Burden-Bearing," in *Metropolitan Tabernacle Pulpit*, 49:234.

and leave him writhing in pain, often for hours at a time. It must be remembered that many of the medications people now take to manage pain were unavailable in the nineteenth century. The medical and pharmaceutical interventions at hand for Spurgeon were quite primitive by today's standards. Often, he simply had to ride out the pain, sometimes for days on end.

These twin trials of kidney disease and gout frequently forced Spurgeon out of the pulpit and required him to pursue seasons of extended rest and recuperation. From 1867 on, he would retreat annually to Menton, France, a charming seaside town situated on a picturesque strip of the French Riviera. His typical pattern was to go there either in the winter or when he was most unwell and spend about a month or two benefiting from the warmer weather, the salt water, and the sunshine. He greatly cherished his retreats to Menton and often used the time there to pursue needed spiritual renewal and refreshment, even as he sought to recover physically.

The status of Spurgeon's health would often be reported in the press to inform visitors to London if they could expect to hear him preach that week. Whether or not he would take the pulpit at the Metropolitan Tabernacle could sometimes become a weekly drama, particularly in the final decade of his life.[6] Whenever he was away, Spurgeon made a habit of writing letters to his congregation not only to update them on his condition but also to express his pastoral affection for them and to provide them with words of encouragement and exhortation in his absence.[7]

Mental Suffering

Spurgeon's physical suffering could be debilitating and, at times, intensely painful. Yet to him, these forms of bodily suffering paled in comparison to the acute mental anguish that often visited him in the

---

6. Morden, *Communion with Christ and His People*, 259–60.
7. *The Suffering Letters of C. H. Spurgeon*, ed. Hannah Wyncoll (London: Wakeman Trust, 2007).

form of spiritual depression. It is clear from the available evidence that Spurgeon struggled with some form of depression for his entire adult life, and perhaps even as a youth as well. In his experience, the darkest nights and deepest valleys he faced did not come as the result of gout or kidney disease but because of spiritual and mental dejection. Throughout his life, he made periodic journeys through what he called the "slough of despond" and often found himself sunk so low under depression that he sometimes doubted that he truly was a child of God.[8] At times he even despaired of life itself.

Spurgeon's experiences of spiritual depression led him to conclude that the worst forms of human suffering stem from disorders not of the body but of the mind. Thus, he often made statements such as these:

I am the subject of depressions of spirit so fearful that I hope none of you ever get to such extremes of wretchedness as I go to.[9]

The worst cloud of all is deep depression of spirit accompanied with the loss of the light of God's countenance. Sickness, poverty, slander, none of these things are comparable to depression.[10]

The worst ill in the world is not poverty; the worst of ills is a depressed spirit; at least, I scarcely know anything that can be worse than this.[11]

Personally I know that there is nothing on earth that the human

8. The "Slough of Despond" refers to an episode in John Bunyan's *Pilgrim's Progress* that is often identified as an allegorical portrayal of spiritual depression and melancholy. See John Bunyan, *The Pilgrim's Progress* (London: Hurst, Robinson, 1820), 8–11.

9. C. H. Spurgeon, "Joy and Peace in Believing," in *Metropolitan Tabernacle Pulpit*, 12:298.

10. C. H. Spurgeon, "Our Leader through the Darkness," in *Metropolitan Tabernacle Pulpit*, 59:427.

11. C. H. Spurgeon, "The Fifth Beatitude," in *Metropolitan Tabernacle Pulpit*, 55:401.

frame can suffer to be compared with despondency and prostration of mind.[12]

The mind can descend far lower than the body, for in it there are bottomless pits. The flesh can bear only a certain number of wounds and no more, but the soul can bleed in ten thousand ways, and die over and over again each hour.[13]

We very speedily care for bodily diseases; they are too painful to let us slumber in silence: and they soon urge us to seek a physician or a surgeon for our healing. Oh, if we were as much alive to the more serious wounds of our inner man.[14]

Many people may be surprised to learn that such a mighty man of God struggled so intensely with depression. What is perhaps even more surprising is how extraordinarily transparent and vulnerable Spurgeon was willing to be about these struggles with his congregation and with the public. In our day, it is normal for public figures to open up about mental health issues, and it is not unheard of for pastors to publicly disclose personal battles with anxiety or depression. But this was extraordinarily rare in the nineteenth century.

Because of Spurgeon's cultural and historical context, his public vulnerability regarding his struggles with depression was highly unusual and virtually unprecedented. To start, Spurgeon was British—and not only British but a Victorian. The British in general, and the Victorians in particular, are not known for their emotional transparency and tended to be more reserved in expressing any spiritual or psychological frailty. Furthermore, he was *the* leading preacher in the evangelical world and a highly visible public figure. Many people in Spurgeon's context would have expected someone in his position to downplay his weaknesses and vulnerabilities. It must also be remembered that Spurgeon was often under severe scrutiny,

---

12. C. H. Spurgeon, "The Garden of the Soul," in *Metropolitan Tabernacle Pulpit*, 12:306.

13. Spurgeon, *Treasury of David*, 4:132.

14. C. H. Spurgeon, "Healing for the Wounded," in *New Park Street Pulpit*, 1:403.

was constantly the subject of newspaper articles, and had no shortage of critics. Additionally, he had the responsibility of stewarding public trust, as he led many important organizations that depended on the practical and financial support of literally thousands of people. The risk of sharing publicly about his inner battles with depression and despondency was great. But out of love for his flock and a sincere desire to be genuinely useful to them, he decided to disclose his struggles in order to help people who suffered with their own mental, spiritual, and psychological battles.

Though the precise cause of a person's depression can be hard to trace, and though various causes may be intertwined, some mental health experts have suggested that there are two basic types of depression.[15] The first may arise from external influences, such as one's environment or circumstances. Such external influences may include relational conflict, financial stress, or some personal trauma or tragedy. These influences may bring someone under prolonged depression, but the depression may abate once the negative external influence is removed. A second form of depression appears to arise from within a person regardless of his or her circumstances. This kind of depression is not necessarily attached to any external influence but rather seems to be in some way endemic to the individual. Whether through some sort of imbalance in the brain or some type of psychological or emotional disorder, such depression can emerge at any time for no apparent reason at all.

Though Spurgeon's depression was certainly aggravated by external factors (e.g., overwork, criticism, and poor physical health), it nonetheless seems clear that Spurgeon suffered, at least to some degree, from this second kind of depression. Spurgeon appeared to have an inward tendency toward melancholy that would visit him at random intervals. He was subject to mood swings and bouts of despondency that could rush over him without warning, seemingly

---

15. Morden, *Communion with Christ and His People*, 261–62. Morden cites his personal discussions with a professional psychiatrist concerning Spurgeon's case.

unattached to any obvious outward circumstances. At times Susie would find him at the foot of the stairs weeping, completely unable to identify the reason why. Speaking of this kind of depression in an 1877 sermon, Spurgeon said, "Quite involuntarily, unhappiness of mind, depression of spirit, and sorrow of heart will come upon you. You may be without any real reason for grief, and yet may become among the most unhappy of men because, for the time, your body has conquered your soul."[16]

It is not known when Spurgeon first began to struggle with depression. There are indications he might have developed a tendency toward melancholy while still a boy. Though he would later become something of an extrovert, usually being found in the company of others, Spurgeon always had a streak in his personality that led him on occasions to retreat from others and into himself. His tendency toward periodic social and psychological withdrawal, when paired with his vast emotional capacity, could make him unusually vulnerable to despondency. This vulnerability can be seen to some degree in his earliest days as a young child in his grandparents' home in Stambourne. It can also be seen in the five-year period of doubt and despair over the state of his soul that he experienced from the ages of ten to fifteen.

The signal event that most heavily affected Spurgeon's mental equilibrium was the disaster at the Surrey Gardens Music Hall (see chapter 6). Susannah wrote that as a result of this traumatic episode, "my beloved's anguish was so deep and violent, that reason seemed to totter in her throne, and we sometimes feared that he would never preach again."[17] Spurgeon himself spoke of his mind and spirit being like broken glass and molten lava.[18] Though he may have always had a native bent toward depression before this, the episode at the Surrey Gardens greatly deepened and intensified his

---

16. C. H. Spurgeon, "The Saddest Cry from the Cross," in *Metropolitan Tabernacle Pulpit*, 48:520.

17. *C. H. Spurgeon's Autobiography*, 2:192.

18. Spurgeon, *Saint and His Saviour*, 341–42.

struggle. He would never truly recover from the trauma of October 19, 1856, and would always bear the emotional and psychological scars of that terrible night.

Most ministers with significant experience in true pastoral work know that some of God's people are troubled by mental and spiritual difficulties of various kinds that leave them unusually liable to despondency and despair. God's children, though saved, still live in a sin-cursed world and are subject to various disorders of the mind and body. Spurgeon was no exception. Yet a consideration of what he learned from his battles with depression can help Christians today as they navigate their own inward struggles of various kinds.

Treasures of Darkness

To understand Spurgeon, we must recognize that although he suffered greatly, he suffered successfully as a child of God. Much of his piety as a Christian and as a minister was forged in the fires of distress and affliction. Moreover, perseverance through suffering became a part of the savor of his ministry and a major motif in his preaching. Sufferers went to hear Spurgeon because they recognized in him a fellow traveler who understood them and could show them the way through their sorrows to Christ.

One of the reasons for Spurgeon's ongoing relevance nearly a century and a half after his death surely has to do with his immense suffering and his extraordinary ability to apply comfort and consolation to those who experience similar affliction. Those who wrestle with depression, chronic pain, isolation and loneliness, and a thousand other sorrows have a sympathetic companion in Charles Spurgeon. Moreover, his unusual transparency and candor about his suffering have the effect of inviting fellow sufferers to listen to him and to find help in the midst of their trials. Millions have found in Spurgeon consolation for their sorrows and have been led by him to better appreciate and trust the promises of God's word for those who suffer. Spurgeon was like a person who plunged into caves of deep darkness and returned with priceless treasures to share with suffering Christians everywhere. Of the many treasured lessons Spurgeon discovered in his suffering, three in particular should be inspected more closely, as they can especially help those who suffer in various ways today.

Spurgeon in his study,
probably in the late 1870s or early 1880s

The first lesson Spurgeon learned in his suffering is that trials are intended by God to sanctify His people. He came to see that God is pleased to use affliction and adversity to refine, humble, and sanctify His children and to make them more like Christ. Suffering for the Christian is never for nothing, and in Spurgeon's case, it was one of the chief ways God sanctified him both as a Christian man and as a minister of the gospel. Spurgeon observed,

I am sure that I have run more swiftly with a lame leg than I ever did with a sound one. I am certain that I have seen more in the dark than ever I saw in the light,—more stars, most certainly,—more things in heaven if fewer things on earth. The anvil, the fire, and the hammer, are the making of us; we do not get fashioned much by anything else. That heavy hammer falling on us helps to shape us; therefore let affliction and trouble and trial come.[19]

A second lesson Spurgeon gleaned is that suffering is meant to lead the Christian to deeper experiences of communion with God. He recognized that God purposes to use suffering to draw believers into a richer relationship with Him and a deeper experience of His love. Spurgeon learned that God perfects His power in the weaknesses, sorrows, and sufferings of His people, and He is pleased to make their suffering an occasion for the display of His matchless grace and glory. Further, he came to appreciate that suffering has the effect of revealing deeper aspects of God's character and His heart for His people. He learned that it is when walking under the weight of suffering that God's children most clearly perceive Him to be their soul's greatest helper, rock, and refuge. In an 1881 sermon he said,

> I the preacher of this hour, beg to bear my little witness that the worst days I have ever had have turned out to be my best days, and when God has seemed most cruel to me he has then been most kind. If there is anything in this world for which I would bless him more than for anything else it is for pain and affliction. I am sure that in these things the richest, tenderest love has been manifested towards me.... Our Father's wagons rumble most heavily when they are bringing us the richest freight of the bullion of his grace. Love letters from heaven are often sent in black-edged envelopes. The cloud that is black with horror is big with mercy.... Fear not the storm, it brings healing in its wings, and when Jesus is with you in the vessel the tempest

---

19. Spurgeon, "Christ's Yoke and Burden," in *Metropolitan Tabernacle Pulpit*, 49:249.

only hastens the ship to its desired haven. Blessed be the Lord, whose way is in the whirlwind, and who makes the clouds to be the dust of his feet.[20]

The third lesson Spurgeon learned through suffering is how to sympathize with other sufferers. Spurgeon's experiences of physical pain, depression, and other forms of distress created within him compassion for the afflicted and downcast. He was extraordinarily gentle with bruised reeds and faintly burning wicks (Isa. 42:3). He urged others to show similar tenderness and kindness to those who walk in the midst of suffering and sorrow:

> [A Christian] understands that as his Lord and Master sought after that which was wounded, bound up that which was broken, healed that which was sick and brought again that which was driven away, even so ought all His servants to imitate their Master by looking with the greatest interest after those who are in the saddest plight. O children of God, if ever you are hardhearted towards any sorrowful person, you are not what you ought to be! You are not like your Master![21]

Spurgeon urged those among his congregation who were unacquainted with great affliction and trial not to judge harshly those who suffer: "Especially judge not the sons and daughters of sorrow. Allow no ungenerous suspicions of the afflicted, the poor, and the despondent. Do not hastily say they ought to be more brave, and exhibit a greater faith. Ask not—why are they so nervous, and so absurdly fearful? Nay.... I beseech thee, remember that thou understandest not thy fellow-man."[22]

Spurgeon's ministry was profoundly shaped by suffering. All his preaching of the gospel, of God's surpassing love for sinners in Christ, of the daily need for divine mercy and grace, of the challenges

---

20. C. H. Spurgeon, "Ziklag; or, David Encouraging Himself in God," in *Metropolitan Tabernacle Pulpit*, 27:373.

21. Spurgeon, "Fifth Beatitude," in *Metropolitan Tabernacle Pulpit*, 55:402.

22. C. H. Spurgeon, "Man Unknown to Man," in *Metropolitan Tabernacle Pulpit*, 35:195.

and trials of the Christian life, and of the hope of the life to come were conditioned by his own experience of suffering in a fallen world. To the end of his life, Spurgeon exemplified persevering faith through extraordinary hardships and trials, and in this he shows believers a way forward through their own suffering to the hope of the gospel and the God of all grace.

Helpers in Ministry

As these significant illnesses emerged in Spurgeon's life in the late 1860s, it became clear that he needed more help in managing the work of his growing church. As seen in the last chapter, by the end of the 1860s, numerous ministries, agencies, and institutions had grown up around Spurgeon and the ministry of the Metropolitan Tabernacle. With less than reliable health and ever-multiplying demands on his time, he found himself in urgent need of support.

Associate Pastor

Help would arrive through hiring a new associate pastor, Spurgeon's brother James Archer Spurgeon.[23] James had served for a few years as a pastor in Southampton and had lately been serving as the pastor of another London church in Bayswater near Kensington Palace.[24] In 1868 the Tabernacle invited him to serve alongside his brother as co-pastor. James's

James Archer Spurgeon,
likely in the 1880s

---

23. *C. H. Spurgeon's Autobiography*, 3:30–36. The church had enjoyed the ministries of at least two previous associate pastors during Spurgeon's tenure, but both served in the role for only one to two years before leaving to pastor other churches.

24. Nicholls, *Lights to the World*, 57–58.

influence eventually extended to practically every corner of the church's ministry. Some of his regular responsibilities included chairing members' meetings, supervising several of the church's ministries, interviewing and baptizing new members, assisting in the work of the Pastors' College, and occasional preaching.

James Archer Spurgeon would prove to be an invaluable and irreplaceable companion to his brother in the work of the Metropolitan Tabernacle. Together they forged an extraordinarily effective and constructive partnership that would facilitate the church's long-term fruitfulness for the next quarter century. Had James not joined the work, it is quite likely Charles's health would have deteriorated further and the ministry of the Tabernacle would have atrophied. Charles would always be the senior man, with James serving under his direction, but the two were nonetheless true fellow laborers. They cheerfully worked in concert with one another for the good of the church.

Elders and Deacons

Spurgeon also received further help and support from his fellow elders and deacons of the Tabernacle. When Spurgeon arrived at New Park Street in 1854, the church had no elders, though it had several deacons. In the days of Spurgeon's predecessor Benjamin Keach, in the seventeenth century, the church benefited from the ministry of a plurality of elders who were, as a body, responsible for the oversight and care of the church. By the nineteenth century, however, most Baptist churches in England rejected the office of elder, viewing it as a presbyterian institution.[25] They instead preferred to employ a sole pastor who was supported by a plurality of deacons.

In studying the matter for himself, Spurgeon came to embrace the plain teaching of the New Testament, which holds that the office

---

25. Presbyterians throughout the centuries have taught that churches should be governed by a plurality of elders.

of elder is indispensable to the proper care and leadership of the local church. Thus, in 1859 he led his congregation to reestablish the office of elder.[26] All elders were voted on by the congregation and served one-year terms, with no limit on the number of terms they could serve. By 1869 the church had twenty-three elders; a decade later there were thirty.[27] These elders were responsible, alongside Spurgeon, for the oversight and leadership of the church body. This involved holding interviews with incoming members to hear their testimonies, regular visitation of members for pastoral care, and at least monthly elders' meetings for prayer and discussion of the health of the flock. In order to provide for the needed oversight and care of so massive a congregation, Spurgeon would come to depend heavily on the help of his fellow elders.

The deacons of the church were fewer but served lifetime appointments.[28] They were in some ways more pivotal to the day-to-day operations of the church than the elders. Spurgeon's deacons were some of his dearest friends and most trusted advisors. They were involved at some level in practically every aspect of the church's life and ministry. They had responsibility for the care of the poor, visitation of the sick, oversight of the church's finances and facilities, superintendence of many of the church's core ministries (especially its Sunday schools and street missions), and participation in regular deacons' meetings, which were often chaired by Spurgeon.[29]

Spurgeon was a champion for the vital ministry of faithful deacons. With reference to his first pastorate in Waterbeach, he extolled the value of the deacons who served alongside him, writing, "The deacons of our first village ministry were in our esteem the excellent of the earth, in whom, we took great delight.... In our idea they

---

26. Chang, *Spurgeon the Pastor*, 146–50.

27. Chang, *Spurgeon the Pastor*, 157.

28. By 1868 there were ten deacons. See Chang, *Spurgeon the Pastor*, 160–63; and DiPrima, *Spurgeon and the Poor*, 157–60.

29. Hayden, *History of Spurgeon's Tabernacle*, 59–65.

were as nearly the perfection of deacons of a country church as the kingdom could afford."[30]

When Spurgeon moved to London, he found himself again serving alongside deacons of superlative character and ability. He described them as "peculiarly lovable, active, energetic, warm-hearted, generous men, every one of whom seems specially adapted for his own particular department of service."[31] In 1868 he published an article in the *Sword and the Trowel* titled "The Good Deacon." In it he wrote,

> The church owes an immeasurable debt of gratitude to those thousands of godly men who study her interests day and night, contribute largely of their substance, care for her poor, cheer her ministers, and in times of trouble as well as prosperity remain faithfully at their posts.... Deprive the church of her deacons and she would be bereaved of her most valiant sons; their loss would be the shaking of the pillars of our spiritual house and would cause desolation on every side.[32]

The greatest among Spurgeon's deacons was Thomas Olney. He was at New Park Street when Spurgeon first came to London, and besides Spurgeon, no one exerted a larger influence on the church than "Father" Olney (he was called Father Olney to distinguish him from his son William, who also served as a deacon). Eric Hayden wrote, "[Spurgeon] seemed to hold Thomas Olney in highest regard" of all his office bearers.[33] In Thomas Olney's sixty years as a member of the church, he served the congregation variously as a deacon, an elder, and the church's treasurer. After his death in 1869, Spurgeon published a eulogy to him in the January 1870 issue of the *Sword and the Trowel*:

---

30. C. H. Spurgeon, "The Good Deacon," *Sword and the Trowel* (June 1868): 244.
31. *C. H. Spurgeon's Autobiography*, 3:18.
32. Spurgeon, "Good Deacon," *Sword and the Trowel* (June 1868): 243; and *C. H. Spurgeon's Autobiography*, 1:255.
33. Hayden, *History of Spurgeon's Tabernacle*, 60.

Of his love and devotion to both the pastor and the church we all are witnesses. His greatest pride, we might almost use that word, was the work of God at the Tabernacle. He gloried and rejoiced in all that concerned the church. Every institution received his cordial co-operation; he loved college, orphanage, and almshouses, and helped them all to the extent of his ability.... In our departed "Father" the poor have lost a friend. The poor, especially the poor of the church, always found in him sincere sympathy and help. By all his children his name will live in lasting remembrance and loving regard.[34]

As commitments and obligations mounted for Spurgeon, he depended on the deacons of the Tabernacle as his trusted deputies. If he was the captain, they were his lieutenants. His trust in them was complete, and his affection for them grew with each passing year. Where other pastors may have found themselves constantly at odds with their deacons, Spurgeon and his deacons worked in perfect harmony as true partners in the work of the gospel and the ministry of the church.

Members

Though Spurgeon received enormous help from his brother as associate pastor and from his many elders and deacons, the most significant support he received in the work of the ministry came from his many members. Spurgeon believed in what today might be called an "every-member ministry." He believed each member of the church had a vital part to play in the ministry of the church and should be actively engaged in the church's work. Spurgeon frequently referred to the Tabernacle as a "working church,"[35] and by this he meant that the members were not merely casual attenders drifting in and out

---

34. C. H. Spurgeon, "Sketch of the Late Mr. Thomas Olney's Life," *Sword and the Trowel* (January 1870): 23.

35. For examples, see C. H. Spurgeon, "The Arrows of the Lord's Deliverance," in *Metropolitan Tabernacle Pulpit*, 10:276; "A Bright Light in Deep Shades," in *Metropolitan Tabernacle Pulpit*, 18:274; and "Plea for the Pastors' College," *Sword and the Trowel* (June 1875): 253.

but rather were all active workers for Christ who vigorously served, supported, and advanced the ministry and mission of the church.

Membership at the Tabernacle was a serious commitment, and this began with the membership process itself. Geoff Chang helpfully outlines the six main steps involved in joining the membership of the church.[36] The first step was to sit for an interview with an elder, in which the elder would inquire about the prospective member's personal testimony along with his or her understanding of the gospel and Christian discipleship. After the elder interview would come the interview with Spurgeon, who, after reviewing the notes from the elder interview, would pose questions of his own and follow up on particular points as he saw fit. The third step was the proposal of the prospective member to the assembled church at one of the regular congregational members' meetings. At this meeting, a "visitor" would be assigned to make inquiries concerning the member candidate's manner of life. The visitor was usually an elder or a deacon, though occasionally an ordinary member who had the responsibility of visiting the prospective member's neighborhood, home, or place of work to inquire concerning his or her reputation and character. The visitor inquiry itself constituted the fourth step in the membership process. The penultimate step was a public interview of the incoming member before the gathered church at a congregational meeting, followed by a congregational vote on the member candidate. The sixth and final step was baptism, admittance to the Communion table, and extending the right hand of fellowship.

Spurgeon organized such a rigorous membership process first because he believed theologically that the church in the new covenant was meant to be a committed community of believers who were genuinely born again. Thus, he believed it was part of his and the church's stewardship to ensure as best as they could that the membership of the church was truly regenerate. But also Spurgeon took great care in the membership process because he viewed

---

36. Chang, *Spurgeon the Pastor*, 113–16.

membership in the church as a serious and vital calling. He maintained high expectations for his members that he believed were derived from the Bible. Members of the church were called to submit to the church's leadership, to live in mutual accountability with one another, and to actively engage in serving the church body and the local community. Church membership was not a casual affair, and therefore the membership process could not be anything less than careful and deliberate.

The church's success depended on an active membership. The multiplying ministries and institutions associated with the Tabernacle could never have been sustained apart from a high volunteer ethic among the members of the congregation. It would perhaps be impossible to calculate with precision how many volunteers were needed to support the expansive work of the church. Practically every member was engaged in some form of Christian service during the week or on Sundays. One of the deacons estimated that on Sunday afternoons alone, over one thousand members filtered out into the streets of London to hold meetings of various kinds in the surrounding neighborhoods.[37] They served in Sunday schools, Bible classes, new church plants, street missions, and ministries to the disabled. Members of the Tabernacle were often to be found all over the city doing practical good to needy people.

Among the membership were some individuals who stood out for their exceptional service to the church and the community. One such member was Lavinia Bartlett, who led an extraordinary ministry to women through the church.[38] Lavinia began teaching women's Sunday school in 1859 with around a half dozen women. Within a few months, the class grew to fifty women, and eventually she was forced to relocate to one of the main halls to accommodate the seven hundred to eight hundred women who attended regularly. Some

---

37. Dallimore, *Spurgeon: A New Biography*, 159.

38. For a detailed account of Lavinia Bartlett's ministry, see Edward H. Bartlett, *Mrs. Bartlett and Her Class at the Metropolitan Tabernacle: A Biography by Her Son* (Cannon Beach, Ore.: Move to Assurance, 2018).

have estimated that as many as a thousand members were added to the Tabernacle through her ministry, including a number of the city's prostitutes who came to faith in Christ through Lavinia's witness.[39] Though Spurgeon did not endorse female deacons (few did in nineteenth-century England), in reference to Lavinia, Spurgeon was fond of saying, tongue in cheek, that his best deacon was a woman.[40]

The church building became a bustling hub of activity for various ministries, all staffed by members of the church eager to serve Christ. The building was open seven days a week, from seven in the morning to eleven at night.[41] Practically every square foot was used for ministry in some form or fashion. The Tabernacle became the informal headquarters for most of the church's ministries, societies, and institutions, and its rooms were often let out for their use. Throughout the week, the Tabernacle hosted numerous teas, lunches, meetings, classes, fund-raising events, and a host of other gatherings connected to the church's ministries. The building site essentially became a factory for Christian work. Literally thousands of members contributed their time, energy, and gifts to help the sacred machinery do its work of promoting the gospel and helping the needy.

Even with the tremendous leadership of Spurgeon and the congregation's other officers, the vast and expansive ministries of the church could not have been sustained without the contribution of thousands of committed members working behind the scenes. Though Spurgeon was often the man out in front, he knew the ministry of the Tabernacle would crumble if not sustained by a vibrant every-member ministry. As he sought to lead the church amid many difficulties and limitations because of his poor health, the members of the congregation bore him up and supported the work of the church through their cheerful activism and devoted support.

---

39. Chang, *Spurgeon the Pastor*, 212–13.
40. *C. H. Spurgeon's Autobiography*, 3:36.
41. Dallimore, *Spurgeon: A New Biography*, 155.

Suffering and Succeeding

It has been said that the best of men are men at best. Though Spurgeon may appear to some people as a kind of superhero of church history, he was still made of flesh and bone like everyone else. His extraordinary life was punctuated by many trials, struggles, and difficulties. He was a man familiar with human weakness and frailty. Yet Spurgeon's great suffering did not disqualify him from usefulness in Christ's kingdom. His successful perseverance through trial made him more effective as a minister, and his suffering became a platform for the display of God's faithfulness, grace, and power.

Spurgeon was enabled to endure the difficulties brought on by poor health, melancholy, and other personal challenges because he enjoyed the aid of numerous helpers, colleagues, and friends in ministry. He depended on his brother, elders and deacons, and many church members to sustain and advance the work of the Metropolitan Tabernacle. The combination of the church's biblical leadership structure and its membership culture served to facilitate the growth and health of the congregation throughout the 1860s and into the 1870s. Spurgeon, his fellow officers, and the Tabernacle congregation entered a new decade with fresh zeal and resolve to serve Christ and promote the spread of the gospel in London and beyond. What was built in the 1860s would grow and mature in the 1870s. Though Spurgeon would continue to experience trials of ill health, the next decade would nonetheless come to represent one of the most fruitful periods of his life.

12

In Labors More Abundant

Spurgeon entered the 1870s with the main pillars of his ministry well established. He continued his unceasing labors in preaching and publishing, caring for his growing church, and leading the Pastors' College, the Stockwell Orphanage, and numerous other organizations and ministries connected with the Metropolitan Tabernacle. This decade would represent a new phase of ministry for Spurgeon, defined less by new efforts and more by maturation and progress in the major works already begun. On the whole, these were peaceful and fruitful years for Spurgeon, undisturbed by controversy, crisis, or division. Though poor health continued to trouble him, he nonetheless kept his hand to the plow and did not relent from the active labors that had always characterized his ministry.

Worship in the Tabernacle

By the 1870s, Spurgeon had become the most well-known and beloved preacher in the English-speaking world. His published sermons were selling twenty-five thousand copies per week and well over one million per year.[1] Visitors came from around the globe to hear him preach and to experience worship at the Metropolitan Tabernacle. For some, the Tabernacle may have been nothing more than a tourist attraction. Yet for the vast majority of those who came to the church in South London, it was to drink from the fountain of divine blessing that poured forth Sunday by Sunday.

---

1. Spurgeon, "To You," *Sword and the Trowel* (January 1871): 1–3.

Numbers of those who visited the church during these years left a record of their impressions of the worship services. A fairly representative report comes from a visiting minister from Boston:

The first prayer was short and general in character, but very devout. No fooling here, we are met to worship God. The first hymn was sung with a will. No chanting or piping organ, no choir to attract attention, but one grand purpose to glorify our Christ. We sang out of "Our Own Hymn Book." Everything has Mr. Spurgeon's imprint. If you don't like it you can leave it; here is a concern big enough to run without your help. Fall into the current or be swept away. I fell in with my whole heart, as happy as a seraph.

Then came the reading of the Scriptures. Time enough. No hurry. How those English people did enjoy the word of God! The second prayer followed. That was my prayer, because it was everybody's cry. His prayer was greater to me than his sermon. In his sermon he talked with men. In his prayer he communed with God. When he described the coming of Christ to the soul, it seemed to me I saw for the first time The King in His beauty. The supplicant was forgiven. With his face streaming with tears, and with tones so full and rich that they swept through every heart, as a breath of perfumed air floats through the halls of a palace, this divine atmosphere possessed our hearts when he cried: "We love thee. Thou knowest it. We love not because thou art great, but because of the inestimable gift of thy only begotten Son. Lift us up O God. Take us out of the dust. Let us by faith come to the fountain and be washed. We come. We feel that thou hast washed us. We are clean. Yes, we are clean. Blessed be the Lord our God. Make us young again. Wake us up. Let us not sleep. We thank thee for our troubles, for all that makes us conscious of our alienation from thee. Bless our Orphanage, our College, our Retreat," and so on he went, enumerating every claim, and presenting the requests so naturally that every heart joined in the up going petition. The close of the prayer lingers as a memory which does not die.

"We close our prayer as to the words. We have been with thee. We know it. Thou hast heard us and blessed us. We feel it.

We retire from the mercy-seat thanking thee for audience and praying for thy blessing on us all."

Another hymn better than the first, because now all were in a worshiping mood, was sung. In the singing he was an inspiration. His happy look, his determined air, his wonderful voice rang out sweeter and grander than any organ-peal I ever listened to at home or abroad.

His step was light and free. His gestures were graceful and telling. His text was found in Psalm 42:1 "As the hart panteth after the water brooks so panteth my soul after thee, O God." It was suited to the highest and best form of dramatic art. I can see him now, as without a pulpit or a note he stood before 6,000 people, every eye on him, picturing that hart on the mountain's brow, thirsty, ears back, tongue out, hunted and almost famishing from thirst, seeing the brook running through the valley in the distance, and then without a care making for it by leaping from crag to crag until he reaches the stream there to slake his burning thirst. The entire audience drank with the hart, and were refreshed. After this in love he portrayed the Christian thirst. How dry we became. Then he uncovered the fountain in Christ. It seemed to me that I had never seen my Christ before. There he was in his beauty. That morning all saw him and were refreshed. It was good to be there.[2]

This account highlights a few distinctive features of the Tabernacle's worship services that consistently impressed visitors. The first was the church's spectacular congregational singing, which was entirely unadorned by any musical accompaniment. Both the volume and quality of the Tabernacle's a cappella singing could have an overwhelming effect on the listener. Many could not help themselves from getting caught up in the rushing sound of thousands of voices rendering praise to God with one heart. The whole congregation seemed to sing with a will and a wonderful sense of purpose. One visitor wrote to a friend, "You would like to hear all the people

2. Justin D. Fulton, *Spurgeon, Our Ally* (Brooklyn, N.Y.: Pauline Propaganda, 1923), 220–23.

sing together, Susie; for they sing as though they enjoyed it. I liked it better than I did the music in [Westminster] Abbey, for at Mr. Spurgeon's church I could sing, too."[3] Another observer wrote,

> To any one who has not been in a similar scene, a hymn sung by a full congregation at the Metropolitan Tabernacle has a thrilling effect. It is no ordinary thing to see four and a half thousand people rise simultaneously to their feet, still less to hear them sing. For a moment during the giving out of the hymn it occurred to us to look wildly round for the organ, which surely must be the only instrument which could lead all those voices. There is none.... A gentleman steps forward to Mr. Spurgeon's side...and at once raises a familiar tune. What is our delight when not only is the tune taken up in all its harmonics, but with perfect time and expression! The slight waving of the precentor's book regulates that huge chorus, as a tap will regulate an engine. The thing is simply wonderful. We feel that tight sensation of the scalp and that quiver down the spine which nothing but the combination of emotion and excitement can produce. We are scarcely able for a while to add our voices to that huge sea of melody which rises and falls and surges and floods the place.... 'Now, quicker,' cries Mr. Spurgeon, as we reach the last verse; and it is wonderful to notice the access of spirit which this produced. We sit down, deeply impressed. After all, what instrument or orchestra of instruments can equal in effect the concert of the human voice, especially in psalmody?[4]

A second feature that stood out to visitors was the spiritual intensity and authenticity of the public prayers, which were typically led by Spurgeon. He always gave a place of special priority to his public prayers and viewed them as the most important portion of the entire service. In his lecture titled "Our Public Prayer," given to the students of the Pastors' College, he said, "I am not able to see any reason for depriving me of the holiest, sweetest, and most

---

3. W. L. Gage, *Helen on Her Travels: What She Saw and What She Did in Europe* (New York: Hurd & Houghton, 1868), 48.

4. Quoted in Fullerton, *C. H. Spurgeon: A Biography*, 146–47.

profitable exercise which my Lord has allotted me; if I may have my choice, I will sooner yield up the sermon than the prayer."[5] Spurgeon generally avoided written prayers, as he believed they tended toward formalism, and he felt their force was weakened by premeditation. He instead aimed to offer impromptu prayers conditioned by the moment, representing as much as possible authentic engagement and communion with God. He said, "Let the Infinite Jehovah be served with our best; let prayer addressed to the Divine Majesty be carefully weighed, and presented with all the powers of an awakened heart and a spiritual understanding."[6]

A third characteristic of the Tabernacle services that regularly impressed visitors was the prominence of the person and work of Christ in Spurgeon's sermons. As noted in previous chapters, this was the dominant motif in Spurgeon's preaching. Members and visitors alike often commented on the ways in which the services of the Tabernacle brought them to deeply cherished experiences of the love and mercy of Christ and real communion with God through congregational worship. This, after all, was Spurgeon's goal in his arrangement of the services at the Tabernacle. He wanted people to walk away with the highest possible thoughts of the love of God in Christ and a sense of having experienced God's presence among them in worship. To see Christ clearly and to treasure Him as Lord and Savior was the grand object of the Tabernacle's worship gatherings.

Spurgeon believed the regular Sunday services of the Metropolitan Tabernacle were the nerve center of the entire church. They shaped the congregation's life and fueled its mission more than anything else. Thus, he gave his all to leading God's people in worship through his selecting of songs, leading in prayer, and preaching of the word. Spurgeon believed the gathering of the saints for the worship of God was the most important hour of the week, demanding his very best.

---

5. Spurgeon, *Lectures to My Students*, 1:60.
6. Spurgeon, *Lectures to My Students*, 1:60.

Services During the Week

Beyond the Sunday services, the church gathered for at least two other weekly meetings. The first was the main corporate prayer meeting on Monday nights. Of these gatherings Spurgeon scholar Geoff Chang writes,

> After the Sunday services, the most important gathering of the church was the church prayer meeting, held on Monday nights in the main auditorium. While dozens of smaller prayer meetings were held throughout the week in homes and before the services, this was the weekly meeting where the whole church came together to pray. More than a thousand members regularly attended, along with visitors and other Christian workers. After a hymn and Scripture reading with commentary, the chair (often Spurgeon, sometimes a deacon or an elder) read through requests for prayer or called on someone to share about particular requests. As requests were shared, various church officers and members of the church, including Spurgeon, led in prayer for those items. The congregation participated in the prayers, voicing their Amens. After a lengthy time of sharing and prayer, a brief address was given (often by Spurgeon), and before long, it was 8:30 p.m. and the meeting was concluded.[7]

A second gathering during the week took place on Thursday nights and amounted to another churchwide evening service. The meeting included singing, prayer, and a sermon, normally preached by Spurgeon. This sermon was usually more extemporaneous in nature, with Spurgeon speaking out of the overflow of his heart with no notes at all. Many of the church's members regularly attended these gatherings along with several current and former students of the Pastors' College. These services also enjoyed the presence of a large number of visitors from the community, including several ministers from other churches in the area. Often, visitors from the Continent and from America who had been turned away on the

---

7. Chang, *Spurgeon the Pastor*, 58–59.

previous Sunday because of capacity issues attended these Thursday night services as well.

Writing and Publishing

Alongside his regular preaching ministry and his leadership of the Tabernacle, Spurgeon enjoyed a thriving publishing ministry. His literary output was simply enormous. The most significant publishing ventures of his life came in the form of the regular weekly publication of *The Metropolitan Tabernacle Pulpit* and the monthly publication of the *Sword and the Trowel*. Beyond these mammoth projects, Spurgeon published numerous other books that not only found a wide readership in his own lifetime but still enjoy popularity today. The interval between 1865 and the early 1880s was the period of greatest productivity in Spurgeon's writing career. Several of his most well-known books came to life during this period. A few deserve special comment.

The late 1860s saw the publication of Spurgeon's classic devotional texts *Morning by Morning* (1866) and *Evening by Evening* (1868), which have since been compiled in a single volume titled *Morning and Evening*. These devotionals took the popular format of short commentaries on various Scripture texts that focus on daily encouragement, devotion, and worship. In the preface to *Morning by Morning* Spurgeon wrote,

Spurgeon in his study in Westwood in the mid- to late 1880s

In penning these short reflections upon certain passages of Holy Writ, the Author has had in view the assistance of the private meditations of believers.... May we not hope that, by the Holy Spirit's grace, as the reader turns morning by morning to our simple page, he will hear in it a still small voice whose speech shall be the word of God to his soul.... We have written out of our own heart, and most of the portions are remembrances of words which were refreshing in our own experience, and therefore we hope the daily meditations will not be without savour to our brethren; in fact, we know they will not if the Spirit of God shall rest upon them.[8]

Today, Spurgeon's devotional material continues to be among the most widely read of all his works.

In 1869 Spurgeon published the first volume in a series that many regard as his magnum opus, titled *The Treasury of David*. This enormous project, providing commentary on the entire Psalter, would come to span seven volumes, with the final issue appearing in 1885. *The Treasury of David* is considered by many not only to be a useful commentary on the Psalms but also a rich devotional resource. Of all Spurgeon's published works, the volumes of *The Treasury of David* received the best of his attention and care, and they showcase more than any other book his exceptional literary gifts.[9] In the preface to the first volume he wrote, "The delightful study of the Psalms has yielded me boundless profit and ever-growing pleasure; common gratitude constrains me to communicate to others a portion of the benefit, with the prayer that it may induce them to search further for themselves."[10] Spurgeon believed Christians should constantly read the Psalms because they speak more to Christian experience than any other book of the Bible: "No man needs better company than the Psalms; therein he may read and commune with friends human and divine; friends who know the heart of man towards God, and the

---

8. Spurgeon, *Morning by Morning*, vi.

9. For more information on the writing and composition of *The Treasury of David*, see Morden, *Communion with Christ and His People*, 131–35.

10. Spurgeon, *Treasury of David*, 1:v.

heart of God towards man; friends who perfectly sympathise with us and our sorrows, friends who never betray or forsake."[11]

The 1870s also saw the publication of what continues to be one of Spurgeon's most important works, *Lectures to My Students*. First published in a series of three volumes, *Lectures to My Students* is a collection of Spurgeon's Friday afternoon lectures to the assembled body of the students at the Pastors' College. There he gave some of his most famous addresses such as "The Call to Ministry," "The Minister's Fainting Fits," and "The Blind Eye and the Deaf Ear." These lectures show Spurgeon at his finest as he spoke extemporaneously on matters related to pastoral theology, as well as on practical pastoral subjects. His seasoned wisdom, sound judgment, and veteran experience are on full display in these lectures. They also provide characteristic specimens of Spurgeon's quick wit and playful sense of humor, as he often provided hilarious critiques of the typical preaching of the day.

Spurgeon's Westwood study, which housed most of his twelve-thousand-volume library

---

11. Spurgeon, *Treasury of David*, 6:vii.

Spurgeon's published books were immediately popular in his own day if for no other reason than they bore his name. But the true test of their worth is the enduring favor they enjoy among contemporary readers. Some of his books have become genuine Christian classics and have blessed millions of believers all over the world. For those who wish to understand the reason for Spurgeon's extraordinary reach, they need only take up one of his many books and read. He sparkles on the page as he did in the pulpit, and those very traits that made him so winsome as a preacher are evident in his writing as well.

Mrs. Spurgeon's Book Fund

The reach of Spurgeon's publishing ministry was further extended through an unplanned yet welcome new venture. Though often confined to the home because of chronic health issues, Charles's wife, Susie, nonetheless engaged eagerly in all kinds of Christian work. She made the Spurgeon home a hub for hospitality and an informal headquarters for her many benevolent efforts among the church and in the community. She was also an active supporter of many of the Tabernacle's formal ministries, such as the Pastors' College, the Poor Ministers' Clothing Society, and the Tabernacle Flower Mission.

Susie was especially concerned about the progress of the gospel both in England and around the globe. She prayed fervently for the work of church planting and international missions carried on through the Metropolitan Tabernacle and the Pastors' College. She was known as the "College Mother" and cared deeply for Charles's students. They were the special objects of her generosity and care and the frequent subjects of her prayers.

In the summer of 1875, Susie expressed to her husband her concern that many ministers had little to no access to good books to assist them in their ministries because most could not afford them. Charles had just published the first volume of *Lectures to My Students*, and Susie wished she could provide a copy to every pastor in the country. Charles, with characteristic spontaneity, challenged her to make it a reality. Though somewhat shocked and surprised by her husband's seemingly impractical suggestion, she began to give it serious thought. She said, "I was ready enough to *desire* the distribution of the precious book; but to *assist* in it, or help to pay for it, had not occurred to me."[12]

Ever the activist, Susie immediately got to work and started to organize what came to be known as Mrs. Spurgeon's Book Fund, a ministry whose sole design was to supply poor pastors with excellent literature entirely free of charge. The ministry started off small but quickly grew, and soon Susie found herself receiving applications

Susannah Spurgeon in middle age

12. Susannah Thompson Spurgeon, *Ten Years of My Life in Service of the Book Fund* (London: Passmore and Alabaster, 1887), 5.

from pastors across the country on a daily basis. Thousands of them would receive packages of books from her over the years, from old Puritan classics to Charles's new releases, which were flying off the press. A characteristic letter of thanks from one such pastor reads as follows:

> My dear Mrs. Spurgeon,—Last night I received the parcel of books, and what shall I say? I hardly know how to express my thanks to you and your excellent husband for such generous and Christian kindness. As I could do nothing else, I asked the Lord to bless you and reward you most amply for such a valuable gift. I can say it is to me better than thousands of silver and gold could be; for I could never get from earthly riches what I this morning obtained from reading Mr. Spurgeon's comment on Psalm xxiii. The books may well be called the *Treasury of David*; I shall keep it as a "Treasury" for my own use, and will never let it go out of my family, the Lord so helping me.[13]

Susie stipulated only three qualifications for pastors wishing to receive books from her fund: (1) they must be poor (earning less than 150 pounds per year), (2) they must be evangelical, and (3) they must be leaders of congregations "wholly devoted to the ministry."[14] Susie was normally generous in her application of these qualifications. She stated the mission of the book fund in this way: "The Book Fund aims at furnishing the bare bookshelves of poor pastors of every Christian denomination with standard works of divinity by various authors; books full of the glorious gospel of Jesus Christ, the study of which shall enrich their minds, comfort their hearts, quicken their spiritual energy, thereby enable them to preach with greater power and earnestness 'all the words of this life.'"[15]

---

13. C. H. Spurgeon, "How the Book Fund Prospers," *Sword and the Trowel* (August 1878): 350.

14. Rhodes, *Susie*, 140.

15. C. H. Spurgeon, "Mrs. Spurgeon's Book Fund," *Sword and the Trowel* (February 1878): 75.

Mrs. Spurgeon's Book Fund became one of the most successful and celebrated ministries of the Metropolitan Tabernacle. Spurgeon often promoted it in the pages of the *Sword and the Trowel*, and evangelical leaders from various denominations across the country applauded Susie for her extraordinary work in supporting pastors and promoting the cause of the gospel. From its beginning in 1875 to Susie's death in 1903, the fund distributed over two hundred thousand books to pastors across the country.[16]

Inventory of Mrs. Spurgeon's Book Fund

A Benevolent Ministry

In addition to the Mrs. Spurgeon Book Fund, the Tabernacle continued to see an explosion of other gospel agencies and institutions devoted to ministries of various kinds in the 1870s. Foremost among them were the many Sunday schools, ragged schools, and street missions that operated all over the city. The Tabernacle Sunday

---

16. Rhodes, *Susie*, 140.

schools were not identical to contemporary Sunday schools. They operated on Sundays but typically took place in the afternoon and drew children from both within the congregation and the surrounding community. Moreover, many of the Tabernacle Sunday school classes were held outside the building in neighborhoods throughout the city.

These Sunday school classes were designed to provide children with a thorough education in the Bible. But the classes were about more than merely teaching children well-known Bible stories. The primary focus of the Sunday school classes was to introduce the children to the person of Jesus Christ and the good news of salvation found in Him. The chief goal was to provide children with clarity on the gospel and to persuade them that they could come to Jesus just as they were, trusting in Him alone to save them from their sins.

Spurgeon was a tremendous advocate for Sunday school ministry, viewing it as one of the most important dimensions of church work and also one of the most strategic ways to reach the local populace with the gospel. He encouraged all his members to engage in ministering to needy children in this way. In an 1878 sermon Spurgeon said, "Can you see these streets swarming with children and not come forward to help the Sunday-school? Can you watch the multitudes of boys and girls streaming out of the Board School and not say to yourself, 'What is done with these on the Lord's day? Others must be hard at work with them, why am I not doing something?'"[17]

Alongside these Sunday schools, the Tabernacle promoted ragged schools, which provided free education to children during the week in subjects such as reading, writing, and arithmetic. For most of Spurgeon's life, there existed no program of government-sponsored education, and thus the education of the poor often fell to

---

17. C. H. Spurgeon, "With the King for His Work!," in *Metropolitan Tabernacle Pulpit*, 24:115.

charitable organizations such as churches.[18] The Tabernacle sought to meet this need and help poor children achieve a basic education that would serve them well in life and help them rise above their difficult circumstances. Moreover, the ragged schools put needy children in direct contact with loving Christians who were able to show the love of Christ to them in a personal way. By the end of Spurgeon's life, the Metropolitan Tabernacle supported twenty-seven Sunday and ragged schools, with 612 teachers and over 8,000 children enrolled.[19]

Perhaps the church's most significant endeavors in evangelism and benevolence were embodied in its many street missions. The street missions typically involved some combination of gospel preaching, organized worship services, and mercy ministry in target neighborhoods and communities across the city. These mission stations were often served by students at the Pastors' College, and many of them eventually turned into new church plants. At any given time, the Tabernacle had roughly ten to twenty street missions in operation.

In 1879 the Stockwell Orphanage, which up to that point had served as an institution exclusively for boys, opened a wing for girls. The orphanage continued to receive fatherless children from all over the country, but especially from London. After the Pastors' College, Spurgeon gave more attention and energy to the orphanage than any other ministry. He treasured his time with the orphans, continuing to visit them on weekends and holidays, writing them letters to be read aloud to them, and purchasing gifts to be sent to the boys and girls. In his later years in ministry, many looked to Spurgeon as one of the greatest philanthropists of the age as he gave himself to mercy ministry among the needy of London with unparalleled energy and compassion.

---

18. DiPrima, *Spurgeon and the Poor*, 189–93.
19. *C. H. Spurgeon's Autobiography*, 4:336.

By the 1880s, the total number of active ministries operating out of the Metropolitan Tabernacle reached sixty-six.[20] They included ministries that provided education for children, subsidized housing for destitute widows, care for the disabled, food for the hungry, clothing for the needy, and evangelistic outreaches to the lost all over London. There were targeted ministries to orphans, widows, police officers, prostitutes, sailors, immigrants, the sick, and the blind. The Tabernacle's benevolent enterprises addressed practically every area of human need, and the congregation gained the reputation of being a church zealous for good works.

Taking Stock

As one decade closed and another opened, Spurgeon reached some significant personal landmarks. In 1879 he completed his twenty-fifth year as the pastor of the Metropolitan Tabernacle, and in 1881 he completed his twenty-fifth year of marriage. In between these two years, in 1880 the Spurgeons moved into their third and final home, which they called Westwood, located on Beulah Hill in Upper Norwood. The home was quite large and became, like their previous homes, a center for ministry. They entered their new residence with a quarter century of shared life and ministry behind them, the joy and happiness of their marriage only enriched by the passing of the years. By this time their boys, Thomas and Charles, whom Spurgeon had the joy of baptizing in 1874, were out of the home and heavily engaged in ministry. To see their sons occupied in preaching and pastoral work, just like their father, only compounded Charles's and Susie's joy.

These years also ushered Spurgeon into a new phase of his life. The boy preacher of the fens had given way to the veteran pastor of the Tabernacle. The young man who first took the city by storm had become a seasoned minister and an elder statesman within British

---

20. *Memorial Volume, Mr. Spurgeon's Jubilee*, 7–8; and Spurgeon, "Mr. Spurgeon's Jubilee Meetings," *Sword and the Trowel* (July 1884): 373.

evangelicalism. Whereas Spurgeon once made his way through the world with an explosive combination of youthful pluck, zeal, and spontaneity, he now stepped into the final decade of his life with a quieter dignity and resilience, becoming a man of years.

By 1884, having completed thirty years as the church's pastor, Spurgeon reached another significant milestone; on June 19 of that year, he turned fifty years old. Given his significant health issues, this was no mean achievement for him. To commemorate the occasion, the Metropolitan Tabernacle organized a special two-night event they called the Pastor's Jubilee Celebration. The occasion was anticipated for months in advance and was reported widely in the press. At the first of the two nights, June 18, thousands attended, including members and officers of the Metropolitan Tabernacle, as well as numerous friends from across London and the rest of the country.

The Spurgeons' third and final home, called Westwood

In many ways this event was about marking and celebrating the evident work of God the congregation had witnessed over the course of Spurgeon's long ministry as the church's pastor. By this time Spurgeon had been ministering in London for three decades.

The Tabernacle had experienced extraordinary blessing under his ministry, and the people desired to publicly honor their pastor and to express thanks to the Lord for His abundant kindness to them during these years.

Numerous people spoke on this occasion, including Tabernacle elders and deacons, visiting ministers from other churches, and old friends from all over England. The event was chaired by the Earl of Shaftesbury, Anthony Ashley-Cooper (known to history as Lord Shaftesbury). He was the leading social reformer of the day and a dear friend to Spurgeon. In the wake of Lord Shaftesbury's death a year later in 1885, Spurgeon referred to him as "the best man of the age."[21]

As part of the ceremonies, a register of the sixty-six benevolent ministries that operated out of the Metropolitan Tabernacle was read aloud:

> The Almshouses; the Pastors' College; the Pastors' College Society of Evangelists; the Stockwell Orphanage; the Colportage Association; Mrs. Spurgeon's Book Fund and Pastors' Aid Fund; the Pastors' College Evening Classes; the Evangelists' Association; the Country Mission; the Ladies' Benevolent Society; the Ladies' Maternal Society; the Poor Ministers' Clothing Society; the Loan Tract Society; Spurgeon's Sermons' Tract Society; the Evangelists' Training Class; the Orphanage Working Meeting; the Colportage Working Meeting; the Flower Mission; the Gospel Temperance Society; the Band of Hope; the United Christian Brothers' Benefit Society; the Christian Sisters' Benefit Society; the Young Christians' Association; the Mission to Foreign Seamen; the Mission to Policemen; the Coffee-House Mission; the Metropolitan

---

21. C. H. Spurgeon, "Departed Saints Yet Living," in *Metropolitan Tabernacle Pulpit*, 31:541–42. Spurgeon said of Shaftesbury in this message, "We shall not know for many a year how much we miss in missing him; how great an anchor he was to this drifting generation, and how great a stimulus he was to every movement for the benefit of the poor. Both man and beast may unite in mourning him: he was the friend of every living thing. He lived for the oppressed; he lived for London; he lived for the nation; he lived still more for God."

Tabernacle Sunday School; Mr. Wigney's Bible Class; Mr. Hoyland's Bible Class; Miss Swain's Bible Class; Miss Hobbs's Bible Class; Miss Hooper's Bible Class; Mr. Bowker's Bible Class for Adults of Both Sexes; Mr. Dunn's Bible Class for Men; Mrs. Allison's Bible Class for Young Women; Mr. Bartlett's Bible Class for Young Women; Golden Lane and Hoxton Mission (Mr. Orsman's); Ebury Mission and Schools, Pimlico; Green Walk Mission and Schools, Haddon Hall; Richmond Street Mission and Schools; Flint Street Mission and Schools; North Street, Kennington, Mission and Schools; Little George Street Mission, Bermondsey; Snow's Fields Mission, Bermondsey; the Almshouses Missions; the Almshouses Sunday Schools; the Almshouses Day Schools; the Townsend Street Mission; the Townley Street Mission; the Deacon Street Mission; the Blenheim Grove Mission, Peckham; the Surrey Gardens Mission; the Vinegar Yard Mission, Old Street; the Horse Shoe Wharf Mission and Schools; the Upper Ground Street Mission; Thomas Street Mission, Horselydown; the Boundary Row Sunday School, Camberwell; the Great Hunter Street Sunday School, Dover Road; the Carter Street Sunday School, Walworth; the Pleasant Row Sunday Schools, Kennington; the Westmoreland Road Sunday Schools, Walworth; Lansdowne Place Sunday School; Miss Emery's Banner Class, Brandon Street; Miss Miller's Mothers' Meeting; Miss Ivimey's Mothers' Meeting; Miss Francies' Mothers' Meeting.[22]

After the list was read, Lord Shaftesbury announced, "What a tale of his agencies [was] read to you just now! How it showed what a powerful administrative mind our friend has. That list of associations, instituted by his genius, and superintended by his care, were more than enough to occupy the minds and hearts of fifty ordinary men."[23]

By any measure, Spurgeon's ministry was spectacularly fruitful—perhaps one of the most fruitful in Christian history. The jubilee

---

22. *Memorial Volume, Mr. Spurgeon's Jubilee*, 7–8; and Spurgeon, "Mr. Spurgeon's Jubilee Meetings," *Sword and the Trowel* (July 1884): 373.

23. Pike, *Life and Works of Charles Haddon Spurgeon*, 6:275.

celebration provided a special occasion for the congregation to look back on all that God had done to advance the cause of the gospel over the course of Spurgeon's years among them. Though Spurgeon enjoyed an abundance of divine blessing on his ministry, it was not one without its trials and sorrows. Over the decades, he had weathered many storms and faced numerous difficulties in his service to Christ. Yet as he reached his fiftieth year of life and his thirtieth year as pastor of the Tabernacle, he little knew that the greatest trial of his life still lay ahead of him. As Spurgeon's extraordinary career reached its final stages, God would require him to wear the crown of suffering before He would give to him the crown of glory.

13

The Downgrade Controversy

"I am quite willing to be eaten of dogs for the next fifty years, but the more distant future shall vindicate me."[1] Spurgeon spoke these fateful words in 1889 at the conclusion of his presidential address at the annual College Conference, a gathering of current and former students of the Pastors' College. At the time, he had been embroiled for two years already in what was unquestionably the greatest controversy of his entire ministry. He was tired, discouraged, and disillusioned yet also calm, resolute, and sure. He had made his stand for the truth, and he felt certain he could endure whatever opposition would come, confident in the knowledge that he had his Lord's approval. Less than three years after he made this famous statement, he would be dead. Susie would later suggest that his death was hastened in part by this controversy, which she described as the "deepest grief of his noble life."[2]

What has come to be known as the Downgrade Controversy defined the final years of Spurgeon's life and in many ways still shapes his legacy today. The issues at stake were chiefly doctrinal. The conflict pitted Spurgeon against the leaders of his denomination, the Baptist Union, and presaged similar conflicts that would erupt in denominations across the United Kingdom and America in the generations that followed. Spurgeon's church had been part of

---

1. C. H. Spurgeon, *An All-Round Ministry: Direction, Wisdom, and Encouragement for Preachers and Pastors* (Edinburgh: Banner of Truth, 2018), 281.
2. *C. H. Spurgeon's Autobiography*, 4:255.

the Baptist Union long before he arrived. Former pastor John Rippon was pivotal to the union's founding in 1813, and the church was actively involved in the new denomination from that point forward. Spurgeon participated enthusiastically in the meetings of the Baptist Union throughout the 1850s, 1860s, and 1870s, but his posture would change as he entered the 1880s, which would become the most controversial decade in the union's history.

To this day, the Downgrade Controversy remains to some degree shrouded in a historical haze, primarily because of the fragmented documentary record, the intense polemics on either side of the conflict, and the sheer complexity of the whole affair.[3] Spurgeon scholar Mark Hopkins comments tongue in cheek, "Participants were quite as lost at the time as historians have been since."[4] This chapter does not attempt a contribution to ongoing scholarly discussions surrounding the subject but rather aims to chart the broad movements of the controversy that are known and documented and to provide some insight into how this episode affected Spurgeon.

In the Downgrade Controversy, Spurgeon sought to defend orthodox Christianity against what he regarded as the incursions of serious doctrinal error in the Baptist Union and evangelical circles more broadly. The influences of incipient modernism; new scientific theories, such as Darwinian evolution; and emerging liberal theological movements, such as German Higher Criticism, had begun to exert considerable influence on Victorian Christianity. The age of doubt had arrived. Its roots had begun spreading under the surface as early as the 1850s. By the 1880s, its buds were in full bloom. Over the course of Spurgeon's ministry, the ground had slowly moved under his feet almost without his notice, and he found himself confronting errors in the final years of his life that he could not have imagined

---

3. To date, the most significant scholarly treatment of the Downgrade Controversy is found in Hopkins, *Nonconformity's Romantic Generation*, 193–248.

4. Hopkins, *Nonconformity's Romantic Generation*, 193.

addressing when he first arrived in London. That they would appear in his own denomination left him astonished and appalled.

Spurgeon in his midfifties

Spurgeon's defense of several core doctrines of the faith did not ultimately take the shape of a full-blown reform movement. Rather, he mounted a simple protest against approaching error that he believed threatened to hollow out Christianity of its substance and power. This protest would lead finally to his resignation from the Baptist Union.[5] Spurgeon foresaw the looming collapse of the main evangelical denominations and endeavored to alert not only the Baptists but all Christians to the enemies crouching at the gate.

---

5. Hopkins was the first to advance the view that Spurgeon's aim in the Downgrade Controversy was not reform, but protest and withdrawal.

History's hindsight has vindicated Spurgeon's foresight. In the penultimate chapter of his life, Spurgeon was called on to play the part of denominational dissenter, one he never wished to play. Though his stand would cost him much, it has cemented his legacy as a defender of orthodoxy and a faithful steward of the evangelical gospel.

Opening Salvos

Typical accounts of the Downgrade Controversy date its beginning to a series of articles published in the *Sword and the Trowel*, the first appearing in March 1887. But this approach to the narrative misses significant context and fails to account for growing tensions between Spurgeon and the Baptist Union going as far back as 1883. Spurgeon was aware as early as the late 1870s that there were some in the Baptist Union who appeared to be drifting into serious theological error, but he was content at the time to believe their number did not rise above a small handful of men who could be safely ignored.[6] By 1883, however, he could see the problem was becoming far more widespread as he became increasingly aware of men retreating from orthodoxy and embracing theologically liberal approaches to the Bible and the Christian faith. At that time, Spurgeon began to express his concerns quietly but firmly to denominational leaders in the Baptist Union. He usually kept to a policy of privacy with respect to these concerns, but occasionally he allowed himself to make revealing, though cryptic, public statements. Commenting on the meeting of the Baptist Union in Leicester in late 1883 (which he did not attend), he wrote, "Certainly the bonds of unity have suffered a severe strain.... When truths which are viewed as vital by a large portion of any society are trifled with by others, there is so far an end of fellowship, or else of conscientiousness. I, for one, have no Christian fellowship with those who reject the Gospel of our Lord Jesus Christ, neither will I pretend to have any."[7]

---

6. Hopkins, *Nonconformity's Romantic Generation*, 195.

7. C. H. Spurgeon, "Notes," *Sword and the Trowel* (November 1883): 607.

Though he was not prepared to formally resign, Spurgeon began at this time to steadily withdraw from the Baptist Union and ceased to attend its meetings altogether. Union leaders understood they had a problem on their hands and did what they could to mollify Spurgeon, even as he continued to express concerns to them privately. Tensions would continue to build over the coming years, however, eventually leading to a point of unavoidable conflict.

Nonetheless, it would seem that as early as 1883, Spurgeon saw the writing on the wall and knew he would be forced to resign from the denomination at some point. In November 1883 he wrote to his brother-in-law, "I think I must personally withdraw from the Baptist Union. I do not care to fight, but can be rid of the responsibility by retiring."[8] From the available historical data, it does not appear that he ever seriously contemplated mounting a thoroughgoing reform movement within the Baptist Union. Both Spurgeon's assessment of the situation as well as his native temperament led him to prefer a program of protest and withdrawal. He found denominational politics distasteful and was somewhat inept when it came to the subtleties of diplomatic procedure. He seemed ready to cut his losses and move on from denominational life. At this late stage of his ministry, Spurgeon's ambitions for what he might achieve in that world were noticeably more temperate than they had been in his younger years. By 1886 he said,

> Our day-dreams are over: we shall neither convert the world to righteousness, nor the church to orthodoxy. We refuse to bear responsibilities which do not belong to us, for our real responsibilities are more than enough. Certain wise brethren are hot to reform their denomination. They ride out gallantly. Success be to the champions! They are generally wiser when they ride home again. I confess great admiration for my Quixotic brethren, but I wish they had more to show for their valour. I fear

---

8. C. H. Spurgeon to William Jackson, November 8, 1883, quoted in Ernest A. Payne, "The Down Grade Controversy: A Postscript," *Baptist Quarterly* 28, no. 4 (1979): 149.

that both church and world are beyond us; we must be content with smaller spheres. Even our own denomination must go its own way. We are only responsible so far as our power goes, and it will be wise to use that power for some object well within reach. For the rest, let us not worry and weary about things beyond our line.[9]

With dignified resignation, Spurgeon was preparing himself to embrace voluntary exile in independence.

By spring 1887, the issues in the denomination had only become more aggravated, and Spurgeon decided to raise his objections more forcefully, this time in public in the *Sword and the Trowel*. In March and April of that year, two anonymous articles appeared under the title "The Down Grade."[10] These articles, though sanctioned by Spurgeon, were not actually written by him. The author was Spurgeon's friend Robert Shindler. Both articles charted the history of doctrinal decline in various denominations and movements in England's history and suggested that something similar was beginning to happen in the present day among the Baptists. Though both articles instantly caught the attention of leaders in the Baptist Union, they did not immediately spark controversy, and they were generally treated with nervous silence by union officials.

Conflict erupted when Spurgeon contributed his own article in August, followed by three more articles in the next three successive months. They forthrightly stated the concerns that he had been expressing privately for years and did so with intense opprobrium. From the first paragraph of the first article, the battle lines were drawn:

> No lover of the gospel can conceal from himself the fact that the days are evil.... Read those newspapers that represent the Broad School of Dissent and ask yourself, How much farther could they go? What doctrine remains to be abandoned?

---

9. C. H. Spurgeon, "What We Would Be," *Sword and the Trowel* (June 1886): 255.
10. [Robert Shindler], "The Down Grade," *Sword and the Trowel* (March 1887): 122–26; and "The Down Grade: Second Article," *Sword and the Trowel* (April 1887): 166–72.

What other truth to be the object of contempt? A new religion has been initiated, which is no more Christianity than chalk is cheese; and this religion, being destitute of moral honesty, palms itself off as the old faith with slight improvements, and on this plea usurps pulpits which were erected for gospel preaching. The atonement is scouted, the inspiration of Scripture is derided, the Holy Spirit is degraded into an influence, the punishment of sin is turned into a fiction, and the resurrection into a myth, and yet these enemies of our faith expect us to call them brethren, and maintain a confederacy with them![11]

In his conclusion to the article he wrote,

A little plain-speaking would do a world of good just now. These gentlemen desire to be let alone. They want no noise raised. Of course thieves hate watch-dogs, and love darkness. It is time that somebody should spring his rattle, and call attention to the way in which God is being robbed of his glory, and man of his hope. It now becomes a serious question how far those who abide by the faith once delivered to the saints should fraternize with those who have turned aside to another gospel.[12]

By the last of the four articles, published in November, Spurgeon's sense of alarm had not abated, and to some he had begun to sound excessively censorious: "We have before us the wretched spectacle of professedly orthodox Christians publicly avowing their union with those who deny the faith, and scarcely concealing their contempt for those who cannot be guilty of such gross disloyalty to Christ. To be very plain, we are unable to call these things Christian Unions, they begin to look like Confederacies of Evil."[13]

---

11. C. H. Spurgeon, "Another Word concerning the Down-Grade," *Sword and the Trowel* (August 1887): 397.

12. Spurgeon, "Another Word concerning the Down-Grade," *Sword and the Trowel* (August 1887): 400.

13. C. H. Spurgeon, "A Fragment upon the Down-Grade Controversy," *Sword and the Trowel* (November 1887): 558.

Spurgeon left no room for ambiguity or nuance in his protest. For a denomination to tolerate serious doctrinal error and allow it to go unchecked was irresponsible at best and reprehensible at worst. To align oneself with such a denomination became an untenable position for him. To do so would be to dishonor the gospel and give cover to wolves. "To pursue union at the expense of truth," he said, "is treason to the Lord Jesus."[14] This led Spurgeon to advocate for a clear policy of separation from a denomination that he felt had been infected with serious theological error. He would later write, "The bounden duty of a true believer towards men who profess to be Christians, and yet deny the Word of the Lord, and reject the fundamentals of the gospel, is to come out from among them."[15]

A Matter of Orthodoxy

Spurgeon had two main grievances with his denomination. The first was that there were a growing number of men who were preaching serious doctrinal error. This point was simply irrefutable and well known by many in the denomination. The second was that leaders of the Baptist Union seemed determined not to address such men for fear of alienating them and provoking their departure from the denomination.

It is important to appreciate the discrete doctrinal issues that provoked Spurgeon to sound the alarm on those he regarded as theologically dangerous. We are not to imagine that Spurgeon made his protest over secondary issues or matters of marginal doctrinal import. He was animated by matters of basic orthodoxy. Though some accused him of prejudice against non-Calvinists and those who did not bear his Puritan stamp, these doctrinal distinctives were not the grounds for his dissent. Though at times tangential issues intruded into the conflict, matters of Christian fundamentals

---

14. Spurgeon, "Fragment upon the Down-Grade Controversy," *Sword and the Trowel* (November 1887): 558.

15. Spurgeon, "Notes," *Sword and the Trowel* (October 1888): 562.

were always at the heart of the debate. Spurgeon was chiefly concerned that a growing number of men within the denomination were either flirting with, or in some cases openly promoting, the following errors:

- the denial of the inspiration and infallibility of Scripture;
- the denial of the necessity and substitutionary nature of Christ's atonement;
- the denial of eternal punishment for the impenitent; and
- the affirmation of some form of universalism.[16]

In the second of the four Downgrade articles Spurgeon authored he wrote, "We cannot hold the inspiration of the Word, and yet reject it; we cannot believe in the atonement and deny it;…we cannot recognize the punishment of the impenitent and yet indulge the 'larger hope.' One way or the other we must go. Decision is the virtue of the hour."[17]

At least two things should stand out regarding this list. First, all four of the errors are doctrinal issues. Second, not only are they doctrinal, but they are each a matter of basic Christian orthodoxy, of first importance, and have to do with doctrines that have been universally affirmed by the church throughout history. The inspiration and infallibility of Scripture, the necessity and substitutionary nature of the atonement, the existence of an eternal hell reserved for the wicked, and the exclusivity of Christ are doctrines as old as Christianity itself. To deny them is to deny some of the basic tenets of the Christian faith. In other words, what must be understood and appreciated is that the Downgrade Controversy was a debate not

---

16. All four of these issues are mentioned in the four main Downgrade articles authored by Spurgeon. See Spurgeon, "Another Word Concerning the Down-Grade," *Sword and the Trowel* (August 1887): 397–400; "Our Reply to Sundry Critics and Inquirers," *Sword and the Trowel* (September 1887): 461–65; "The Case Proved," *Sword and the Trowel* (October 1887): 509–15; and "Fragment upon the Down-Grade Controversy," *Sword and the Trowel* (November 1887): 557–60.

17. Spurgeon, "Our Reply to Sundry Critics and Inquirers," *Sword and the Trowel* (September 1887): 465.

over obscure theological matters but over the very heart of orthodox Christianity. These were the main issues that led Spurgeon first to protest and then to withdraw from his denomination.

That last sentence is important. Many may assume that before the 1880s, Spurgeon did not have any disagreements with those in his denomination, but as soon as he did, he decided to depart. This would be wrong—spectacularly so. The truth is Spurgeon maintained many disagreements with men in his denomination on a host of secondary doctrinal and practical issues for decades before the Downgrade Controversy. For example, Spurgeon, a vocal proponent of Calvinism, was content to remain in fellowship with men of a more Arminian persuasion. He disagreed with such men publicly and passionately, yet he continued to associate with them and seemed happy in doing so. He disagreed with men over the use of instruments in worship, whether Communion should be open or closed, and how evangelism should best be conducted. He disagreed with some over various social and political issues, such as British foreign policy, the relative utility of public schools, the temperance movement, and which political candidates should be supported.

These and many other lower-level disagreements could be enumerated, yet none of them ever suggested to Spurgeon that he should divide from the men in his denomination. None of them created the same crisis of conscience for him. Spurgeon was perfectly content to be in denominational and associational fellowship with men with whom he held disagreements over secondary doctrinal and practical matters. What animated Spurgeon in the Downgrade Controversy was his concern that the very heart of the Christian faith was being tampered with, and even repudiated, by some:

> The largest charity towards those who are loyal to the Lord Jesus, and yet do not see with us on secondary matters, is the duty of all true Christians. But how are we to act towards those who deny his vicarious sacrifice, and ridicule the great truth of justification by his righteousness? These are not mistaken friends, but enemies of the cross of Christ. There is no use in

employing circumlocutions and polite terms of expression: where Christ is not received as to the cleansing power of his blood and the justifying merit of his righteousness, he is not received at all.[18]

The Vote of Censure

On October 29, 1887, Spurgeon officially resigned from the Baptist Union. He announced his resignation in the November issue of the *Sword and the Trowel*.[19] His concerns, first raised privately for a number of years and then publicly for a number of months, had gone largely unheard and ignored. Spurgeon could see the denomination was essentially uninterested in addressing the serious problems he had identified. Moreover, Spurgeon was not motivated to stay in the denomination to try to reform it from within. Whether this was due to his assessment of the bleak prospects of a successful reform movement or his sense that he was not well suited to lead such a movement himself, Spurgeon decided to resign instead. But it was impossible that the departure of so visible and influential a figure as C. H. Spurgeon could go without some kind of formal response from the leaders of the denomination. Yet the course that their response would ultimately take would leave Spurgeon completely blindsided and disoriented.

Almost as soon as Spurgeon resigned, he left for the French Riviera for his annual retreat to Menton. At the same time, leaders in the Baptist Union began to make overtures to Spurgeon, requesting a meeting between him and four union officials: James Culross (president), John Clifford (vice president), S. H. Booth (secretary), and Alexander McLaren (former president). This delegation was intent on pursuing a closed-door meeting with Spurgeon in order to challenge the grounds of his resignation and somehow induce him to

---

18. Spurgeon, "Fragment upon the Down-Grade Controversy," *Sword and the Trowel* (November 1887): 559.

19. Spurgeon, "Fragment upon the Down-Grade Controversy," *Sword and the Trowel* (November 1887): 557–60.

withdraw his charges and return to fellowship with the union. These intentions were not made clear in their communications with Spurgeon, though he immediately suspected their aims. He wrote to his wife in December that he feared they meant "to fix on me the odium of being implacable."[20]

Spurgeon made clear to the delegation that he had no interest in discussing the past, nor was he interested in reconsidering his resignation. The only subject he was interested in discussing with leaders of the Baptist Union was the prospect of establishing a solid evangelical course for the denomination's future. Regrettably, Spurgeon never received final clarity on the agenda for the meeting. After a complicated and unsatisfying correspondence between Spurgeon and union officials, he finally agreed to attend a private meeting with them on January 13, 1888, in London, choosing to trust in the good faith of the delegation. But he had fallen into a trap that had been cleverly set for him by men more skilled in denominational diplomacy than he.[21]

When the meeting finally occurred, it became clear that the parties were at cross-purposes with one another.[22] Contrary to Spurgeon's plainly expressed conditions and requests, the delegation indeed scrutinized him over his resignation and pressed him to reconsider his withdrawal from the union. The committee successfully shifted the focus to the veracity of Spurgeon's charges and insisted that he substantiate his accusations by providing a full list of the names of those he believed represented the progressive drift he had alleged was taking place in the denomination. Spurgeon was determined to resist this ploy. The names were already well known to the Baptist Union. But he knew that if he was coaxed into actually

---

20. C. H. Spurgeon to Susannah Spurgeon, December 14, 1887, quoted in *C. H. Spurgeon's Autobiography*, 4:257.

21. Hopkins, *Nonconformity's Romantic Generation*, 209–13.

22. James Culross, John Clifford, and S. H. Booth attended the meeting with Spurgeon. Alexander McLaren did not attend because of ill health. See Hopkins, *Nonconformity's Romantic Generation*, 213.

providing a written list, those named would immediately be turned into martyrs. Moreover, no one stood to gain from a heresy trial. The denomination would only suffer further, and Spurgeon would be painted as disagreeable, uncharitable, and domineering. He would not allow them to portray him as a kind of Baptist pope, making categorical and authoritarian pronouncements over other men's ministries. At the same time, Spurgeon knew that if he failed to provide names at the request of union leadership, they could then easily represent themselves as sincerely interested in investigating his charges and Spurgeon as stridently unwilling to cooperate. That Spurgeon's charges had been ignored to this point immediately exposes the union's posture as disingenuous. Nonetheless, Spurgeon knew he was caught in an impossible situation. In the end, he chose not to provide names, though it is possible he hesitated over what was the best course of action.[23]

Spurgeon's desire had been to withdraw into a peaceful independence. He thought that by resigning his membership in the denomination, the matter could be put to rest, his conscience being appeased and the union free to proceed as it wished, untroubled by his dissent. He was clearly not interested in ongoing warfare with the Baptist Union. But he was already engaged in war, whether he wanted it or not. He would not be allowed to retreat quietly.

Less than a week after the tense and unfruitful meeting with the union delegation, Spurgeon was dealt a blow that caught him completely off guard. On January 19, the Baptist Union Council, made up of nearly one hundred members, passed a resolution known thereafter as the "vote of censure," which publicly reprimanded Spurgeon for what they regarded as divisive conduct and unfounded allegations. In the resolution, they specifically cited Spurgeon's failure to supply

---

23. In a fascinating section of his retelling of the controversy, Hopkins suggests Spurgeon contemplated revealing the names of several men at a later stage of the controversy. He speculates about a particular note that was discovered with the names of several men on it. See *Nonconformity's Romantic Generation*, 217–18.

a list of names to support his charges.[24] Spurgeon was floored. He felt such an action was unconscionable and borderline vindictive. Union leaders, for their part, felt they were only defending their denomination from Spurgeon's accusations made public in the *Sword and the Trowel* the previous summer and autumn. The conflict had taken a bitter turn, making any reunion of fellowship practically impossible.

The later stages of the Downgrade Controversy were complicated and drawn out. Over the following months, various articles were traded between the two sides as numerous other spectators and commentators weighed in as well. Privately, there was a movement among men within the Baptist Union who were sympathetic to Spurgeon to push the denomination toward making a clear and thorough statement outlining its commitment to orthodox and evangelical theology. After months of private discussion and debate, a somewhat vague and unsatisfying statement was advanced and swiftly ratified by an overwhelming majority.[25] Though many were ready to declare the controversy ended, a significant contingent

Spurgeon with men from the College Conference, 1888

---

24. Ernest A. Payne, *The Baptist Union: A Short History* (London: Carey Kingsgate Press, 1959), 136.

25. Hopkins, *Nonconformity's Romantic Generation*, 224–26.

remained disappointed with the union's public declaration as well as their treatment of Spurgeon. Instead of a decisive movement toward resolution and reconciliation, open wounds were left to fester for years after the vote of censure.

Spurgeon would never fully recover from his treatment during the Downgrade Controversy, and some even testified that his health suffered as a result. At one point, feeling exhausted and defeated, he confided to a friend, "The fight is killing me."[26] Though he felt certain he was right, he was nonetheless deeply grieved and personally discouraged by the whole affair. It was without question the greatest sorrow of his life. His opponents caricatured him as uncharitable and embittered, and for many of those less informed about the twists and turns that took place behind the scenes, the portrait stuck. His sorrow was further compounded because some of his former students turned against him in the controversy and sided with the Baptist Union. Spurgeon would spend the next few years bearing the reproach that was heaped on him by members of the press, fellow ministers, and several men he had formerly regarded as close friends. In all this, Spurgeon kept to a policy of a "generous silence" and did not reveal publicly all that he had witnessed privately.[27] Spurgeon would indeed allow himself "to be eaten of dogs" and would look to the last day for vindication.

Spurgeon, the Controversialist

The Downgrade Controversy provides significant insight into Spurgeon's personality and illuminates several important dimensions of his character. It also offers a number of intriguing interpretive angles on his life and ministry. Five are briefly noted.

First, in the Downgrade Controversy, Spurgeon displayed his characteristic commitment to conviction over pragmatism. Spurgeon was thoroughly committed to his convictions. His devotion to

---

26. Quoted in Fullerton, *C. H. Spurgeon: A Biography*, 206.
27. *C. H. Spurgeon's Autobiography*, 4:254.

the revealed will of God was paramount, and when he felt scriptural truth was being undermined or denied, he could defend the truth with unmatched courage, zeal, and determination. This devotion to the cause of truth could drive him to extreme lengths. He was willing to endure criticism, lose friends, and make enemies if he felt he was in the right. Spurgeon's stand in the Downgrade Controversy was not a pathway to greater influence or popularity. Rather, it would cost him deeply. It would hurt his standing in the public eye and require him to enter a lonely and uncertain exile. He would become estranged and alienated from some of his closest friends and valued partners in ministry. He would lose public support for some of his most treasured ministries. Spurgeon was not driven ultimately by pragmatism, however, but by conviction. This was the case throughout his ministry. The Downgrade Controversy was merely the final chapter in a lifetime devoted to standing for the truth regardless of the consequences.

Second, Spurgeon's conduct in the Downgrade Controversy was not a symptom of some kind of shift or evolution in his character. He was the same man in the Downgrade as he ever was, just older, wiser, and perhaps less of an idealist. The Downgrade Controversy should not be interpreted as a departure from Spurgeon's typical modus operandi. Rather, Spurgeon acted entirely in accord with his nature. His passionate devotion to sound doctrine, his commitment to moral integrity, his total intolerance of every form of duplicity, and his congenital and inalterable determination to speak his mind at all times directly and forthrightly were all on full display in the Downgrade Controversy. Though some tried to forward a narrative that Spurgeon had fundamentally changed and had become more impatient, tribal, and embittered with age, a more accurate reading finds Spurgeon in these years much as he ever was. He was fundamentally the same man and behaved in the Downgrade as he would have at any other stage of his life.

Third, the Downgrade Controversy, much like the Baptismal Regeneration Controversy of 1864, demonstrated that Spurgeon was not well suited for conflict. His former student, friend, and biographer W. Y. Fullerton made this point:

> Mr. Spurgeon was too earnest, too intent on the eternal meaning of things, too sure of his own standing, to be a good controversialist. His instinct led him to conclusions that others approached only by logic, and he was therefore not apt to be too patient with those who debated every step of the way, or lost themselves in details, failing, as he judged, to see the wood because of the trees, and the city because of the houses. He was a witness, not a debater.[28]

He was not always at his best when engaging in polemics. He often seemed impervious to the assumed rules of engagement and displayed little tolerance for the subtleties and nuances of polite debate. Furthermore, some of Spurgeon's native weaknesses put him at a disadvantage when it came to public controversy. At times he could be too sharp and overly dogmatic in ways that could unnecessarily alienate his opponents. He also had a tendency toward overstatement and exaggeration in some of his public comments, which often got him into trouble. His zeal for the truth inclined him to make excessive and intemperate statements that tended to inflame rather than illuminate. He struggled with empathy toward his opponents and often projected his own feelings and intuitions onto other people. On occasion, this could lead him to be guilty of imputing motives to others uncharitably. Though one of Spurgeon's strengths was his sense of moral clarity and doctrinal conviction, it seemed at times as though his color palette was limited to only two shades: black and white. He rarely saw room for gray.

If one were to compare Spurgeon's conduct in the Baptismal Regeneration Controversy with his conduct in the Downgrade Controversy, he would doubtless appear more noble in the latter than in the former. Spurgeon's behavior in 1864 is much harder to defend than his behavior in 1887 and 1888. In the Baptismal Regeneration

---

28. Fullerton, *C. H. Spurgeon: A Biography*, 199.

Controversy, Spurgeon appeared to be deliberately tribal and divisive, whereas in the Downgrade Controversy, he made a good-faith effort to avoid division through private entreaty. Nonetheless, the latter episode still displayed some of his native weaknesses. Though Spurgeon's protest in the Downgrade Controversy was doubtless justified, it is likely that the collateral damage stemming from the conflict would have been better contained if his leading traits were temperance and moderation.

Fourth, the controversy made plain that Spurgeon was most at home as a pastor, and not as a denominational statesman. He was in his element as the strong and dynamic leader of a vital and active urban megachurch but was ill-suited for a career in denominational politics. There was never much of a chance Spurgeon would embrace the role of the slow reformer of the Baptist Union. It would require him to defer, concede, and compromise in ways his conscience could not tolerate. Spurgeon was at his best when he could speak openly, lead freely, and direct affairs in accord with his convictions.

Finally, it would be a severe misjudgment to conclude from this consideration of the Downgrade Controversy that Spurgeon possessed the isolationist or separationist impulse that would later become characteristic of fundamentalists in the twentieth century. Spurgeon was not naturally oriented toward faction and division. Nor did he view independency as a desirable course for his church. Rather, throughout his life, Spurgeon was heavily invested as an active collaborator and participant in many meaningful expressions of broad Christian fellowship. He delighted in being part of visible manifestations of evangelical unity. He collected friends from across denominational lines, pursued intimate fellowship with men of differing convictions, and eagerly participated in various evangelical groups, denominations, and associations. Though a staunch Calvinist, Spurgeon enjoyed denominational and associational fellowship with many Arminians. Though a convinced Baptist, he happily hired paedobaptists to lead the Pastors' College and the Stockwell Orphanage. Though a proud Nonconformist, he even counted some

Anglicans among his closest friends. Spurgeon gloried in the gospel unity he shared with Christians with whom he differed on issues such as predestination, baptism, and church polity. He was never so narrow-minded as to believe unity required uniformity nor so fragile as to think that fellowship cannot tolerate differences. It was important to him to manifest wider fellowship with Christians of every stripe. He was a man oriented toward broad Christian unity.

Spurgeon did not gravitate toward conflict. In fact, in his forty years in pastoral ministry, he participated in only two major controversies (the Baptismal Regeneration Controversy and the Downgrade Controversy). Spurgeon hated war and loved peace. He entered the former with great reluctance; the latter was always his aim. The Downgrade Controversy was agonizing for Spurgeon at the deepest possible level. Even when a break became necessary, Spurgeon found separation from his Christian brothers in the Baptist Union exceedingly painful. Ultimately, the controversy left him pining for the decisive end of all strife and division that he knew would come on the last day. "Oh, that the day would come," he said, "when, in a larger communion than any sect can offer, all those who are one in Christ may be able to blend in manifest unity!"[29]

Lessons from the Downgrade

The Downgrade Controversy remains relevant today and will be as long as truth and error are opposed to one another. Well over a century later, it is still debated and discussed among scholars, pastors, and church leaders in various quarters of the Christian world. There is also a great deal left to uncover and explore in relation to the controversy, including yet-to-be-consulted documentary material, fuller studies of various major and minor actors in the drama, as well as the aftermath for many of Spurgeon's former students, some of whom supported him and some of whom did not. The foregoing

---

29. Spurgeon, "Fragment upon the Down-Grade Controversy," *Sword and the Trowel* (November 1887): 560.

sketch of the controversy is not offered as a major contribution to scholarly debates. That work is left to others.[30] I close this chapter by briefly drawing a few pastoral lessons from the controversy that are worth considering as historians and theologians continue to grapple with the ongoing implications of the Downgrade Controversy.

The first is the most obvious and surely the most important: orthodoxy must be jealously guarded and maintained. Churches and denominations do not *drift* into faithfulness but into error. It is through active exertion and effort that the truth is preserved. False teaching in a church or denomination, even in small doses, is cancerous, and if left ignored and unchecked will always metastasize. The rank error Spurgeon encountered among certain ministers in the Baptist Union in the 1880s was virtually unheard of in the 1850s and even in the 1860s. The Downgrade Controversy is evidence that doctrinal drift is an ever-present threat, and it can cover enormous ground in a short time. Tragically, after Spurgeon's death, almost all his prophecies proved true—doctrinal decline continued apace in the Baptist Union over the following century as core doctrines continued to be denied. In contrast, the Metropolitan Tabernacle has remained faithful to the biblical gospel for over 130 years since Spurgeon's death. Spurgeon understood that the faith once for all delivered to the saints must be protected, preserved, and passed down from generation to generation. It was this awesome responsibility that propelled him to contend for orthodoxy against the approaching tide of error. As he saw the clouds forming on the horizon, Spurgeon said in an 1880 sermon,

> How are we to expect the gospel to be kept alive in the world if we do not hand it on to the next generation as the former generation handed it down to us.... Oh, shall it ever be said a century hence, "The people of 1880 never thought of us of 1980? They let the gospel go: they allowed the doctrines to be

---

30. There is still need of a doctoral dissertation devoted entirely to the Downgrade Controversy.

denied one after the other, and here are we without it to perish in the darkness"?... Oh let it never be so. May God grant that we may be clear of the blood of souls. What a crime it will be if we murder generations of men by our cowardly silence![31]

A second lesson from the Downgrade Controversy is that when private doctrinal debates advance to the point of public controversy, the discussion can quickly become shrouded in procedural obfuscation, tangential disputes, and conflicting egos and personalities. The original concern in the Downgrade Controversy was clear enough: men in the denomination had begun to tamper with cardinal doctrines of the faith. Yet before long, the controversy became as much about personality clashes and denominational procedure as anything else. Spurgeon repeatedly tried to bring the debate back to the particular doctrinal issues that first prompted his objections; the politicization of the whole affair, however, eventually obscured the doctrinal matters at stake and amplified numerous micro dramas that distracted from Spurgeon's chief concerns. Such is the typical course when a matter of doctrinal disagreement becomes a matter of public controversy; the possibility of thoughtful, productive, and linear debate is greatly jeopardized, and the main issues can quickly become confused. Perhaps it was impossible that the Downgrade Controversy would ever remain a private matter. Nonetheless, there is still value in recognizing the challenges that typically attend public controversy and anticipating them before they appear.

The final lesson is especially relevant for pastors: none of Christ's ministers are guaranteed a glorious finale in this life. Spurgeon's ministry was, as one famous man of the day put it, "a career... unparalleled in the history of ministers."[32] In 1884, on the occasion of his fiftieth birthday celebration, Spurgeon found himself surrounded by manifold evidence of a long and fruitful pastorate. He had the

---

31. C. H. Spurgeon, "Cheer for the Worker, and Hope for London," in *Metropolitan Tabernacle Pulpit*, 26:619.

32. Gough, *Sunlight and Shadow*, 407.

joy of seeing sinners converted, pastors trained, churches planted, widows and orphans rescued, books published, and untold thousands blessed by his ministry throughout the world. It would seem as though Spurgeon had reached the mountaintop. And yet the final years of his life were not spent atop the mountain but in the deepest valley he had ever known. They were indeed the saddest years of his life, filled with immense sorrow and suffering. Surely the lesson to be learned is that even the most faithful servants of Christ do not always go out to the sound of trumpets. Some of the greatest men and women of the faith die with broken hearts.

Spurgeon did not look to this world for his ultimate reward. His hope was not in some sort of grand or triumphant ending to a long and faithful ministry. The prize for Spurgeon was far greater. He looked finally to the resurrection from the dead, when he, along with all the faithful, would receive the unfading crown of life from Jesus Christ. If the pathway to glory required him to pass through one last long vale of tears, he could bear it as long as his Savior waited for him on the other side. Though he was discouraged and disillusioned by so much around him, he continued to preach with indomitable zeal the same hope he had preached for four decades, perhaps clinging to it himself more tightly than he ever had. Spurgeon seemed to recognize the fight was nearly over and that he was coming to the end of his race. Unto the last, he would keep the faith.

14

Final Days

On June 7, 1891, Spurgeon preached his final sermon in the Metropolitan Tabernacle. He did not know then that it would be his last. He would live another eight months, and during that time he entertained the hope that he would return again to preach. But it would not be so. This would be the final time he would address his flock from the pulpit he had occupied for thirty-seven years as their pastor. His last words on that day were quintessentially Spurgeon:

> What I have to say lastly is this: how greatly I desire that you who are not enlisted in my Lord's band would come to him because you see what a kind and gracious Lord he is! Young men, if you could see our Captain, you would down on your knees and beg him to let you enter the ranks of those who follow him. It is heaven to serve Jesus.... Every man must serve somebody.... Depend upon it, you will either serve Satan or Christ, either self or the Saviour. You will find sin, self, Satan, and the world to be hard masters; but if you wear the livery of Christ, you will find him so meek and lowly of heart that you will find rest unto your souls. He is the most magnanimous of captains. There never was his like among the choicest of princes. He is always to be found in the thickest part of the battle. When the wind blows cold he always takes the bleak side of the hill. The heaviest end of the cross lies ever on his shoulders. If he bids us carry a burden, he carries it also. If there is anything that is gracious, generous, kind, and tender, yea lavish and superabundant in love, you always find it in him. These forty years and more have I served him, blessed be his name!

and I have had nothing but love from him. I would be glad to continue yet another forty years in the same dear service here below if so it pleased him. His service is life, peace, joy. Oh, that you would enter on it at once! God help you to enlist under the banner of Jesus even this day! Amen.[1]

As Spurgeon had done for nearly four decades, he once more extolled the beauty, centrality, and all-sufficiency of Christ. This theme had been the keynote of his entire ministry. His message had been from the first about the surpassing loveliness and worthiness of Jesus and His readiness to save sinners by His blood. Thirty-seven years later, nothing in Spurgeon's message had changed.

Spurgeon himself had changed, though. He was no longer the vigorous and sprightly youth of the 1850s. He was an older man, encumbered and weighed down by suffering, sickness, and age. Though his inner man was being renewed day by day, his outer man was wasting away (2 Cor. 4:16), and he could feel it. He never stopped praying for healing and never ceased to hope that he would recover, but he seemed to know the end was near. His health was rapidly declining; his chronic kidney disease was worse than ever, and the attacks of gout occurred more often and with greater intensity. Moreover, his health problems were exacerbated by the ongoing stress, pressures, and tensions extending from the Downgrade Controversy, which persisted and continued to cause him pain even beyond the climactic battles of 1887–88. The man who had once boasted about breaking down his own constitution through his ceaseless activity for Christ had, indeed, broken it down irreparably.

The Last Visit to Menton

In the final years of Spurgeon's life, he made more frequent trips to Menton, France, which had become to him a quiet refuge and a home away from home. As he neared the end, his visits there became all

---

1. C. H. Spurgeon, "The Statute of David for the Sharing of the Spoil," in *Metropolitan Tabernacle Pulpit*, 37:323–24.

the more essential and would last longer as he sought the rest and recuperation he so badly needed. In autumn 1891, Spurgeon left London for the last time and made his way to the French Riviera as he had done dozens of times. But on this final visit, at long last, Susie was able to join him.[2] In the past, Spurgeon had written

The view of Menton from the garden of one of Spurgeon's friends

hundreds of love letters to her from Menton, declaring how he so dearly wished that she could be with him on his retreats. He wanted to show her all his favorite walks, the many beautiful and exotic flowers that grew in the South of France, and the spots where he loved to sit to take in the sunshine and the ocean air. Finally, in the last three months of his life, his wish would come true. The loving couple would know the joy of spending their final days on earth together, hidden from the world in a delightful little corner of paradise.

They stayed at Spurgeon's usual haunt, the Hôtel Beau Rivage, which "soon began to give evidence of a lady's presence," as Susie seamlessly made the rooms their own.[3] The couple was joined, as Spurgeon usually was, by a small cadre of his close friends and secretaries. Though he was quite limited physically, he still managed to enjoy afternoon carriage rides in the warm sunshine as well as short walks with Susie down by the water's edge. Except when extreme pain prevented him, he would usually sit in the corner of their room in the morning and engage in work of various kinds. Susie had rearranged the room to accommodate a makeshift office for him. The sounds of the waves and the smells of the sea breeze that wafted in from an open window transformed the room into a charming and peaceful

---

2. *C. H. Spurgeon's Autobiography*, 4:365.

3. *C. H. Spurgeon's Autobiography*, 4:365.

hideaway. In the company of one of his secretaries, Spurgeon was usually able to engage in work in this happy environment for several consecutive hours.

Spurgeon would occasionally edit one of his sermons for publication or perhaps an article or two for the *Sword and the Trowel*. He also penned book reviews and notices for insertion in the magazine. By far his most significant writing project during this time was his devotional exposition of Matthew's Gospel, *The Gospel of the Kingdom*, which would be the last book he ever wrote.[4] He also wrote numerous letters to friends and family, as well as to his officers at the Metropolitan Tabernacle. Even from afar, he was still engaged in the leadership and direction of the church.

One of the greatest treasures that remains from Spurgeon's latter visits to Menton is a collection of letters he wrote to his congregation to be read aloud on Sunday mornings. On numerous occasions, he would sit at his desk and simply pour out his pastoral heart to his flock in these exceedingly open and affectionate missives. In one such letter, from November 5, 1891, he concluded with these words:

> I am writing in the early morning of a warm day of brilliant sunshine; and the very thought of your holy assembly and your loving thoughts of me makes all this tenfold more powerful to cheer and to restore me. If I had not such an attached people I should miss my greatest earthly joy and succumb to the depression which physical weakness is so apt to produce. My dear brother will soon be with you to report of my behaviour, but I am doubly happy in having my beloved wife as my watchful companion,—a joy specially given in this peculiar hour of need.
>
> The Lord himself bless every one of you, and specially those who minister in word and doctrine.
>
> Your loving friend,
> C. H. Spurgeon[5]

---

4. C. H. Spurgeon, *The Gospel of the Kingdom: A Popular Exposition of the Gospel according to Matthew* (London: Passmore and Alabaster, 1893).

5. *Suffering Letters of C. H. Spurgeon*, 111.

In a December 10 letter he began,

> Beloved friends,
>
> Every message from home concerning the work at the Tabernacle comforts me. Your unity of heart, and prayerfulness of spirit, are a joy to me. How much I wish that I could look you in the face, and lead you in prayer to the throne of the heavenly grace.[6]

On January 6, 1892, less than four weeks before his death he wrote,

> On looking back upon the valley of the shadow of death through which I passed so short a time ago, I feel my mind grasping with firmer grip than ever that everlasting gospel which for so many years I have preached to you. We have not been deceived. Jesus does give rest to those who come to him, he does save those who trust him, he does photograph his image on those who learn of him. I hate the Christianised infidelity of the modern school more than ever, as I see how it rends away from sinful man his last and only hope. Cling to the

Susannah Spurgeon in older age   *Spurgeon in Menton*

---

6. *Suffering Letters of C. H. Spurgeon*, 113.

gospel of forgiveness through the substitutionary sacrifice, and spread it with all your might, each one of you, for it is the only cure for bleeding hearts.[7]

On Sundays, and at other times during the week, the Spurgeons and their little company would gather in one of the main common rooms, along with any hotel guests who wished to join them, for a short worship service. These were especially sweet and simple times of prayer, singing, and consideration of God's word. Spurgeon would often lead in prayer at these services and even managed to preach a short message on a couple of occasions.

On the evening of January 17, 1892, two weeks before he died, Spurgeon participated in the last worship service of his life, which was held in his room.[8] Before closing in prayer, he announced the final hymn as he had done thousands of times before. The hymn that evening could not have been more appropriate, as his life was drawing to a close. He chose Samuel Rutherford's classic hymn "The Sands of Time Are Sinking," whose first verse reads,

> The sands of time are sinking;
> The dawn of heaven breaks;
> The summer morn I've sighed for,
> The fair, sweet morn awakes;
> Dark, dark hath been the midnight,
> But dayspring is at hand,
> And glory, glory dwelleth
> In Immanuel's land.

The last words Spurgeon ever sang in the company of other worshipers on earth were these:

> The bride eyes not her garment,
> But her dear bridegroom's face;
> I will not gaze at glory,

---

7. *Suffering Letters of C. H. Spurgeon*, 118–19.

8. *C. H. Spurgeon's Autobiography*, 4:370; and Fullerton, *C. H. Spurgeon: A Biography*, 335.

But on my King of grace;
Not at the crown He giveth,
But on His pierced hands;
The Lamb is all the glory
Of Immanuel's land.[9]

A few days later on Wednesday afternoon, a severe attack of gout forced Spurgeon into his bed, this time never to leave it. For the next several days, he went in and out of sleep and spent many hours in the night awake and in pain. On January 26, Spurgeon had the presence of mind to remember that the Metropolitan Tabernacle was holding a special thank offering that day for the support of the church and its many ministries. He purposed to give a generous gift of one hundred pounds for the offering. The final telegram he ever sent read, "Self and wife, £100, hearty thankoffering towards Tabernacle General Expenses. Love to all friends." Spurgeon's secretary, Joseph Harrald, recorded, "That was his last generous act, and his last message."[10] Shortly after this, Spurgeon went into a coma and never regained consciousness. He died at 11:05 p.m. on the Lord's Day, January 31, 1892. After a brief prayer of thanks to God for the great gift her husband had been to her for thirty-five years, Susie sent a message to her son Thomas: "Father in Heaven. Mother resigned."[11]

*One of the last photographs
taken of Spurgeon*

---

9. Anne R. Cousin, "The Sands of Time Are Sinking," in *The Baptist Hymnal: A Collection of Hymns and Spiritual Songs* (London: E. Marlborough, 1879), no. 916. The lyrics of Cousin's hymn are based on the letters of Samuel Rutherford.

10. *C. H. Spurgeon's Autobiography*, 4:371.

11. *C. H. Spurgeon's Autobiography*, 4:371.

Final Farewells

Word of Spurgeon's death immediately reached London. From there telegrams were sent around the world bearing the news that the greatest preacher of the age had died. Newspapers across the globe carried the story, and literally thousands of tributes, eulogies, and articles poured forth in gazettes, magazines, and periodicals everywhere. Memorial services were held in major American cities, such as New York, Boston, Philadelphia, and Chicago. The entire Christian world was united in mourning the loss of the Prince of Preachers.

Ministers of the gospel as well as ministers of Parliament shared their public remembrances of Spurgeon. Great men of the age, such as William Gladstone, John Ruskin, and William Booth, mourned Spurgeon's passing. Even the Prince of Wales, who would one day be crowned Edward VII, king of England, offered his condolences. The entire nation, it seemed, recognized it had suffered a monumental loss.

A week after Spurgeon's death, the Metropolitan Tabernacle held a series of memorial services, with no less than a hundred thousand people attending to pay their respects and to listen to the many moving tributes that were offered.[12] A striking sense of gravity and glory hung over these services. W. Y. Fullerton recorded, "None who were there will ever realise more concentrated emotion than then."[13]

At one time, Spurgeon had expressed the wish to be buried in the middle of the Stockwell Orphanage grounds. Given his international fame, he knew many would come from far and wide to visit his grave. He hoped that when they did, they would see the plight of the poor children and be moved to make contributions to the orphanage to sustain the work in his absence. This was eventually rendered impractical, however, because of the interference of the South London Electric Railway. Spurgeon later requested that he be buried in Norwood Cemetery, "so that, in death, as in life, he might

---

12. Carlile, *C. H. Spurgeon: An Interpretive Biography*, 11.
13. Fullerton, *C. H. Spurgeon: A Biography*, 335.

be surrounded by his church-officers and members, many hundreds of whom are buried there."[14] It was heartily agreed on by his family and fellow church officers that this should be his final resting place.

On Thursday, February 11, 1892, Spurgeon's body was transported along a five-mile route from the Metropolitan Tabernacle to Norwood Cemetery in South London. A thousand police officers were on hand to tend to the procession, with hundreds of thousands of people gathered along the route to watch as the hearse was carried to its destination followed by a cavalcade of forty-one carriages.[15] Shops and public houses along the way were closed, and traffic halted to a standstill.

At one point during the waning days of Spurgeon's life, as he saw his death fast approaching, he whispered to his secretary, "Remember, a plain stone. C. H. S. and no more; no fuss."[16] But in the words of one of his biographers, "Love denied the last request."[17] Spurgeon's tomb, though still modest, included more than merely his initials. The front of the grave bore the simple inscription,

Here lies the body of
Charles Haddon Spurgeon
Waiting for the appearing of his
Lord and Saviour
Jesus Christ.

Etched on the side of the grave were the final two verses of William Cowper's classic hymn "There Is a Fountain Filled with Blood," which Spurgeon had quoted hundreds of times in sermons, articles, and letters:

E'er since by faith I saw the stream
Thy flowing wounds supply,

---

14. *C. H. Spurgeon's Autobiography*, 373.

15. Charles Ray, *The Life of Charles Haddon Spurgeon: With an Introduction by Pastor Thomas Spurgeon* (London: Passmore and Alabaster, 1903), 482; and *Suffering Letters of C. H. Spurgeon*, 121.

16. Carlile, *C. H. Spurgeon: An Interpretive Biography*, 266.

17. Fullerton, *C. H. Spurgeon: A Biography*, 339.

Redeeming love has been my theme,
And shall be till I die....

Then in a nobler, sweeter song
I'll sing Thy power to save,
When this poor lisping, stammering tongue
Lies silent in the grave.[18]

Atop the grave rested a sculpture of a Bible opened to 2 Timothy 4:7–8: "I have fought a good fight, I have finished my course, I have kept the faith: henceforth there is laid up for me a crown of righteousness, which the Lord, the righteous judge, shall give me at that day: and not to me only, but unto all them also that love his appearing."

As Spurgeon was laid to rest, members of the family and close friends huddled around the grave, with about a thousand onlookers enclosed in the cemetery grounds and thousands more still standing on the streets outside the cemetery. Archibald G. Brown, the most eminent of Spurgeon's former students and one of his dearest friends, offered a memorable farewell at the graveside:

Beloved President, Faithful Pastor, Prince of Preachers, Brother Beloved, Dear Spurgeon,–We bid thee not "farewell," but only for a little while "good-night." Thou shalt rise soon, at the first dawn of the resurrection day of the redeemed. Yet is not the "good-night" ours to bid, but thine. It is we who linger in the darkness; thou art in God's own light. Our night, too, shall soon be past, and with it all our weeping. Then, with thine, our songs shall greet the morning of a day that knows no cloud nor close, for there is no night there.

Hard Worker in the field, thy toil is ended! Straight has been the furrow thou hast ploughed. No looking back has marred thy course. Harvests have followed thy patient sowing, and Heaven is already rich with thine ingathered sheaves, and shall be still enriched through years yet lying in eternity.

---

18. William Cowper, "There Is a Fountain Filled with Blood," in *Our Own Hymn-Book: A Collection of Psalms and Hymns for Public, Social, and Private Worship*, ed. C. H. Spurgeon (London: Passmore and Alabaster, 1866), no. 288.

Champion of God, thy battle long and nobly fought is over! The sword, which clave to thine hand, has dropped at last; the palm branch takes its place. No longer does the helmet press thy brow, oft weary with its surging thoughts of battle; the victor's wreath from the Great Commander's hand has already proved thy full reward.

Here for a little while, shall rest thy precious dust. Then shall thy Well-beloved come, and at His voice thou shalt spring from thy couch of earth, fashioned like unto His glorious body. Then spirit, soul, and body shall magnify thy Lord's redemption. Until then, beloved, sleep! We praise God *for* thee; and, by the blood of the everlasting covenant, we hope and expect to praise God *with* thee. Amen.[19]

Spurgeon's funeral train entering Norwood Cemetery

---

19. *C. H. Spurgeon's Autobiography*, 375–76.

A Burning and Shining Lamp

Charles Haddon Spurgeon was without question the greatest preacher of the nineteenth century, and some would argue, of any century. His extraordinary preaching abilities, his genius for administration, and his massive global influence set him apart as a leader of rare brilliance. His place is well secured among church history's greatest men, and his outstanding legacy will continue to attract grateful praise and admiration for years to come.

Spurgeon's career was wholly unique. Yet many people have attempted to draw comparisons, nonetheless. Some have suggested a resemblance to George Whitefield, but the likeness is not a good one. Whitefield was an itinerant evangelist who constantly preached to new crowds in new locations. He was not a pastor of a church, nor did he publish copious works or lead numerous organizations. Spurgeon was a pastor who stayed in the same church and shepherded the same people for two generations. Like Whitefield, he was certainly able to draw new crowds anywhere at any time, but unlike Whitefield, he managed to keep essentially the same (though ever-growing) crowd together for thirty-eight years. He also published more words in English than any other Christian writer and bore the sole responsibility for the management of dozens of organizations and ministries.

Others have compared Spurgeon to the Puritans, and certainly there is a kinship between him and them, particularly in terms of the shared body of doctrine to which he and they were devoted. But there is no Puritan who enjoyed even half the popularity Spurgeon achieved, nor did any of them realize as wide a reach. Furthermore, many of the Puritans were theologians trained at Oxford or Cambridge; Spurgeon never went to college. Most of the Puritans pastored small to midsize churches, many in rural areas; Spurgeon pastored a megachurch in the heart of London. The Puritans were not known for their evangelical activism; Spurgeon was an evangelical activist par excellence.

Spurgeon occupies a wholly unique place among ministers of the gospel. He stands apart as a burning and shining lamp whose light has gone out across the world, blessing literally millions of people. His extraordinary biography, his incomparable preaching, his massive corpus, and his scores of devoted followers who continue to promote his ministry place him in a class of his own.

Much of Spurgeon's fruitfulness, in the providence of God, was tied to circumstances peculiar to nineteenth-century England. He emerged at a time when the nation's Christian heritage was still intact, though about to begin its slow decline. Spurgeon's particular approach to preaching thrived in a context in which people were at least nominally familiar with Christian doctrine, morality, and thought. The popular religious imagination had, for previous years, atrophied because of the stolid and pedantic preaching of the day, which seemed to lecture the people but did nothing to inspire Christian piety and devotion. Spurgeon was able to successfully tap into the culture's religious consciousness, reawaken it, and direct it to his ends. With unmatched skill and exceptional brilliance, Spurgeon was capable of breathing new life into the old categories and of recapturing the spiritual attention of men and women who for years had been slowly losing their religion or had perhaps dismissed Christianity altogether as irrelevant and devoid of power. Spurgeon was able to lay hold of something deep within the country's long Christian memory and pull it into the present, bringing it to the people in a way that was fresh and compelling. The old religion of the English Reformation and of the Puritans was given new life again largely thanks to Spurgeon.

The status of Victorian Nonconformity around the middle of the nineteenth century also created an auspicious context for Spurgeon's rise to prominence. At just that time, Nonconformity had reached the zenith of its national influence, and no voice among the Nonconformists carried more weight than Spurgeon's. It is unlikely Spurgeon could have achieved the same status in the religious world of England in the century before or after the nineteenth century. If a Nonconformist was to become the country's greatest preacher, it would happen during the period of Victoria's reign.

A further factor that advanced Spurgeon's popularity was the country's surging industrialization, mechanization, and urbanization, which forced people into cities like London, causing its many boroughs to explode with population growth. This created a context in which such people could be reached en masse by the concentrated efforts of individual ministries and churches like never before. The population growth in London was predominately among the lower and middle classes. The Victorian era was in many ways the age of the common man. Spurgeon was eminently a man of the people, and he possessed a special aptness for reaching the working-class poor. He was their advocate, sympathizer, and friend. David Bebbington writes, "[Spurgeon] was one of the most articulate—perhaps the most articulate of all—in arguing the claims of the people against the elite. His immense popularity therefore flowed not only from his pugnacious loyalty to the basics of the gospel. It was also a result of his doughty championship of the common man."[20]

When Spurgeon arrived in London, it was primed and ready for him. The population hungered for preaching like his. The masses of common people, long forgotten by London's more sophisticated ministers, wanted a preacher who would speak frankly, earnestly, and lovingly to them about the intimate concerns of their souls. Spurgeon was indeed the "people's preacher."[21] His sermons, marked by their simplicity, plainness, and directness and enriched by a compelling mastery of the English of Shakespeare and the King James Version, went to the heart of the people and made them alive once again to the things of God.

Yet it must be said that Spurgeon was not simply the product of auspicious social and cultural circumstances. His success as a

20. Bebbington, "Spurgeon and the Common Man," 75.
21. Eva Hope, *Spurgeon: The People's Preacher* (London: Walter Scott Publishing, n.d.); and Morden, *C. H. Spurgeon: The People's Preacher*.

minister of the gospel was the result of a divine anointing that manifestly rested on him. The Spirit of God sanctified Spurgeon's ministry and empowered and blessed his many efforts at doing good. God's hand was on Spurgeon in a way that was powerfully evident to tens of thousands who heard him preach. And thus, it is to God we should turn in thanksgiving and praise for the surpassing gift Spurgeon has been to so many.

As long as his name remains in living memory, Charles Haddon Spurgeon will be honored as a preacher utterly devoted to one essential message—the good news of salvation for sinners through the blood of the Lord Jesus. He was determined to publish this news

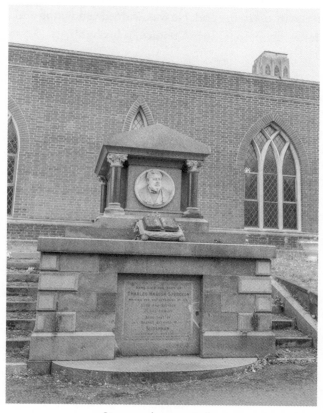

Spurgeon's grave today

as widely as possible and to invite men and women wherever he found them to come to the Savior in repentance and faith. Spurgeon was altogether absorbed in the person and work of Christ. He was a dedicated preacher of the old evangelical gospel, and his one great passion was the proclamation of the truth of the abiding and enduring word of God. Throughout the generations of the church, many Christians will highly esteem him for his searching and penetrating preaching, for his evangelistic zeal, for his earnest devotion, for his vigorous experimental piety, for his pastoral tenderness, for his compassionate benevolence, for his moral courage, for his undaunted leadership, for his unflagging integrity, for his unshaking conviction, for his evangelical catholicity, for his warm love for family, and for his faithful witness to the end. He was, indeed, a burning and shining lamp. May many more come to rejoice in his light.

Timeline

June 19, 1834 — Charles Haddon Spurgeon is born in Kelvedon, Essex, to John and Eliza Spurgeon.

August 1835 — Spurgeon moves in with his grandparents in Stambourne, where he lives between the ages of one and six years old. He is first introduced to the writings of the Puritans in his grandfather's study.

1840 — Spurgeon returns to his parents' home, now in Colchester.

1849 — Spurgeon is sent to board at Newmarket Academy, just outside Cambridge.

January 6, 1850 — Spurgeon is converted at the age of fifteen in a Primitive Methodist Chapel through a sermon from Isaiah 45:22 delivered by a preacher whose identity remains unknown.

May 3, 1850 — Spurgeon is baptized at Isleham Ferry, a few miles outside of Cambridge, by the Reverend W. W. Cantlow.

June 17, 1850 — Spurgeon moves to Cambridge.

Winter 1850–51 — Spurgeon begins preaching in a local Cambridge lay preachers' association; he preaches his first sermon in Teversham Cottage.

October 1851 — Spurgeon accepts the call to pastor Waterbeach Baptist Chapel, just outside of Cambridge, at the age of seventeen.

December 18, 1853 — Spurgeon preaches his first sermon at New Park Street Chapel in London.

April 19, 1854 — At the age of nineteen, Spurgeon officially accepts the call to pastor New Park Street Chapel.

1855 — Spurgeon republishes the Second London Baptist Confession of 1689 with his own preface.

January 1855 — Spurgeon begins publishing weekly sermons, which he would continue to do for the rest of his life. His sermons would be published weekly even after his death until 1917, when a paper shortage during WWI brought an end to their publication.

July 1855 — Spurgeon begins to mentor T. W. Medhurst, who is eventually the first student in the Pastors' College.

January 8, 1856 — Spurgeon marries Susannah Thompson, and the couple settle in a home on New Kent Road.

September 20, 1856 — Susannah gives birth to twin boys, Charles and Thomas.

October 19, 1856 — Disaster at the Surrey Gardens Music Hall occurs; seven people die, and twenty-eight are injured.

1857 — The Spurgeons move to a home they call Helensburgh House on Nightingale Lane. They live there until 1880.

1857 — The Pastors' College is officially established.

October 7, 1857 — Spurgeon preaches to 23,654 people at the Crystal Palace, the largest recorded congregation he ever addressed.

August 16, 1859 — The foundation stone of the Metropolitan Tabernacle is laid.

March 25, 1861 — Spurgeon preaches his first sermon in the newly erected Metropolitan Tabernacle.

June 5, 1864 — Spurgeon preaches his controversial sermon "Baptismal Regeneration." It would go on to be Spurgeon's best-selling sermon.

January 1, 1865 — Spurgeon begins publishing his monthly magazine, *The Sword and the Trowel*, which he publishes until the end of his life. It would continue in publication long after his death.

August 1866 — Anne Hillyard and Charles Spurgeon meet, and plans for the Stockwell Orphanage are put in place.

November 1, 1866 — The Colportage Association is founded for the widespread distribution of affordable Christian literature.

September 9, 1869 — The Stockwell Orphanage officially opens.

September 1875 — Mrs. Spurgeon's Book Fund is founded. It continues in operation until the end of her life in 1903.

1879 — The Girls' Orphanage is established.

1880 — The Spurgeons move to a home they call Westwood in Beulah Hill. This is their final home.

June 18–19, 1884—The Metropolitan Tabernacle holds a special Jubilee Service to celebrate the pastor's fiftieth birthday and to commemorate his (then) thirty years of ministry among them.

1885—Spurgeon publishes the final volume of his magnum opus, *The Treasury of David* (7 volumes in all).

March 1887—The Downgrade Controversy commences with two articles published in *The Sword and the Trowel*.

October 29, 1887—Spurgeon officially resigns from the Baptist Union.

January 19, 1888—The vote of censure against Spurgeon is taken by the council of the Baptist Union.

June 7, 1891—Spurgeon preaches his last sermon at the Metropolitan Tabernacle.

January 31, 1892—Spurgeon dies peacefully in Menton, France, surrounded by his wife and a few of his closest friends and associates.

February 11, 1892—Spurgeon is laid to rest in West Norwood Cemetery.

Bibliography

Albert, William Brian. "'When the Wind Blows Cold': The Spirituality of Suffering and Depression in the Life and Ministry of Charles Spurgeon." PhD diss., Southern Baptist Theological Seminary, 2015.

Baker, Susan Valerie. "'Susannah and the Lemon Tree': Mrs. C. H. Spurgeon's Book Fund." *Baptist Quarterly* 48, no. 4 (2017): 159–67.

The Baptist Hymnal: A Collection of Hymns and Spiritual Songs. London: E. Marlborough, 1879.

Bartlett, Edward H. *Mrs. Bartlett and Her Class at the Metropolitan Tabernacle: A Biography by Her Son*. Cannon Beach, Ore.: Move to Assurance, 2018.

Bebbington, David W. *The Dominance of Evangelicalism: The Age of Spurgeon and Moody*. Downers Grove, Ill.: InterVarsity Press, 2005.

———. *Evangelicalism in Modern Britain: A History from the 1730s to the 1980s*. London: Routledge, 1989.

———. "The Political Force." *Christian History* 10, no. 1 (1991): 36–37.

———. "Spurgeon and the Common Man." *Baptist Review of Theology* 5, no. 1 (Spring 1995): 63–75.

———. *Victorian Nonconformity*. Revised ed. Eugene, Ore.: Cascade Books, 2011.

Beeke, Joel R., and Michael Reeves. *Following God Fully: An Introduction to the Puritans*. Grand Rapids: Reformation Heritage Books, 2022.

Breimaier, Thomas Andrew. *Tethered to the Cross: The Life and Preaching of C. H. Spurgeon*. Downers Grove, Ill.: IVP Academic, 2020.

Briggs, J. H. Y. *The English Baptists of the Nineteenth Century*. Didcot, UK: Baptist Historical Society, 1994.

Brown, Kenneth D. *A Social History of the Nonconformist Ministry in England and Wales 1800– 1930*. Oxford: Clarendon, 1988.

Brown, Steward J., Peter B. Nockles, and James Pererio, eds. *The Oxford Handbook of the Oxford Movement*. Oxford: Oxford University Press, 2017.

Bunyan, John. *The Pilgrim's Progress*. London: Hurst, Robinson, 1820.

Candlish, J. S., ed. *The British and Foreign Evangelical Review*. London: James Nisbet, 1877.

Carlile, J. C. *C. H. Spurgeon: An Interpretive Biography*. London: Kingsgate Press, 1933.

Chadwick, Owen. *The Victorian Church*. Part 1, *1829–1859*. 3rd ed. London: SCM Press, 1971.

———. *The Victorian Church*. Part 2, *1860–1901*. 2nd ed. London: SCM Press, 1972.

Chandler, Tertius, and Gerald Fox. *3000 Years of Urban Growth*. New York: Academic Press, 1974.

Chang, Geoffrey. "The Militant Ecclesiology and Church Polity of Charles Haddon Spurgeon." PhD diss., Midwestern Baptist Theological Seminary, 2020.

———. "New Insights into the Formative Influence of Spurgeon's Early Years." *Themelios* 47, no. 3 (December 2022): 500–512.

———. *Spurgeon the Pastor: Recovering a Biblical and Theological Vision for Ministry*. Nashville: B&H Academic, 2022.

Colquitt, Henry Franklin. "The Soteriology of Charles Haddon Spurgeon Revealed in His Sermons and Controversial Writings." PhD diss., University of Edinburgh, 1951.

Conwell, Russell. *Life of Charles Haddon Spurgeon: The World's Greatest Preacher*. Philadelphia: A. T. Hubbard, 1892.

Dallimore, Arnold. *Spurgeon: A New Biography*. Edinburgh: Banner of Truth, 1985.

Davies, Horton. *Worship and Theology in England: From Watts and Wesley to Martineau, 1690–1900*. Grand Rapids: Eerdmans, 1996.

Day, Richard E. *The Shadow of the Broad Brim: The Life Story of Charles Haddon Spurgeon, Heir of the Puritans*. Philadelphia: Judson Press, 1934.

de Quincey, Thomas. *Autobiographic Sketches*. Boston: Ticknor, Reed, and Fields, 1853.

Dickens, Charles. *Oliver Twist*. 2nd ed. London: Richard Bentley, 1839.

———. *The Personal History of David Copperfield, in Two Volumes*. London: Chapman and Hall, 1874.

DiPrima, Alex. *Spurgeon and the Poor: How the Gospel Compels Christian Social Concern*. Grand Rapids: Reformation Heritage Books, 2023.

Douglas, James. *The Prince of Preachers: A Sketch and an Appreciation by One Who Knew Him Well*. London: Morgan and Scott, [1893].

Drummond, Lewis A. *Spurgeon: Prince of Preachers*. 3rd ed. Grand Rapids: Kregel, 1992.

Edwards, David L. *Christian England*. Vol. 3, *From the 18th Century to the First World War*. Grand Rapids: Eerdmans, 1984.

Eliot, T. S. *The Waste Land*. New York: Penguin Random House, 2021.

Ellison, Robert H. *Victorian Pulpit: Spoken and Written Sermons in Nineteenth-Century Britain*. London: Associated University Press, 1998.

Eswine, Zachary W. *Spurgeon's Sorrows: Realistic Hope for Those Who Suffer from Depression*. Fearn, Ross-shire, Scotland: Christian Focus, 2014.

Flanders, Judith. *The Victorian City: Everyday Life in Dickens' London*. New York: St. Martin's Griffin, 2015.

Fullerton, W. Y. *C. H. Spurgeon: A Biography*. London: William and Norgate, 1920.

Fulton, Justin D. *Spurgeon, Our Ally*. Brooklyn, N.Y.: Pauline Propaganda, 1923.

Gage, W. L. *Helen on Her Travels: What She Saw and What She Did in Europe*. New York: Hurd & Houghton, 1868.

George, Christian. "Jesus Christ, The 'Prince of Pilgrims': A Critical Analysis of the Ontological, Functional, and Exegetical Christologies in the Sermons, Writings, and Lectures of Charles Haddon Spurgeon (1834–1892)." PhD diss., University of St. Andrews, 2011.

Gill, John. *A Body of Doctrinal and Practical Divinity; or, A System of Practical Truths. Deduced from the Sacred Scriptures*. London: Whittingham and Rowland, 1815.

Gough, John B. *Sunlight and Shadow; or, Gleanings from My Life Work*. Hartford, Conn.: A. D. Worthington, 1881.

Halliday, Stephen. *The Great Stink of London: Sir Joseph Bazalgette and the Cleaning of the Victorian Metropolis*. Gloucestershire: History Press, 2001.

Hart, D. G., and R. A. Mohler Jr., eds. *Theological Education in the Evangelical Tradition*. Grand Rapids: Baker, 1996.

Hayden, Eric W. "Did You Know?" *Christian History* 29, no. 1 (1991): 1–2.

———. *Highlights in the Life of C. H. Spurgeon*. Pasadena, Tex.: Pilgrim Publications, 1990.

———. *A History of Spurgeon's Tabernacle*. Pasadena, Tex.: Pilgrim Publications, 1971.

Heasman, Kathleen. *Evangelicals in Action: An Appraisal of Their Social Work in the Victorian Era*. London: Geoffrey Bles, 1962.

Hope, Eva. *Spurgeon: The People's Preacher*. London: Walter Scott Publishing, n.d.

Hopkins, Mark. *Nonconformity's Romantic Generation: Evangelical and Liberal Theologies in Victorian England*. Eugene, Ore.: Wipf and Stock, 2006.

Kidd, Thomas. "'John Brown Is Immortal': Charles Spurgeon, the American Press, and the Ordeal of Slavery." *American Nineteenth Century History* (October 2023): 1–17.

Kruppa, Patricia Stallings. *Charles Haddon Spurgeon: A Preacher's Progress*. New York: Garland, 1982.

Larsen, Timothy. *A People of One Book: The Bible and the Victorians*. Oxford: Oxford University Press, 2011.

Lloyd-Jones, Martyn. *Preaching and Preachers*. 40th anniversary ed. Grand Rapids: Zondervan, 2012.

Lorimer, G. C. *C. H. Spurgeon: The Puritan Preacher in the Nineteenth Century*. Boston: James H. Earle, 1892.

Magoon, E. L. *"The Modern Whitfield": Sermons of the Rev. C. H. Spurgeon, of London; With an Introduction and Sketch of His Life*. New York: Sheldon, Blakeman, 1856.

Masters, Peter. *Men of Destiny*. London: Wakeman Trust, 2008.

McLeod, Hugh. *Religion and Society in England, 1850–1914*. New York: St. Martin's Press, 1996.

Meredith, Albert R. "The Social and Political Views of Charles Haddon Spurgeon 1834–1892." PhD diss., Michigan State University, 1973.

Metropolitan Tabernacle. *Memorial Volume, Mr. Spurgeon's Jubilee: Report of the Proceedings at the Metropolitan Tabernacle on Wednesday and Thursday Evenings, June 18th and 19th, 1884*. London: Passmore and Alabaster, 1884.

Moody, William R. *The Life of Dwight L. Moody.* New York: Fleming H. Revell, 1900.

Morden, Peter J. *C. H. Spurgeon: The People's Preacher.* Farnham, UK: CWR, 2009.

———. *Communion with Christ and His People: The Spirituality of C. H. Spurgeon.* Eugene, Ore.: Pickwick, 2013.

Murray, Iain. *The Forgotten Spurgeon.* Edinburgh: Banner of Truth, 1966.

———. *Letters of Charles Haddon Spurgeon: Selected with Notes.* Edinburgh: Banner of Truth, 1992.

———. *Spurgeon v. Hyper-Calvinism: The Battle for Gospel Preaching.* Edinburgh: Banner of Truth, 1995.

Needham, George Carter. *The Life and Labors of Charles H. Spurgeon: The Faithful Preacher, the Devoted Pastor, the Noble Philanthropist, the Beloved College President, and the Voluminous Writer, Author, Etc., Etc.* Boston: D. L. Guernsey, 1887.

Nettles, Tom. *Living by Revealed Truth: The Life and Pastoral Theology of Charles Haddon Spurgeon.* Fearn, Ross-shire, Scotland: Christian Focus, 2013.

Nicholls, Mike. *C. H. Spurgeon: The Pastor Evangelist.* Didcot, UK: Baptist Historical Society, 1992.

———. *Lights to the World: A History of Spurgeon's College, 1856–1992.* Harpenden, UK: Nuprint, 1994.

Oliver, Robert. *History of the English Calvinistic Baptists 1771–1892: From John Gill to C. H. Spurgeon.* Edinburgh: Banner of Truth, 2006.

Packer, J. I. *A Quest for Godliness: The Puritan Vision of the Christian Life.* Wheaton, Ill.: Crossway, 1990.

Payne, Ernest A. *The Baptist Union: A Short History.* London: Carey Kingsgate Press, 1959.

———. "The Down Grade Controversy: a Postscript." *Baptist Quarterly* 28, no. 4 (October 1979): 146–58.

Pike, G. Holden. *James Archer Spurgeon, D.D., LL.D.: Preacher, Philanthropist, and Co-Pastor with C. H. Spurgeon at the Metropolitan Tabernacle.* London: Alexander & Shepheard, 1894.

———. *The Life and Works of Charles Haddon Spurgeon.* 6 vols. London: Cassell, 1894.

Randall, Ian. *A School of the Prophets: 150 Years of Spurgeon's College.* London: Spurgeon's College, 2005.

Ray, Charles. *The Life of Charles Haddon Spurgeon: With an Introduction by Pastor Thomas Spurgeon.* London: Passmore and Alabaster, 1903.

Reeves, Michael. *Spurgeon on the Christian Life: Alive in Christ.* Wheaton, Ill.: Crossway, 2018.

Rhodes, Ray, Jr. *Susie: The Life and Legacy of Susannah Spurgeon, Wife of Charles H. Spurgeon.* Chicago: Moody, 2018.

————. *Yours, till Heaven: The Untold Love Story of Charles and Susie Spurgeon.* Chicago: Moody, 2021.

Rippon, John. *A Selection of Hymns, from the Best Authors, Intended to Be an Appendix to Dr. Watts's Psalms & Hymns.* London: Thomas Wilkins, 1787.

Ryle, John Charles. *Simplicity in Preaching: A Few Short Hints on a Great Subject.* London: William Hunt, 1882.

Shepherd, Peter. "Spurgeon's Children." *The Baptist Quarterly* 42, no. 2 (April 2007): 89–102.

Shindler, Robert. *From the Pulpit to the Palm-Branch: A Memorial of C. H. Spurgeon.* London: Passmore and Alabaster, 1892.

————. *From the Usher's Desk to the Tabernacle Pulpit: Pastor C. H. Spurgeon, His Life and Work.* London: Passmore and Alabaster, 1892.

Spurgeon, C. H. *All of Grace: An Earnest Word with Those Who Are Seeking Salvation by the Lord Jesus Christ.* London: Passmore and Alabaster, 1897.

————. *An All-Round Ministry: Direction, Wisdom, and Encouragement for Preachers and Pastors.* Edinburgh: Banner of Truth, 2018.

————. *C. H. Spurgeon's Autobiography, Compiled from His Diary, Letters, and Records by His Wife and His Private Secretary.* Vols. 1–4. London: Passmore and Alabaster, 1897–1899.

————. *"Come Ye Children": A Book for Parents and Teachers on the Christian Training of Children.* London: Passmore and Alabaster, 1897.

————. *Commenting and Commentaries: Two Lectures Addressed to the Students of the Pastors' College, Metropolitan Tabernacle, Together with a Catalogue of Biblical Commentaries and Expositions.* London: Passmore and Alabaster, 1893.

————. *Evening by Evening: or, Readings at Eventide for the Family or the Closet.* London: Passmore and Alabaster, 1868.

————. *The Gospel of the Kingdom: A Popular Exposition of the Gospel according to Matthew.* London: Passmore and Alabaster, 1893.

————. *Lectures to My Students.* 3 vols. London: Passmore and Alabaster, 1881–1894.

————. *The Lost Sermons of C. H. Spurgeon: His Earliest Outlines and Sermons between 1851 and 1854.* Edited by Christian T. George, Jason G. Duesing, and Geoffrey Chang. 7 vols. Nashville: B&H Academic, 2016–2022.

————. *Memories of Stambourne.* New York: American Tract Society, 1891.

————. *The Metropolitan Tabernacle: Its History and Work, Mr. Spurgeon's Jubilee Sermons, A Memorial Volume.* London: Passmore and Alabaster, 1876.

————. *The Metropolitan Tabernacle Pulpit: Sermons Preached and Revised by C. H. Spurgeon.* Vols. 7–63. Pasadena, Tex.: Pilgrim Publications, 1969–1990.

————. *Morning by Morning: or, Daily Readings for the Family or the Closet.* London: Passmore and Alabaster, 1866.

————. *The New Park Street Pulpit: Containing Sermons Preached and Revised by the Rev. C. H. Spurgeon, Minister of the Chapel.* 6 vols. Grand Rapids: Baker Books, 2007.

————. *Only a Prayer Meeting: Forty Addresses at the Metropolitan Tabernacle and Other Prayer Meetings.* London: Passmore and Alabaster, 1901.

————, ed. *"Our Own Hymn-Book": A Collection of Psalms and Hymns for Public, Social, and Private Worship.* London: Passmore and Alabaster, 1866.

————. *Pictures from Pilgrim's Progress: A Commentary on Portions of John Bunyan's Immortal Allegory.* Pasadena, Tex.: Pilgrim Publications, 1992.

————. *The Saint and His Saviour, or the Progress of the Soul in the Knowledge of Jesus.* New York: Sheldon, Blakeman, 1857.

————. *Smooth Stones Taken from Ancient Brooks.* London: W. H. Collingridge, 1859.

————. *The Suffering Letters of C. H. Spurgeon.* Edited by Hannah Wyncoll. London: Wakeman Trust, 2016.

————, ed. *The Sword and the Trowel.* London: Passmore and Alabaster, 1865–1892.

————, ed. *Thirty-Two Articles of Christian Faith and Practice; or; Baptist Confession of Faith, with Scripture Proofs, Adopted by the Ministers and Messengers of the General Assembly, Which Met in London in 1689, with a Preface by the Rev. C. H. Spurgeon*. London: Passmore and Alabaster, 1855.

———. *The Treasury of David: Containing an Original Exposition of the Book of Psalms: A Collection of Illustrative Extracts from the Whole Range of Literature; A Series of Homiletical Hints upon Almost Every Verse; And List of Writers upon Each Psalm*. 7 vols. London: Passmore and Alabaster, 1869–1885.

———. *Trumpet Calls to Christian Energy: A Collection of Sermons Preached on Sunday and Thursday Evenings at the Metropolitan Tabernacle*. London: Passmore and Alabaster, 1875.

Spurgeon, Susannah Thompson. *Ten Years of My Life in Service of the Book Fund*. London: Passmore and Alabaster, 1887.

Stevenson, G. J. *A Sketch of the Life and Ministry of the Reverend C. H. Spurgeon*. New York: Sheldon, Blakeman, 1857.

Thomas, Amanda J. *Cholera: The Victorian Plague*. Barnsley, UK: Pen and Sword Books, 2015.

Thomas, Geoff. "The Conversion of Charles Haddon Spurgeon: January 6, 1850." January 1, 2000. Banner of Truth. https://banneroftruth.org/us/resources/articles/2000/the-conversion-of-charles-haddon-spurgeon-january-6-1850/.

Tupper, M. F. *The Poetical Works of Martin Tupper: Including Proverbial Philosophy, A Thousand Lines, Hactenus Geraldine, and Other Poems*. Series 1. New York: John Wilen, 1859.

Watts, Michael R. *The Dissenters*. Vol. 2, *The Expansion of Evangelical Nonconformity*. Oxford: Clarendon, 1995.

Wayland, H. L. *Charles H. Spurgeon: His Faith and Work*. Philadelphia: American Baptist Publication Society, 1892.

Wells, H. G. *Mr. Britling Sees It Through*. New York: Macmillan, 1916.

Williams, William. *Personal Reminiscences of Charles Haddon Spurgeon*. London: Religious Tract Society, 1895.

Wolffe, John. *God and Greater Britain: Religion and National Life in Britain and Ireland 1843–1945*. London: Routledge, 1994.